Out of Time

One Woman's Journey on the Camino

KATHARINE B. SOPER

Published by Stellaire Press, Ann Arbor, MI.
Email: stellairepress@gmail.com

All quotations from *The Pilgrim's Guide* are from *The Pilgrim's Guide, A 12th Century Guide for the Pilgrimage to St James of Compostella*, translated from the Latin by James Hogarth, Confraternity of Saint James, London, 1992, and used with the permission of The Confraternity of Saint James.

The lines of Ronsard's sonnet "A sa Maîtresse" are from the translation by Scott Horton, first published in *Harper's* on-line in 2008 (harpers.org/blog/2008); used with the permission of Mr. Horton.

All other translations are by the author.

John Brierley and Camino Guides kindly granted permission to use and adapt for this book the elevation charts in Brierley's *A Pilgrim's Guide to the Camino de Santiago*.

Book design, including the front and back covers, is by Mike Savitski of Savitski Design, in Ann Arbor, Michigan. The front-cover art is a portion of an iron statue depicting medieval pilgrims by Spanish artist Vicente Galbete. In 1996 it was placed at the Alto del Perdón just outside of Pamplona.

The photos on pages 109 and 172 and the photo of the author on the back cover are by Jacques Mouchel; the photo of the statue of Saint James atop the Santiago cathedral on page 264 is by Miguel Castaño. They are used by permission of the photographers. All other photos were taken by the author.

The names and identifying information of many of the pilgrims in this book have been changed to respect their privacy. The people and their stories are real and are told here to the best of the author's recollection.

ISBN 978-0-9911492-0-9

Library of Congress Control Number: 2013953987

Fifth printing, April 2020

For my family, but especially for Philip, with love and thanks

Table of Contents

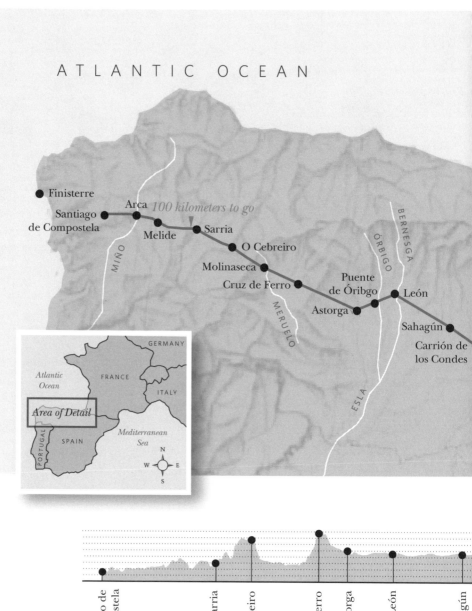

ATLANTIC OCEAN

Finisterre

Arca 100 kilometers to go

Santiago
de Compostela

Melide

Sarria

O Cebreiro

Molinaseca

Cruz de Ferro

Puente
de Óribgo

Astorga

León

Sahagún

Carrión de
los Condes

MINO

MERUELO

ÓRBIGO

BERNESGA

ESLA

GERMANY

Atlantic
Ocean

FRANCE

ITALY

Area of Detail

PORTUGAL

SPAIN

Mediterranean
Sea

N
W   E
S

Santiago de
Compostela

Sarria

O Cebreiro

Cruz de Ferro

Astorga

León

Sahagún

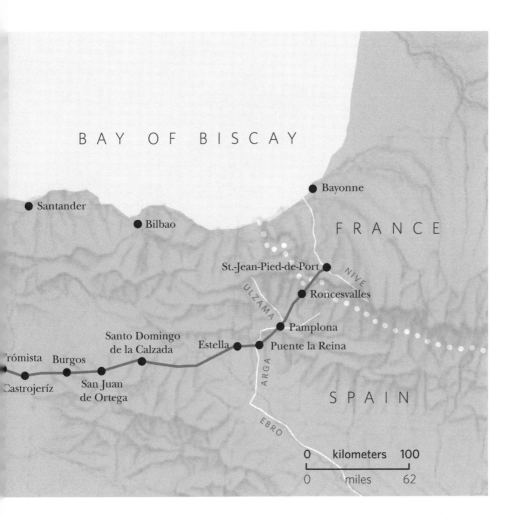

BAY OF BISCAY

Santander

Bilbao

Bayonne

FRANCE

St.-Jean-Pied-de-Port

NIVE

Roncesvalles

ULZAMA

Pamplona

Santo Domingo
de la Calzada

Estella

Puente la Reina

Frómista

Burgos

ARGA

Castrojeríz

San Juan
de Ortega

EBRO

SPAIN

| 0 | kilometers | 100 |
| 0 | miles | 62 |

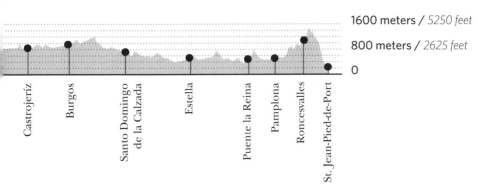

1600 meters / *5250 feet*

800 meters / *2625 feet*

0

Castrojeríz

Burgos

Santo Domingo
de la Calzada

Estella

Puente la Reina

Pamplona

Roncesvalles

St.-Jean-Pied-de-Port

9

Give me my Scallop shell of quiet,
My staffe of Faith to walke upon,
My Scrip of Joy, Immortall diet,
My bottle of salvation:
My Gowne of Glory, hopes true gage,
And thus Ile take my pilgrimage.

Sir Walter Raleigh, "Pilgrimage" (1604)

Prologue

One morning in 1982, I flushed my gold watch down the toilet. Two decades later, the memory of that incident sent me on a five-hundred-mile walk across northern Spain on the centuries-old pilgrim trail to Santiago de Compostela.

That morning in 1982 had been the usual multitasking whirlwind. I had just nursed my infant daughter and with my mind on work and my eyes on my fifteen-month-old son, I was removing my watch before stepping into the shower. Suddenly it slipped through my hands, disappearing down the toilet bowl. I felt terrible about the watch, a lovely birthday gift from my husband, Philip, but I had no time for regrets. I was due in court in forty-five minutes and had to move on. After a quick shower, I struggled into my detested pantyhose, suited up, and crammed the day's pleadings into my briefcase. Then I gathered up my sweet-smelling babies and held them close, loving those few precious moments before the sitter arrived and I had to dash out the door.

The years flew by. Before I knew it, my babies were taller than I was. I'd left practice for an administrative position at the University of Michigan; Philip, a law professor, continued to find satisfaction in his scholarship and teaching. Our marriage had the usual ups and downs as we juggled family life and two demanding careers. But both of us, having escaped unhappy first marriages, knew how lucky we were to have found each other. Life was good.

Still, I was becoming increasingly weary of a life lived in quarter-hour increments of obligations and responsibilities, with every moment scheduled and demanding an accounting. And yet, at the end of the day,

I never seemed to have accomplished everything on my list. Sometimes I would fantasize about leading a simpler, less complicated life. But how? All of the activities and chores that consumed my time were, without question, *essential.* (Not that I ever considered abandoning any of them.) The problem, I would inevitably conclude, came down to simple math: not enough hours in the day. If only I could increase my efficiency.

Every now and then I'd notice a pretty gold watch on a friend's wrist and the memory of mine disappearing down the toilet would return. I'd laugh, recalling how busy my life had been back then. But I was avoiding the truth: my daily pace, if anything, had only accelerated as I grew more adept at multitasking. Sometimes the image of my watch twirling around in the toilet bowl would give me pause—*time disappearing before my eyes,* I'd think—but I'd soon be laughing at myself again, this time for even considering the absurd possibility that my drowned watch signaled anything other than clumsiness.

Then my father died. Dad had been a loving presence in my life since the day he returned from World War II to meet his year-old daughter (me) for the first time. The oldest of three girls, I inherited my father's adventurous temperament. He introduced me to many of his interests, which led to my life-long passions for traveling, walking, jazz, skiing, and gourmet pleasures. For more than fifty years, Dad was my cheerleader, sounding board, reality check (well, he tried), and a great role model for how to embrace life to the fullest. His death left an emptiness that even the demands of my very full life could not fill.

The year after my father died, our son left for college, and the next year, our daughter did the same. Thrilled as I was to see them eager and bright-eyed at this new stage, waves of nostalgia greeted me when I sat down at the breakfast table, still set with four placemats. And the hits kept coming. Leadership changes at the University of Michigan were going to affect my position, but how? I learned that I had osteoporosis, then I was diagnosed with Sjögren's Syndrome, a chronic disease of the immune system. Meanwhile, my sixtieth birthday was looming.

Faced with a milestone birthday, the death of my father, an empty nest, professional uncertainty, and for the first time in my life limitations imposed by health, I suddenly felt vulnerable—and acutely mortal.

Propelled by all of this, along with a series of curious coincidences, I decided to leave everything behind and head for Santiago de Compostela.

Credencial del Peregrino

Ultreïa !

COMP✳STELLE 2000

The cover of my pilgrim passport.

*Quelle force jette ainsi dans l'inconfort assuré,
et les difficultés probables, ces gens considérés
hier encore comme "raisonnables"?*

What force throws people who were only
yesterday considered reasonable into
likely difficulties and certain discomfort?

Jean-Claude Bourlès, *Le Grand Chemin de Compostelle*

Chapter One

I'm Off!

May 26 – 27, 2002, Ann Arbor, Michigan, to Bayonne, France.

I am about to dissolve into a puddle on the pavement, right in front of curbside check-in at Detroit Metro Airport.

"How can you leave me to go walking in Spain for forty days?" Philip demands, glaring at me angrily from the driver's seat.

This is not how I want my trip to begin, I feel like wailing. But I don't say anything. I hesitate a moment, then grab my little purple and gray day pack—my only luggage for the next forty days—from the backseat. My husband gets out of the car and heads for the sidewalk, his face a thundercloud. I brace myself. It's a beautiful spring evening. How can a single human figure, a speck against the vast evening sky, make this lovely night so bleak?

"I would never leave *you* for that long," he accuses as he shoves into my hand the hat I had left on the seat. "Why can't we spend the last weeks of our sabbatical relaxing together in Ann Arbor? Why are you being so unreasonable?"

This has been his refrain all the way to the airport. Granted, Philip has never been what you'd call enthusiastic about my idea of walking the five-hundred-mile pilgrimage trail to Santiago de Compostela. When I first broached the possibility nine months ago, he made it clear that he had no intention of walking this Camino thing with me, whatever it was, and as far as he was concerned, that was that.

But it wasn't. I continued to explore the possibility, leaving books about the Camino around the house and mentioning it from time to time.

I'm Off!

Eventually the objections stopped, and I took his silence as tacit acceptance. After more than two decades together I should have known better, but I was so intrigued by the idea of walking to Santiago that I closed my eyes to the obvious: silence equals brooding. Now, just hours before my departure, all his suppressed unhappiness erupts, catching me by surprise, and we're back to where we were nine months ago: two lawyers making their cases.

Compounding his unhappiness with my plan is the timing. It's not ideal. Only two weeks earlier, we had returned to our Ann Arbor home after a sabbatical in Paris, just in time for our son's college graduation. We'd had a wonderful time abroad, and Philip wanted to ride out the afterglow at home, together. In retrospect, I don't think he believed until today—the day of my departure—that I would turn right around and go back to Europe less than a week after the graduation festivities.

By the time we pull up to the curb, I finally understand that nothing I can say will win his approval. I've lost my case. He can't imagine why anyone would want to walk five hundred miles. In spite of my reassurances (and suggestion that he come with me), it's pretty clear he feels abandoned by my taking off on what he views as a month-long vacation in Europe—for what else could it be?—without him. The only thing that would appease him would be for me to change my mind and stay home. And I can't—I don't want to. I *need* to take this trip, even if I don't (in his opinion) have a rational explanation for why.

"How can you leave me for forty days?" he repeats. "This is crazy."

I know that behind the anger he's also feeling hurt. And worried about me. He keeps dwelling on the time I somersaulted off a trail in the Dolomites and cracked a few ribs before a friend saved me from sailing into oblivion. I wish he'd get over that. I have my concerns, too, and his anger saps my confidence. Now that I'm about to move from planning to execution, the excitement I felt when I stepped into the car to go to the airport has morphed into a knot in the pit of my stomach. What if I can't walk that far? What if I get lost? Or sick? Or tumble down a steep section of the trail with nobody to catch me this time?

What if Philip is right?

We stand together in the unsparing silence. He looks at me; I look at my shoes. A security cop drives by and points first at our car, then at his watch. Tears of frustration and anger drip down my cheeks. Why must expressing my opinions and desires so often result in a battle of wills? I pick up my backpack and start toward the terminal.

"Wait," says Philip, reaching for my arm. "Don't leave like this." He pulls me into an embrace, the anger replaced by another look I can't identify. We hug, awkwardly at first, and then I look up and feel myself sinking into his blue eyes. Sometimes he makes me crazy—sometimes we make each other crazy—but I really do love this man. Perhaps I will just stay here, safely wrapped up in the warmth of his strong, familiar arms.

No you don't! I tell myself. *You've got too much invested in this trip. Get your butt on the plane.* Swiping at my face with my sleeve, I pull away.

He holds out his hands invitingly, then sighs, defeated.

"Call me every day," he says. "Be careful. I love you."

"I love you, too," I sniffle back.

Touching his cheek with my hand, I promise to try to call at least weekly, dig out my passport, and after a last embrace, I'm on my way.

With no luggage but my small pack—not even a purse for the first time in my adult life—I breeze through airport security and head for the gate, both hands free. Other passengers struggle with heavy suitcases and overflowing totes while juggling cell phones, portable media players, and countless other gadgets. That's usually me—more stuff than I can possibly need and way more than I can comfortably carry. I savor the novel feeling of walking unencumbered down an airport concourse, but I'm flattened and demoralized by this last argument with Philip. I can't get beyond a rising tide of doubts. What if my joints act up and I'm miles from medical care? What if I fall and break one of my honeycombed bones? And what was I thinking when I packed one change of clothes for a forty-day trip?

I inhale deeply, reminding myself that I'm taking the first steps of a journey I want to be on, and I'll never know if I can do it unless I try. It would be self-defeating to turn aside my dream of walking the Camino just because of health issues that might—or might not—be a problem. I vow then and there to put Sjögren's and osteoporosis out of my mind until I get home. As for the limited wardrobe, well, there is nothing I can do about my packing decisions at this point, so I'll just have to get used to the clothes I'll be wearing for the next forty days.

A lot can happen in forty days.

Lost in thought, I walk right past my gate—not a great start for someone who expects to navigate her way across Spain. By the time I find it, the Air France jumbo jet to Paris is ready for boarding. I get in line with my four hundred fellow travelers, who push and shove as they jockey for a spot in the overhead compartment for their impossibly large carry-ons. I slip my day pack into a corner of the overhead bin and claim my seat. Surrounded by the depressing solitude of a packed airplane, I sit and brood. I fuss with my water bottle, put my glasses in my shirt pocket, take them out, return them, and, finally, close my eyes to try to sleep. But my mind is racing. What am I doing? Why did I think I could do this? I put my glasses back on and stare out the window into the night.

"Well, folks, we're next for departure," announces the captain.

The whine of the engines escalates to an ominous roar. I think about bolting, but before I can formulate a plan, the plane is airborne. As the lights of Detroit fade away, I'm hit by the same anguish—or is it guilt?—that overtakes me every time I do something for myself, even if it's just stopping by the mall on the way home from work. Philip *is* right, I am being selfish and irresponsible to leave behind family and other obligations and go off on a month-long adventure because of some vague notion that I'm meant to do it. Something awful is bound to happen to one of my children or my husband. Or my elderly mother will become ill and I won't be there to help. And, of course, there's the standard worry about the plane crashing—those several minutes of sheer terror while I careen toward the sea, my body broken into smithereens when I hit the water, leaving my loved ones to pick up the pieces.

My seatmate looks worried, too, as she watches me nervously bouncing my foot back and forth and stares at the shredded boarding pass in my lap. She starts to say something, but changes her mind, turns away, and opens her book. I wish desperately that I had a book to read, then it occurs to me that it's because of a damned book that I'm strapped into this airplane seat. Last September, I had dashed into Borders to pick up a birthday gift and careened straight into a display table that featured Shirley MacLaine's book about her pilgrimage to Santiago de Compostela, *The Camino: A Journey of the Spirit.* The cover stopped me in my tracks. It showed a photo of a solitary figure, presumably MacLaine, striding across a field of tall grass, snow-covered peaks in the background. She was wearing a humongous pack, carrying a pilgrim's staff, and head down, she appeared both purposeful and pensive. This image had made my heart pound. How I longed to be that woman.

As I stared at the photo, I could see myself decades earlier, not yet consumed by all the things I would "achieve"—career, professional and community responsibilities, house and garden, cars, an avalanche of mail, a packed calendar every minute of every day—and caught a glimpse of the freedom and possibility that were so much a part of who I was, the me that used to be. I bought the book and read it straight through that very night.

Pilgrim stories have fascinated me ever since I first learned about the ancient trail to Santiago de Compostela as a graduate student in French literature in the 1970s. But I hadn't known that the trail still existed—and that people continued to walk it—until I read MacLaine's book. A few days later, it hit me. I had a window of opportunity when I could hike this trail, or at least try. In January, I would begin a seven-month leave of absence that would coincide with Philip's upcoming sabbatical. We planned to be in Paris until mid-May, and after that I would have no commitments until early August, when I had to return to work. For the first time in my adult life, I would have over two months with no professional or family obligations, and those two months were prime time for walking the Camino. Nothing stood in the way but my own fears and indecision.

A month after that chance encounter at Borders, I happened upon the pilgrimage trail again, this time during a trip to Oregon with my friend Bee, whom I had first met during my days as a French instructor at Boise State some thirty years earlier. We joined up in Portland, where we planned to spend the day before driving to the Oregon coast for a hiking trip. Bee and I both love bookstores, so our first stop was Powell's, a book-lover's paradise. As always, I headed immediately for the travel section, where a blond pony-tailed young man with intense blue eyes was shelving books.

"Like to walk?" he said, holding out a copy of *The Lonely Planet Guide to Walking in Spain.*

I nodded, startled at his choice of books. How did he know the idea of a trip to Spain was rumbling around in the back of my mind?

"Hang on," he replied, fumbling to find the page he wanted. "You might want to consider this hike," he said, pointing to a long wavy line on a map. "It runs for five hundred miles across northern Spain. It's called the Camino."

Heart pounding, I took the book out of his hands and headed for the check-out counter. The chapter on the Camino captivated me. The walk sounded fantastic, full of historical sites and remarkable scenery, with great food and wine all along the way. It was a bit long, but the terrain sounded easy and the route-finding straightforward. A week later, when I got back to Ann Arbor, still brimming with enthusiasm, I began talking about my idea of walking the Camino with family and friends. To my surprise, they all reacted with some combination of disbelief, ridicule, or confusion. The comment that stung most, however, came from my youngest sister.

"Having a midlife crisis, are we?" she said.

"I'm not in crisis," I huffed, irritated by the suggestion that there was anything wrong with my life. "And, at fifty-seven, it's pretty optimistic to call me middle-aged."

In fact, everyone thought I'd lost my mind—except our two children.

"Go for it, Mom!" they exclaimed when I told them of my plan. *The boundless energy and fearless optimism of youth in action,* I thought. Then I remembered my dad and knew that the willingness to embrace an adventure, to take a chance, was a matter of attitude, not age. He would have loaded my backpack and laughed at my hesitation as he pushed me out the door.

My children's enthusiasm and the memory of Dad helped keep the disparaging comments at bay, and I continued to dream about walking to Santiago. Nevertheless, I was still undecided when we left for our sabbatical in Europe. And that's when another fortuitous event intervened. From *The Lonely Planet Guide*, I had learned about a London-based organization, the Confraternity of Saint James, that offers a range of support to pilgrims to Santiago. As luck would have it, Philip and I had decided to spend ten days in London on the way to Paris, so I tucked the address and phone number of the Confraternity office in my passport, thinking I might give them a call. But when we got to London, I kept finding reasons not to phone. Finally, two days before we were to continue on to Paris, I dialed the number.

"I'm thinking about walking the Camino this spring," I told the woman who answered the phone. "Do you have any information about the route?"

"Yes, indeed," she exclaimed, "and your timing is perfect. Our annual Practical Pilgrim's Day is tomorrow morning, beginning at ten. I think you'd find it well worth your time. Do come! No need to register in advance, just stop by."

I go to enough meetings at work to last me a lifetime, I thought. Why would I go to one for fun? And I don't like large groups, especially when I don't know anyone. Besides, Philip and I had planned to go to the Tate Modern the next day, our last full day in London. But I knew, in my heart of hearts, that this was my moment of truth.

Pilgrim Associations

In 2001, when I was struggling to decide whether to make my first pilgrimage to Santiago de Compostela, information about the Camino was not readily available. There were no Camino associations in North America and online resources were just catching on. By chance, I stumbled on the London-based Confraternity of Saint James (csj.org.uk). This serendipitous encounter was instrumental in my decision to walk to Santiago, alone and on foot.

Today, many organizations throughout the world promote and facilitate the pilgrimage to Santiago de Compostela. English language Camino associations include American Pilgrims on the Camino (americanpilgrims.org), the Canadian Company of Pilgrims (Santiago. ca), the Confraternity of St. James South Africa (csjofsa.za.org), and the Camino Society Ireland (caminosociety.ie). Most European countries have at least one, if not several, active Camino associations. There are also many in South America, and one each in Japan, South Korea, and the Philippines. For a list of confraternities and associations in non-English speaking countries, go to the Santiago Pilgrim Office website (oficinadelperegrino.com/en), select "preparation," then select "confraternities worldwide."

The following morning, Philip headed for the Tate—alone—while I went to the Confraternity office on Blackfriars Road.

From the minute an enthusiastic Confraternity member greeted me at the door, I knew I'd made the right decision. Patient and helpful veteran pilgrims answered questions from would-be pilgrims on a range of topics for over two hours: route-finding, health and safety issues, finances, when to go, what to bring, whether to stay in the primitive pilgrim shelters called *refugios*, and more. Several women asked whether it was safe to walk alone, a concern I shared. The no-nonsense advice of a twinkly eyed, gray-haired English woman who had walked just about every route to Santiago more than once put that fear, if not to rest, at least in perspective.

"You're better off going alone," she laughed. "You can't know what you're getting into with someone else, especially a spouse. Be your own good company and get to know yourself."

Also at the Practical Pilgrim's Day, I learned of a twelfth-century book about the pilgrimage to Santiago that is sometimes referred to as the world's first travel guide. Written in Latin around 1140, *The Pilgrim's Guide* describes the four main pilgrimage trails to Santiago from France and gives advice about the route. The book addresses concerns so eternally human that the nine-hundred-year-old account seems astonishingly contemporary. I loved the author's tales of marauding robbers, poisonous waters, and treacherous ferrymen, as well as his colorful descriptions of the landscape, people, food, and places to visit along the way. The pull of the trip was becoming irresistible. I left the Confraternity meeting with a growing confidence I could do it, a confidence based on facts and detailed information that bolstered my gut sense that I should not let this opportunity slip.

Once Philip and I got to Paris, my encounters with things Camino accelerated, and I soon decided they were not coincidences but rather signs all pointing me toward Santiago de Compostela. These included running into a French woman about my age at *Compostelle 2000*, the Parisian equivalent of the Confraternity of Saint James. She had just returned from walking to Santiago from Paris, a journey of over one thousand miles. We talked for most of an hour—*femme à femme*, as she put it—and as we parted ways, she invited me to call her with any questions. Then, sensing my hesitation, she offered words of encouragement that I would recall several times during my pilgrimage.

"Don't be afraid," she said. "There really is a force that looks out for you. The Camino is more than a place. You'll see what I mean."

Finally, one decisive Friday, after three random encounters with the pilgrimage to Santiago in a twelve-hour period, I jumped off the emotional fence, once and for all, and phoned for a round-trip plane ticket to Europe, leaving Detroit in late May and returning forty days later. Later that week, I started brushing up on my Spanish, compiling my packing list, and taking daily cross-Paris walks to break in my new shoes and get in shape to walk five hundred miles.

And here I am, I think, *Santiago-bound.* The captain announces that we've reached cruising altitude. My foot tapping has stopped; a grumbling stomach reminds me I haven't had any dinner, a casualty of all that arguing. As I stare out the window into the void, an unexpected grin comes over my face. I *love* adventures, and I have a feeling this will be a doozy. I put my glasses in my shirt pocket, pull a blanket around my shoulders, and, finally, fall fast asleep.

I wake to the sound of rain against the window and the captain's announcement that we're on our final approach. Minutes later, we land at Charles de Gaulle Airport, right on time. It's an easy trip on the RER train from the airport into central Paris, then a short Metro ride to the Gare Montparnasse, where I will meet Juliette, a French friend and my last-minute traveling companion.

Until two weeks ago, I expected to walk to Santiago de Compostela alone, not by choice, but because I couldn't persuade anyone to come with me. Nobody I knew had the time or slightest interest, especially after I went into the details—like the distance involved and the primitive dormitory-style accommodations. Eventually, bolstered by the comments of the English woman at the Confraternity of Saint James and the French woman at *Compostelle 2000*, I convinced myself that it was OK—and maybe even preferable—to walk alone.

Then, just days before Philip and I returned home from our Paris sabbatical, a conversation with Juliette at a favorite bistro led me to reconsider my decision. She and I first met decades ago, when I was a college student on a junior year in France and she was a skinny, buck-toothed ten-year-old. Our fathers were business acquaintances who had become friends, so when her family learned I was studying in Paris, they invited me to their home in the heart of Burgundy, and that was the beginning of my long relationship with the entire family.

Initially, Juliette had been like a kid sister, but gradually our ten-year age difference mattered less and less, and we became friends. Our adult lives have had striking parallels—we are both professional women who have survived painful divorces, we had babies about the same time, and we share a love of good food and good books. We discovered something else in common over lunch at that Paris bistro, when I casually mentioned my plans to walk the Camino.

"Can I come?" Juliette blurted out in French. "I've been thinking about making this pilgrimage for some time. Now would be perfect. I really need a break. Would you mind?"

Hardly anyone I had talked with in the United States had ever heard of the pilgrimage to Santiago, so I was astonished that she not only knew all about it, but actually wanted to go. On reflection, I should not have been surprised. This pilgrimage has been part of French cultural heritage since the year 950, when a bishop named Godescalc walked to Santiago from central France. French pilgrims have been going there ever since, so of course Juliette knew about the pilgrimage and even had friends who had walked it.

Now what? By the time of our bistro lunch, I had gotten used to the idea that I would go alone and it felt right. Yet the Camino is a public path open to everyone. Besides, Juliette was reeling from the breakup of a relationship, and maybe a pilgrimage was just what she needed to help put her life back together.

"Think about it," she said. "Call me tomorrow after you've slept on the idea, and we can talk."

When I told Philip about her proposal and that she planned to take a cell phone (an item I felt unnecessary), he jumped on the idea.

"At least I'd have a way to reach you," he said, "and someone would be there if you had a problem."

That night, as I was trying to figure out what to do, my eyes settled on a French priest's account of his Camino journey that I was reading at the time.

"*Il faut se laisser faire*," he kept repeating, loosely translated as, "Chill out and let things happen."

What a concept. And one that was utterly foreign to me. He was referring to nothing less than letting go of control over my life—checking out, to my pre-pilgrimage way of thinking. But I had to admit that there would be many things I simply could not control while on the pilgrim trail—like the weather or how my body would react to walking all day every day for a month. Or whether I would make it home in one piece (a bit dramatic, perhaps, but the possibility did cross my mind). *Maybe I need to be a little more flexible*, I thought. *Maybe this development with Juliette is the first test of my readiness to walk the pilgrimage trail.*

The next morning, I accepted her proposal to accompany me.

"But can you get ready in time?" I asked, knowing that it had taken me months to compile a packing list and train for the walk.

"*Bien sûr*," she replied without missing a beat.

That settled, we agreed to meet in fourteen days at a Paris train station and travel together to Saint-Jean-Pied-de-Port, a French village at the foot of the Pyrenees where we would begin walking.

On the appointed day, I arrive at the Gare Montparnasse about three hours before our scheduled departure, happy for the chance to walk around the neighborhood and stretch my legs after some nine hours jammed into an economy seat on an overbooked plane. Later, I have lunch at a sidewalk cafe before returning to the cavernous station where I join the hordes waiting in front of an electronic bulletin board for their tracks to be posted. The numbers on the board twirl around noisily every five minutes for what seems like forever. Finally—in reality, after less than half an hour—a number is posted in front of the *TGV* (*train de grande vitesse* or high-speed train) to Bayonne, where we will catch the connecting train to Saint Jean.

I go to the track and look around. No Juliette. Ten minutes pass, and still no sign of her. I begin to wonder if she changed her mind. It all happened so fast, this decision to walk the Camino together. I can't call her since I don't have either a cell phone or a French phone card, so I go over the reasons I had wanted to walk alone, just in case. The loud speaker announces our train's imminent departure, I get on the train— and there she is, installed in her seat.

Thirty years ago, the gangly kid had blossomed into a beautiful woman, and today, as usual, Juliette looks fabulous—all smiles and very elegant. Her blond highlighted hair is perfectly coiffed, her makeup exquisitely subtle. Exuding charm, she wears slim khaki pants, a freshly ironed white shirt tucked in to show off her tiny waist, and a red sweater tied casually around her shoulders. Gold earrings, a stack of gold bracelets, and new gray hiking boots trimmed in red complete her outfit. She has somehow managed to hoist onto the luggage rack her enormous backpack, also new. I try to slide it over to make room for my pack but it won't budge. It appears to be filled with poured concrete.

I'm happy to see my long-time friend, but next to such glamour, I feel incredibly dumpy. Actually, I always feel that way in Paris, even though I usually dress several steps above "Ann Arbor casual" when I go to France. I tower over most French women (and men). I'm not a size zero. I don't wear stilettos anymore because they hurt my feet. My naturally curly mop is not in style, and I wear glasses, also not stylish. But this time, especially after spending the night on an airplane, I'm downright embarrassed by my appearance. My khaki hiking pants are rumpled, my baggy blue hiking shirt untucked. I wear the ugliest footware I've ever owned, a pair of sensible English walking shoes that look like clown shoes on my size eleven feet. Second thoughts creep in about my decision to bring only functional clothes and not to take any jewelry or makeup.

Juliette seems not to notice my new look. She rushes up, offering a flourish of greetings. After quickly kissing each other on both cheeks, we take our seats as the train pulls out of the station. We begin to catch up on family news but I soon crash, exhausted from the long flight and lulled by the soothing whisper of the train. Juliette wakes me at sunset as we arrive in Bayonne, a bustling town in the heart of the French Basque country. We couldn't get there in time to catch the last connecting train to Saint-Jean-Pied-de-Port, so we have reserved a room for the night in a charming hotel in the old part of town (and while we were at it, we also reserved a hotel for the next night in Saint-Jean-Pied-de-Port, so we could get off to a good start). We'll have a nice dinner, then take the first train to Saint Jean in the morning.

And tomorrow, the adventure begins.

. . . le sac léger pour ne pas trop oublier
que je ne suis sur terre que de passage et
n'emporterai là-haut comme seul bagage
que l'amour donné ici-bas.

. . . a light pack to remind me that I
am only passing through this world
and that the only baggage I will take
up there is the love I gave down here.

Luc Adrian, *Compostelle: Carnet de route d'un pèlerin*

Chapter Two

Decisions, Decisions

May 28, Bayonne to Saint-Jean-Pied-de-Port.

Despite sleeping through two alarm clocks, Juliette and I somehow manage to throw on clothes and dash to the station in time to catch the 7 a.m. train. The dilapidated one-car local is packed, but two heavyset American men in their fifties move their gear off the wooden bench and make a space for us. Within minutes we are in the midst of lush green mountains as we rattle past fast-flowing streams and an occasional hamlet. The hillsides are speckled with gently swaying white dots—grazing sheep, it turns out.

An hour later, the little train bounces into the medieval village of Saint-Jean-Pied-de-Port. Nestled in the gentle curves of the Pyrenees, the village on this beautiful morning looks like a travel poster for southwest France. Window boxes crammed with colorful summer flowers perch on the sides of centuries-old half-timbered houses. The town's cobblestone streets wind past the fourteenth-century Gothic church and along the banks of the River Nive, while the hazy blue Pyrenees stand guard over Saint-Jean-Pied-de-Port's two thousand inhabitants.

The name translates as "Saint-John-at-the-Foot-of-the-Pass" and reflects the town's location on a twelfth-century pilgrimage trail as it goes over a pass in the Pyrenees to reach Spain. From there, the trail crosses three more mountain ranges and a vast plain called the *meseta* before reaching its destination, the shrine of Saint James in Santiago de Compostela. In centuries past, this little town offered respite to weary European pilgrims who arrived on foot from their homes before they began the difficult and often dangerous crossing of the Pyrenees. These days, some Europeans still start walking from their doorsteps, and for them, Saint-Jean-Pied-de-Port continues to be a stop on the way to Santiago. Tens of thousands more arrive each year from all over the world via twenty-first century transportation to start their pilgrimage in Saint Jean, on the route that has become known as the *Camino francés* or simply the Camino.

Saint Jean is just waking up when we arrive. Merchants raise iron security grates and sweep the steps in front of their stores; café waiters in black pants and white shirts set out sidewalk tables and chairs; townspeople walk briskly to work. Our first order of business is breakfast. Wandering through town, we discover an open pastry shop with outdoor tables and a sign proclaiming that it specializes in *gâteaux basques*, delicious butter cakes with a custard filling. *Parfait!* We take the table next to a massive planter of fire-engine-red geraniums and settle in, sampling pastries and drinking one excellent coffee after another while we enjoy the morning quiet and write in our journals.

The journal is an idea I picked up at the Practical Pilgrim's Day in London. All the experienced pilgrims I met at that event insisted that a journal was standard equipment for a pilgrimage. One man even claimed that a journal was *the* most critical piece of equipment because it would encourage us to reflect upon the journey once we returned home, and these post-trip musings, in his view, were an essential part of the experience. He was persuasive. Although I had not kept a diary since junior high school, I started my new journal that day in London and wrote in it daily over the following months.

The sound of creaky wheels makes Juliette and me look up from our writing. It's the two heavyset men from the train, wobbling past—on bicycles. I do a double take. Enormous, bulging saddlebags are draped over the rear wheels, and deep wicker baskets, also stuffed to overflowing, hang from the front handlebars. These men apparently share Juliette's philosophy of packing. We start to wave, then hesitate because they seem so unsteady and struggle with even the slight incline of this modest slope. Shaking our heads, we exchange smug looks.

"If they can do it, you bet we can," Juliette observes confidently.

I relish the warmth of the sun and the spicy fragrance of the geraniums as I lick my fingers and decide whether to have another *gâteau basque* or try something different, perhaps a chocolate éclair.

"I'm not sure what it's like to be on a pilgrimage, but this feels pretty good," I comment. "I guess we're not going as hard-core pilgrims."

Juliette tosses back her head and laughs. *"Ah non!* Me, I'm more of an epicure," she says, moving her face to catch the sun's rays.

Well, that's a relief, because I don't see myself as a pilgrim either.

A Brief History of the Pilgrimage to Santiago de Compostela

Santiago de Compostela in northwestern Spain has been a popular destination for pilgrims since the early Middle Ages because the crypt of its cathedral is said to contain the bones of Saint James.

James was one of Jesus's twelve disciples (along with his brother, John). After the crucifixion, he was beheaded by Herod in 44 A.D. and, according to the tradition, his body made its way to Spain on a stone boat, which landed on the coast near what is now Santiago. James was buried on a nearby hill by his followers and forgotten until the year 813, when a Christian hermit named Pelayo followed a path of stars to rediscover James's remains. The local bishop authenticated the bones and a chapel was built to house them in what would become the city of Santiago de Compostela. Soon the relics began attracting pilgrims from all over Europe. The name of the city reflects both the name of the saint and the reason the site was chosen: "Santiago" means Saint James in Spanish, and "Compostela" is said to come from the Latin *campus stellae*, or field of stars, in reference to the stars that led Pelayo to discover the relics.

By the eleventh century, the pilgrimage to Santiago de Compostela had grown to become one of the three main pilgrimage destinations in medieval Europe, rivaling those to Rome and Jerusalem. An infrastructure—roads, bridges, towns with an array of services, hospices, churches—soon developed. This not only benefited pilgrims, but also fueled local economies and was a major influence in opening up European trade routes.

Pilgrims traveled to Santiago in large numbers throughout the Middle Ages. During the Reformation, the numbers declined precipitously and then dropped further during the Enlightenment. In the mid-twentieth century, the pilgrimage to Santiago experienced a gradual resurgence, largely due to the efforts of Spanish priests and scholars to promote the centuries-old tradition. The twenty-first century has seen a veritable explosion of interest in this pilgrimage.

From the early days, trails coming from the west, east, and north of Europe led pilgrims to a village at the foot of the Pyrenees in France. From there, the trails merged to become a single route known as the Camino francés, which went over a pass into Spain, then headed west to Santiago. In 1987, the Council of Europe proclaimed the Camino francés Europe's first Cultural Itinerary, in recognition of its historical and cultural importance. UNESCO declared the Camino francés a World Heritage site in 1993, along with such treasures as the Pyramids of Egypt, Peru's Machu Picchu, and the Great Wall of China. Today, the pilgrimage to Santiago attracts visitors from all over the world, who come as tourists, scholars, adventurers, athletes, and yes, even pilgrims.

Everyone knows that pilgrims are religious fanatics who reject the world and turn their backs on all earthly pleasures and responsibilities. A long-lapsed Methodist like me who goes to church on Christmas Eve and Easter (and then only for the music) can't be a pilgrim. Besides, my life as a lawyer and university administrator is firmly anchored in the here and now, in the rational. And yet. And yet, my decision to walk the Camino was not exactly rational. I decide not to worry about this detail and order a strawberry tart. Then Juliette and I talk about some practical considerations.

First is the question of where we'll stay—at the traditional pilgrim shelters called *refugios* or the more comfortable (and more expensive) accommodations along the way, such as *pensiones* and hotels. The refugios, also called *albergues*, offer dormitory-style beds for just a few euros to pilgrims en route to Santiago. But they are reputed to be dirty, crowded, plagued by snorers, and you can't reserve a bed in advance. This last point was a huge hurdle for me as I was contemplating the trip. It took me weeks to get my mind around the idea that if I stayed in refugios, I wouldn't know whether I'd even *have* a bed to sleep in at night, much less *where*. But I finally had to accept that I couldn't reserve ahead in any event because it would be impossible to know how far I would get each day given all the things I couldn't control—the weather, unexpected route changes, an injury or illness, getting lost, and a host of other unforeseen events (attacks by wild dogs?). What got me over this hump was thinking about the hundreds of thousands of pilgrims who had made it to Santiago over the centuries without reservations and survived the experience.

Now, faced with making an actual decision, my ambivalence comes slinking back. I haven't shared a room with a total stranger (much less thirty or more) since my freshman year in college—and that was a disaster. On the other hand, the choice of overnight lodging will have a big impact on my budget. Just as important, I want to experience this journey in the traditional way (even if I'm technically not a pilgrim), and everyone knows that pilgrims stay in refugios.

"Let's try out a refugio tomorrow night," I say to Juliette. "I'm game if you are."

"I have a different idea," she says. "Let's continue staying in hotels at first, while we ease into the trip and, of course, after difficult stages when we'll need our comfort and a reward for hard work. We can try refugios after a few days, once we've found our equilibrium."

My shaky resolve vanishes and I quickly agree. That settled, we turn to the question of what time to start off. We know we must leave early since the first day is such a long one, but we run into a snag over breakfast. Bakeries here don't open until 7:30, so I suggest buying a baguette and some fruit and yogurt today, having breakfast in our room around six, and leaving by seven at the latest. Juliette, however, points out that yesterday's baguette would be stale by morning, and stale bread for breakfast is, in her view, "*Impossible!*"

This is *so* Juliette, I think, half annoyed at her unwillingness to adapt to the realities of a pilgrimage and half agreeing with her that a day-old

Steps Out of Time

baguette—which has the texture of biscotti—is not an ideal way to start the day. Then an image runs through my head of the consequences of starting too late. We are huddled under a tree whose menacing shadow looms over us. The dark sky churns angrily, and it's raining. Draped in a dripping wet designer poncho, Juliette is sitting propped up against her giant pack. I'm soaked to the bone and shivering. Miserable, we wait in the downpour for dawn and enough light to continue.

Meanwhile, the pastry shop waitress overhears our conversation and offers a suggestion.

"*C'est simple*," she says. "Our *gâteaux basques* stay fresh for several days. Take some with you, and you'll have a delicious breakfast tomorrow before you start out. *Et voilà!*" she proclaims, looking quite pleased that she's figured this out for us.

Pastries for breakfast? We instantly agree with her. We also decide that we need to carry food with us each day for lunch in case we aren't near a town with a good restaurant at midday.

"I have some emergency supplies," Juliette volunteers, "just in case. Four boxes of breakfast bars, some chocolates, nuts, and a few other things."

What a great travel companion, I think. Whatever happens, there's no way we'll go hungry. And with business out of the way, we order pastries we haven't yet sampled—a fabulous local specialty made with an almond meringue and praline butter cream called a *Chaumontais* and a *mille-feuille* (aka a Napoleon). It's now mid-morning, and the street is clogged with backpackers who spill over from the jammed sidewalks. They wear scallop shells around their necks or pinned on their hats or packs, a sign that they are pilgrims on the way to the shrine of Saint James in Santiago. Scallops are plentiful on the coast near Santiago, so in the Middle Ages pilgrims would take them home as proof of their journey. (In French, a scallop shell is called a *coquille Saint Jacques*, literally, a Saint James shell.) Modern-day pilgrims have taken to wearing the shells from the beginning of their journey, as a mark of intention rather than completion.

We placidly observe the energetic crowd from our table in the sun. It's hard to move on, but eventually we shoulder our packs and go to our hotel, a small, family-run place in the center of town. A bellboy shows us to our room, suppressing a grunt when he deposits Juliette's pack on the floor. As Juliette unpacks, I see that she is not about to risk being cold, hot, hungry, bedraggled, or bored. In addition to several outfits of various weights and a make-up kit, she has come prepared with large bottles of creams, lotions, and hair products; several books; extra shoes; and her emergency food supply—all items she considers essential. And of course, she has the standard pilgrim equipment of sleeping bag, rain

Tourists strolling down the Rue de Charlemagne in Saint-Jean-Pied-de-Port.

gear, and water bottle. She figures that as long as she can lift her pack, she can carry it on her back. I am astounded at how much stuff she has—and she can't believe all the things I *don't* have.

My approach was admittedly bare bones. I took to heart the recommendations of several Camino guidebooks, all of which urged a very sparse packing list. I also knew from experience that weight in a backpack translates directly into pain. With my osteoporosis and joint problems, I wasn't sure I would make it to Santiago even with a light pack, but I could maximize my chances. I decided to follow the Spartan advice of the Confraternity of Saint James: carry the lesser of eight kilograms or 10 percent of your body weight, which for me was 6.08 kilograms (13.4 pounds).

In the months before my departure, I labored over my packing list, weighing every item on a kitchen scale, then starting over when my pack exceeded the maximum weight I had allowed myself. I don't know if I was diligent or compulsive, but by the end of April, my fully loaded pack weighed 6.165 kilograms, and that included one liter of water, a change of clothes, toiletries for a month, a new extra-lightweight down sleeping bag, and the weight of my pack—everything I would be carrying on my back except for any food I bought along the way. In addition, I prepared a small waist-pack in which I would carry valuables (passport, pilgrim credential,

Steps Out of Time

one family photo, cash, a credit card, and an ATM card), items I needed to have handy (clip-on sunglasses, lip balm, spoon), and a few small but heavy necessities (camera, extra batteries, mini-headlamp). I planned to wear the waist-pack across my stomach for easy access and to keep it with me at all times, even in the shower, so that I wouldn't have to worry about theft of difficult-to-replace items. It weighed 960 grams (2.1 pounds). Not bad.

It was hard—not to mention completely out of character—to pack only one change of clothes, but that was nothing compared to the agonizing question of whether to take books. How could anyone be expected to pack for a forty-day trip, including two transatlantic flights, without books? How to cope with the hassles of traveling, where to go to escape, without books? But books are bulky and heavy—even paperbacks when you are in the mindset of weighing every aspirin. And my pre-trip reading seemed to suggest that stripping down to the essentials meant leaving behind creature comforts. I waffled for days but eventually decided I would go truly bare bones and leave my books at home. Reluctantly and with trepidation, I packed only selected pages torn from a Camino guidebook and a small notebook to serve as my journal, minus the front and back covers to save an ounce or two.

I did make one concession to vanity. Inspired by a character in a novel who made a pilgrimage to Santiago, I mailed a pretty sundress, a pair of strappy sandals, and make-up to the Santiago hotel where I had reserved a room at the end of my trip. "Hold for arrival on June 30," I wrote optimistically on the front of the box in big black letters. After a month of wearing the same clothes every day, I knew I would be desperate for a nice outfit to wear while I explored Santiago and, later, for the trip home and my reunion with Philip.

Juliette looks thoughtfully at my pack and considers the mountain of stuff on her bed. After deliberating a long time, she decides to mail home a few things she can do without—an extra sweater, a large bottle of styling gel, two heavy books, and a few other miscellaneous items for a total of about one-and-a-half kilograms—so off we to go the post office. ("This happens all the time," says the weary clerk.) Then we visit the pastry shop, cheese shop, green grocer, supermarket, and chocolatier, buying provisions for the next day.

Our last stop is the *Accueil des Pèlerins de l'Association des Amis du Chemin de Saint-Jacques/Pyrénées Atlantiques,* a pilgrim welcome center in downtown Saint-Jean-Pied-de-Port, which we must visit so Juliette can get her credential. Also called a pilgrim's passport, this document identifies the bearer as a pilgrim on the way to Santiago. It is a distant cousin of the safe conduct pass that medieval pilgrims secured from local authorities before leaving home and is required for access to the refugios.

My credential, which I obtained at the Paris pilgrim association, came with a curious little observation (or was it a warning?): *"Quelles que soient ta foi et ta relation à Dieu, en partant tu n'es plus le même . . ."* (Whatever your faith, whatever your relationship with God, by your decision to leave [on this pilgrimage], you are no longer the same person . . .)

Refugios and pilgrim centers all along the Camino stamp and date the credentials of passing pilgrims, and these little stamps provide a colorful record of a pilgrim's progress. This record also enables a pilgrim who makes it to Santiago to prove to church authorities that she has walked at least the last one hundred kilometers (or cycled the last two hundred kilometers) to Santiago. That proof, together with a statement that the journey was religiously motivated, earns the pilgrim a second document, called a *Compostela*. Obtaining a Compostela was a major motivation for pilgrims in the Middle Ages because it officially recognized completion of the pilgrimage, and that in turn entitled the successful pilgrim to the remission of all or part of the time spent in Purgatory—essentially a get-out-of-penance-free card. Today, travelers to Santiago remain eager to get their Compostela, though as often as not, I suspect it's because this handsome document in Latin with its official-looking seal is a fine souvenir.

The French pilgrim association is bustling and efficient; Juliette has her credential in no time. A friendly volunteer gives both of us our first stamp, a green one with the image of a medieval pilgrim and mountains in the background.

"¡Buen Camino!" she wishes us as she stamps, dates, and signs our credentials with a flourish. This traditional salutation is the pilgrim equivalent of "happy trails."

She might be more excited about our trip than I am. This small French town is so comfortable with its flower boxes and gardens, friendly merchants, and the buzz of a language I understand. The mountains that we must cross to get to Spain loom over the village. Tomorrow is, in fact, reputed to be the hardest day of the Camino, on a twenty-seven-kilometer trail that takes pilgrims over the Pyrenees and into Spain. But I know from my guidebook that there are two options for our first day of walking: the harder way and the hard way. The harder way, which was the traditional route, originated as a Roman track. Later it became known as the *Route de Napoléon*, when the French emperor began using it in the early nineteenth century. Napoleon was not known for coddling his soldiers. The elevation chart shows exactly what we'd face on that route: a near-vertical climb up and over the Pyrenees at the Cize Pass, then a treacherously steep drop into Roncesvalles (Roncevaux in French).

The author of the twelfth-century *Pilgrim's Guide* has this to say about the Route de Napoléon:

Still in the Basque country, the road to St. James goes over a most lofty mountain known as the *Portus Cisere* [Cize Pass]. . . . It is a journey of eight miles up to the pass and another eight down from it. The mountain is so high that it seems to touch the sky, and a man who has climbed it feels that he could indeed reach the sky with his hand.

The other route, the *Route de Charlemagne*, follows the road for much of the way, stays lower, and crosses the mountains at the Ibañeta Pass. In the early days, either option was dangerous. Pilgrims taking the Route de Napoléon faced deadly, high-mountain weather conditions and risked getting lost in fog or unexpected blizzards. If they took the lower route, they became targets for highwaymen who robbed and murdered them. Today, some nine hundred years later, the lower route, while less dramatic, is not only easier but safer.

We're not sure we're up to the high route on our first day of walking, but when I ask the Association volunteer about the road route, she hands me a one-page description for the Route de Napoléon and denies any knowledge of an alternative. I show her the page in my guidebook describing another option. She backpedals.

"Well, maybe there is a road route. *Mais personne ne la prend*," she insists, "*personne, personne!* (But nobody takes it, absolutely nobody!) You really should take the Route de Napoléon."

"I don't know," I say. "It's our first day."

"*Eh bien*, do as you wish," she concludes, her voice dripping with disapproval. Other volunteers appear, all eager to support their colleague's sound advice. We try to thank her, but by now the volunteers are so engrossed in lively conversation that none of them pays us the slightest attention. (Since then, the Association has changed its advice. Volunteers, of which I am now one, hand out information in a dozen languages describing both routes and telling pilgrims that in case of inclement weather, they must take the lower route.)

As we leave, the words of a British pilgrim who's lounging in the doorway clinch our decision not to take the Route de Napoléon: "Did you hear about the three girls who got lost at the Cize Pass a few weeks ago?" he asks us in a hushed voice. His eyes dart about as if he thinks he's being watched. "They had to be rescued by the mountain patrol," he hisses. "Lucky for them that someone wondered where they were or they'd still be up there."

Juliette and I look at each other, somewhat alarmed. *This guy is weird*, we think, *but what if he's telling the truth?*

"Then there was the Brazilian pilgrim earlier this season who wasn't rescued," he says darkly. "The Association volunteers told him not to attempt the pass that day, given weather conditions, but he wouldn't listen and headed out anyway. They figured he'd made it when he didn't come back, but since nobody was expecting him on the other end, nobody missed him there either. They found this one when the snow melted. Take care."

Well, this exchange puts a damper on our day. Twenty-first century pilgrims aren't supposed to die en route to Santiago. It's a hiking trail, for heaven's sake, and like any other long-established European trail, it's surely safe.

Isn't it?

We walk back to our hotel in silence. When we get there, Juliette goes up to our room. Feeling restless, I take a stroll and end up on the graceful fifteenth-century bridge over the River Nive that we will cross the next morning on our way out of town. I stand there for a long time, leaning against the cool stones and watching the motion of the water. It makes a muffled sound as it tumbles over the rocky stream bed. The silvery shadows of trout flitting about effortlessly create a dappled pattern in the sunlit water, and the stream keeps flowing, steadily, calmly, inevitably. I wonder where my journey will take me. Behind me lies the security of this little thousand-year-old village.

Ahead of me, who can say?

It was no picnic yet, let alone a pilgrimage.

Colin Fletcher, *The Man Who Walked Through Time*

Chapter Three

Nobody Said This Would Be Easy

May 29 – 31, Saint-Jean-Pied-de-Port to Larrasoaña via Zubiri.

Overnight, the weather turns. It's not quite raining when the alarm goes off at 6:30 a.m., but the sky is leaden in anticipation. While we pack up, we talk about our encounter with the spooky Englishman yesterday. His comments were unnerving, but after a good night's sleep and in the light of day, we decide he was just trying to scare us with his tall tales of pilgrim deaths. We enjoy a leisurely snack of buttery gâteaux basques and hand-dipped chocolates, settle our bill, and stride out the door of the hotel at 7:45. It has started to drizzle. We go back inside, dig out our bad-weather gear, and try again.

Within minutes, the drizzle turns into a steady, penetrating rain. No matter, we each have a voluminous, hooded waterproof cape called a *pèlerine* that fits over us and our backpacks and will keep both dry. I wasn't going to buy this traditional pilgrim garment since I already had good rain gear, but the packing lists I consulted recommended taking a pèlerine, so I decided to check out this unfamiliar piece of equipment while we were in Paris. Besides, that gave me an excuse to visit *le Vieux Campeur* (the Old Camper), a series of little shops in the Latin Quarter, each carrying a different type of outdoor equipment. It is my favorite store in all of Paris and is just around the corner from the rue Saint Jacques, the street pilgrims to Santiago have been taking on their way out of Paris since the Middle Ages. Coincidence? Of course not, and it's another reason I was happy to go on this shopping expedition.

When I explained to the Vieux Campeur saleslady that I was thinking about buying a pèlerine for my trip to Santiago de Compostela, her haughty Parisian smirk turned into a warm smile. She had been to Saint Jacques, as she put it, and was eager to help me prepare for my trip. For the next half hour, this enthusiastic clerk was all mine while she detailed the features of the different *modèles,* each of which she insisted I try on.

"A pèlerine is very practical," she explained, "because you can put it on in seconds if a storm comes up. No struggle to get into rain pants and jacket—and don't forget the hassle of putting on a pack cover. By the time you've organized all that, you're soaked."

But the real selling point as far as she was concerned was tradition.

"It's what pilgrims wear," she said, staring straight into my eyes, daring me to disagree. I docilely selected a pale green model that was both waterproof and breathable, and, at 210 grams, the lightest option.

Truth be told, I felt like I was wearing a Halloween costume when I tried this thing on in Paris. On the other hand, it weighed 60 percent less than my backpacking rain gear, so I decided it was worth a try. It only took one cloudburst for me to realize that my pèlerine was a wise purchase, and not just for the weight advantage. Storms move in quickly on the Camino, especially in the mountains and on the meseta. The ease of getting the pèlerine on and off more than compensated for the two occasions when the rain blew sideways and I would have been drier in my rain pants and jacket. As for the Halloween costume issue, I got over that in five minutes on the trail, where comfort and function triumph over style.

So that first morning, looking like pilgrims in our new pèlerines, Juliette and I head confidently out of town. The first few kilometers of the Route de Charlemagne are unsigned, but we know the way, having scouted out the start of the trail the day before. Soon, we're on a quiet country lane that leads us gently up and into the foothills. Low-hanging clouds hide the mountaintops that were so spectacular yesterday, but the lush green valley shimmers in the rain and the swirling mist makes it mysterious and otherworldly. After an hour, we take advantage of a break in the weather to eat our remaining Basque cakes and chocolate, stopping in the little field where we had turned around during our scouting expedition. Then, spirits high, we continue on, now in unknown territory.

Still climbing, the country lane becomes a dirt trail through a little woods, and now the way is well-marked with the traditional sign for the Camino: yellow arrows painted on rocks, trees, pavement, the side of shepherd huts, or anything else that's stationary. I would have preferred a good topo map like I'm used to from backpacking in Idaho or an Ordnance Survey map like the ones available for long-distance footpaths in England. That's not the way of the Camino, where maps are sketchy and not always accurate. The yellow arrows, however, are easy to follow. As long as they don't disappear on us, we'll be fine, but if they do, we're in trouble. Left to rely on my sense of direction, we are certain to head in the wrong direction, every time.

Half an hour later, the pleasant forest path abruptly dumps us onto a busy departmental highway. One side of this narrow, winding two-lane road abuts a fast-moving stream, the other a steep slope. Just as we step onto the pavement, it starts to pour again. Yellow arrows direct us to walk on a foot-wide shoulder, where we are buffeted by traffic with no possible escape from maniacal drivers who appear to make a game of seeing how close they can come without actually striking us.

"We're going to get ourselves killed," groans Juliette, as a furniture delivery truck speeds by, dousing us with a spray of muddy water.

I'm too busy bracing for the next onslaught to reply.

When we reach the Spanish border, the guard house is not staffed, so we walk on by, and that's when things get dicey. The rain has let up, and there are plenty of yellow arrows marking the route, but they are not reliable. They take us into impassible thickets where there is no choice but to retrace our steps or lead us to a crumbling bridge we cannot possibly cross, even though an arrow on the other side of the bridge confirms that it is the correct route. Then we come to a sign (in French, even though we're in Spain) for the Chemin de Saint Jacques, and right next to it, a yellow X painted on a rock, which means we should *not* take that path. Now what? And what were all those people talking about when they assured me that wayfinding on the Camino was easy? After much agonizing, we decide to stay on the road—at least we can't get lost on the highway, which is signed for Roncesvalles. We might get hit by a car, but that's probably preferable to vanishing into the mountains.

Ten minutes later we come to an unambiguously marked and unobstructed path that takes us off the road and steeply uphill into a dense forest. We follow the path all afternoon without seeing another soul. Meanwhile, the weather deteriorates again as heavy rain alternates with periods of pea soup fog. No yellow arrows—at least none that we can see in this weather—reassure us we are on the right route. We don't spot any houses or other signs of life, just a barking dog that we can't see through the dense mist. As it gets later and darker, we become increasingly worried, and Juliette is really struggling under the weight of her pack.

I've resigned myself to a night under a tree in the rain—my nightmare come true?—when, without warning, the path spills us right onto a busy four-lane highway, traffic whizzing by in both directions. The fog is now so thick we can barely see a foot ahead, but somehow we spot a yellow arrow that sends us into the void, and a minute or two later, the shadowy outline of a chapel rises out of the fog. Consulting our guidebooks, we decide this must be Ibañeta Pass, site of an early-twelfth-century pilgrim hospice (a combination hostel and hospital) that was moved to Roncesvalles in 1132 because of the terrible weather at the pass. No kidding. The modern chapel that stands at the summit today is said to have a bell that priests ring to guide pilgrims in bad weather, as has been done since the earliest days of the pilgrimage. Why it is not ringing now is a mystery.

This is also the very spot where Charlemagne's rear guard, commanded by his nephew Roland, was defeated and the entire battalion slaughtered in 778, allegedly by the Moors, who at that time occupied most of Spain. The *Song of Roland,* a masterpiece of medieval literature, commemorates the event. But according to Spanish legend, the real hero of the effort to recapture Spain from the Moorish invaders is not Roland or Charlemagne, but Santiago. He is said to have appeared on a white charger during a decisive battle and saved the day for the Spaniards, hence his other identity as Santiago Matamoros, Saint James the Moor Slayer. For centuries, the image of Saint James, sword in hand and slaying the infidels, was as revered as the image of Saint James, the pilgrim. His persona as a merciless warrior strikes me as completely inconsistent with that of Saint James, the peaceful pilgrim. However, to the medieval pilgrim, these dual identities probably went hand-in-hand: the warrior ridding the land of infidels, the pilgrim leading the way to personal salvation.

Ten minutes later—and nine hours after leaving Saint-Jean-Pied-de-Port—Juliette and I struggle into the medieval monastery complex at Roncesvalles under an icy downpour that pummels our spirits as well as our wet, cold, and tired bodies. A small sign leads us to a massive stone structure—what's left of the medieval hospice. Inside, the old building is light and warm and full of pilgrims speaking Spanish, French, German, Dutch, and a smattering of other languages.

"*Credenciales, por favor,*" says the frazzled priest.

We produce them. He motions for us to sign the pilgrim register, stamps our credentials, and starts to sign us up for the refugio.

"*No, gracias,*" I say, "*no refugio.*" He looks surprised but turns quickly to the next person. We slink out and go to the new hotel on the other side of town where we take a charming twin room with a spotless, tiled bathroom. I say a mental merci to Juliette for pushing a hotel tonight—especially after seeing the refugio—though I feel a little guilty at choosing such luxurious and unpilgrim-like accommodations.

After cleaning up as best we can, we go in search of something hot to drink and discover Spanish bars. What a find! These warm and welcoming places are a lifeline for pilgrims all along the Camino. Though Spanish and English use the same word, their respective concepts of "bar" are quite different. Spanish bars (pronounced with a rolled *r* and an open *a*) are more like French cafés than American bars. Open all day, they offer morning coffee, snacks throughout the day, and sometimes excellent meals, as well as the usual alcoholic beverages. Just as important, Spanish bars provide a place for pilgrims to gather and commiserate, recover, or celebrate, depending on how the day has gone.

Tonight, the scene is subdued. Dozens of shivering, soggy, exhausted strangers wearing scallop shells talk about the hardships of the Route de Napoléon, especially the difficulty of staying on the path. They saw nothing but the inside of clouds the entire way. Other hikers, who also wear scallop shells but are in better shape, arrived here by bus or taxi from Pamplona and will begin walking tomorrow from Roncesvalles, another popular starting point for modern-day pilgrims. In no time, Camino friendships develop and bars become much livelier. But let's face it. This is the beginning of the journey for most of us, and we're a bunch of strangers in shock, wondering what we've gotten ourselves into.

Around 8 p.m., the bar empties out as people walk across the street to the thirteenth-century Collegiate Church to attend the Pilgrim Mass, a popular tradition now as in centuries past. We follow the crowd. There is nothing else to do, not even a book to read. Suddenly I intensely regret my decision not to bring books on my pilgrimage. (But what I would have missed if I'd tucked a good novel in my pack, you, the reader, will soon understand.) Restaurants don't open for dinner before nine or nine-thirty, so eating and going to bed early isn't an option either.

The church is stern from the outside, but inside it is pure Gothic. Candles create eerie shadows and hint at the majesty of the vaulted ceiling, though the soft lighting doesn't reach far enough to illuminate details of the stonework. Large stained-glass windows, no doubt magnificent in the daylight, appear as mysterious black panels. The muggy air smells of damp wool and incense, but the flickering candlelight and murmur of voices make the church feel safe and comforting. Soon, an organ rings out and five priests wearing richly embroidered robes file in. After welcoming us, the presiding priest tells us he has looked at today's pilgrim register and that we are from almost every country in Europe (he names them), as well as the United States, Australia, New Zealand, South Korea, and Chile. Then the priests say Mass in a combination of French and Spanish, and when it's over, the presiding priest returns to the lectern, looks out at his bedraggled flock, and begins to talk with us about our endeavor. We are, it seems, here for a purpose, and he does not suggest that it must necessarily be a religious one, which intrigues me.

"You are setting off," he tells us, speaking slowly and earnestly in French. "You are looking for something, but you don't know what. Perhaps you are searching for yourself, or perhaps someone is looking for you. Be attuned to what the Camino has to teach you. Keep your hearts open. You will find what you seek."

Then he wishes us well and, with a smile, asks us to pray for them when we get to Santiago. A titter goes through the congregation at the thought of the priests needing our prayers. But in fact, over the course of my pilgrimage, many people, including other priests, ask me to pray for them when I get to Santiago. At first, the requests startle me. Then I realize that, in their eyes, I am a pilgrim, and endowed with this special status, I can put in a good word with Saint James.

Finally, the priest invites us to come forward for a blessing that he explains has been bestowed on pilgrims setting out from Roncesvalles since the eleventh century:

> Oh God, who called your servant Abraham out of the town of Ur in Chaldea, watching over him during all his wanderings, and who guided the Jewish people through the desert: we ask you to watch over us, your servants, who for the love of your name make a pilgrimage to Santiago de Compostela.
>
> > Be for us
> > a companion on our journey,
> > a guide at the crossroads,
> > our strength in fatigue,
> > a fortress against danger,
> > a shelter along the way,
> > shade in the heat,
> > light in our darkness,
> > consolation when we are discouraged,
> > and the power of our intention,
>
> so that under your guidance, safe and unhurt, we may reach the end of our journey and, strengthened with gratitude and power, return to our homes, filled with grace and happiness. In the name of Jesus Christ, our Lord. Amen.

It's staggering to realize that hundreds of thousands of pilgrims have been sent on their way by this blessing over the past ten centuries. How has this tradition endured for so long, and why do pilgrims continue to walk to Santiago? What is this world I am entering? One thing is certain: it's a very different world from the one I inhabited just forty-eight hours earlier, before I was plunked down on the Camino, fresh off a jet plane and a high-speed train.

The next morning, we wake around eight to a deserted little settlement. Everyone else managed a more timely departure. The rain has finally stopped, and in the daylight we notice an enormous, unsightly parking lot for tour buses. What dominates, however, is the beauty of the countryside: white sheep grazing on emerald fields, paler green beech forests, and above everything the graceful curves of the Pyrenees peeking out from the mist that cloaks the slate roof of the monastery. The crisp smell of mountain air drifts in through our open window. Bells around the necks of grazing horses jingle; church bells chime. These sensory pleasures dispel yesterday's doubts. Soon the mist will clear, and it will be a fine day, sunny and cool.

After a leisurely breakfast of fruit and yogurt in our room, we leave the hotel at 8:45—then wander around for fifteen minutes trying to find our way out of town. With few exceptions (yesterday being a notable one), the Camino is well marked with yellow arrows once you are under way. But the route out of town, even if it's just a little settlement, is not always apparent. Once we find the path, the first village is just a short stroll away. As we reach the outskirts, a man carrying an armful of fragrant loaves of bread walks toward us.

"Hello, ladies," he booms out in a deep Scottish brogue. Dressed in shorts, flip-flops, an unbuttoned blue plaid shirt, and a captain's hat, he greets us enthusiastically. "Name's Robert," he says, holding out his hand. "Come, let me offer you breakfast."

"He's trying to pick us up," whispers Juliette.

Us? I think. Yeah, right. Juliette may be forty-eight, but she is gorgeous and youthful looking.

He must have heard her. "I have a mission to help pilgrims," he quickly explains, pointing to a beat-up old camper that is parked in the grass by the side of the road.

The smell of fresh bread proves stronger than any suspicions. We walk with him back to his camper, where he produces a card table and three folding chairs that he sets up in the grass beside a bed of blazing red poppies.

"Sit," he says. "I'll be right back."

Within minutes, Robert is serving us a second breakfast of freshly made strong coffee, warm crusty bread, creamy local butter, and tangy strawberry jam. His boom box is playing a tape of Mozart's *Clarinet Quintet in A Major*. The haze has burned off and the mountain views are incredible. Robert takes a chair and leans forward, eager to tell us his story.

"Several years ago, I came to Spain to do the Camino for strong personal reasons," he begins, "but I couldn't complete my pilgrimage."

I start to ask for details, but anticipating my question, he holds up his hand.

"The details aren't important," he says. "All that matters is that I had to go home midway. Yet something kept pulling me back." He stretches out his hands, palms up, and shrugs his shoulders. "I knew I needed to return, but I couldn't walk the Camino, so why would I come back? Finally, it dawned on me. I would upgrade and return as a Samaritan."

I butter another slice of bread, turn away from the lovely mountain views, and try to focus on the conversation. "What exactly does a Samaritan do?" I ask.

"Depends," he says. "Mostly I drive my camper up and down difficult stretches during the high season and rescue pilgrims. You'd be surprised how many are unprepared. They take off without rain gear or are in terrible condition yet expect to walk many miles for days on end. Other times, it's just bad luck. They fall and break something, and I find them sitting in the middle of the trail. On slow days, I serve coffee at problem spots. You know, long stretches without anything or the top of a tough climb."

"Well," he says, looking at us and chuckling, "you probably don't know, but you will."

He also offers advice about the route, some helpful and some unwelcome.

"Women should not do the Camino alone. The younger and prettier, the riskier," he proclaims, looking straight at Juliette. When pressed, he admits it's not so much a safety issue as an annoyance, the biggest problem being flashers.

His advice about refugios is more welcome.

"Be sure to stay at the Trinidad de Arre refugio, just outside of Pamplona," he says. "It's very well-appointed, and you can make it easily for tomorrow night. If you make decent time today."

He looks at his watch. Checking mine, I discover that it's a quarter past ten.

"Best get going," he advises, standing to make his point. And refusing our offer to help with the dishes, he waves us on our way, with a cheery "Good luck. I'll see you again."

On the way out of town, we stock up on bread, cheese, fruit, chocolate, and yogurt. Our pace is a little on the slow side. It's now after eleven, and we've only done three kilometers. On the other hand, yesterday's miseries forgotten, we're having a great time. Leaving town, the path crosses open farmland for a couple of kilometers, then becomes heavily wooded and begins to climb. It takes us through several small villages, each with no more than a dozen stone houses from the sixteenth, seventeenth, and eighteenth centuries, according to dates carved above the doorways. Gorgeous roses frame the massive wooden doors, sometimes in pots, sometimes planted in the earth. Juliette and I admire them in passing and go on automatic pilot, following the yellow arrows and talking nonstop about everything and nothing.

At one village, reached after a particularly hard ascent, we stop for a water break. Just as we are about to start walking again, a well-dressed young woman appears, identifies herself as a reporter for a Spanish magazine, and asks if she can take our picture for a story she is doing on the Camino. It's now mid-afternoon and the sun, so pleasant in the morning, has turned the earth into a giant oven. Sweat is pouring off our foreheads and down our backs, mixing with dust to form grimy streaks. Our faces are red from the heat and the effort, our hair matted. We look at each other and laugh.

"I guess we must look like pilgrims," I say to Juliette in French.

The reporter understands me, smiles, and says, in Spanish, "Of course I know you're pilgrims—it's written all over your faces."

She takes half a dozen shots, wishes us a *¡buen camino!* and gets into a car that is parked nearby. As she drives off, I notice that the car windows are up, which can only mean one thing on a day like this: she has air conditioning. She will arrive at her destination cool, rested, sweet smelling—and soon. I feel a fleeting jolt of unadulterated envy as I watch her drive off. I don't say anything to Juliette, but I see the look of longing in her eyes.

All day today we pass and are passed by two women about our ages, Australian sisters who introduce themselves as Jill and Lil. They walk side by side on the trail, chipper and upbeat in spite of the large shopping bag full of stuff that bounces awkwardly between them.

"We had to do something to lighten our packs," Jill explains. "I guess we didn't do such a good job of packing. Look at all we can do without," she says, pointing to the overflowing bag. "We're going to mail these things home from the next post office."

"That'll be Pamplona," adds Lil. "Another two days. If we can't get that far, we'll start pitching things. One way or the other, we have to eliminate weight."

Their problem resonates with us. Juliette has been experiencing shoulder pain all day, and it's becoming debilitating. I help her re-adjust the straps of her pack so more of the weight rests on her hips, but that brings only temporary relief. Half an hour later, we stop again, this time to re-balance her load. The pain continues unabated. She takes a double dose of ibuprofen; it has no effect. There's no getting around the fact she's carrying too much weight.

My observations over the next weeks will bear out a basic truth of the Camino: less is better, much better. Never once during the course of my journey do I hear a pilgrim complain about a pack being too light. Rather, pilgrims constantly reconsider what is essential as they seek relief from aching backs and tense shoulders. They regularly mail home nonessential items and squeeze out half the contents of jumbo-size tubes of toothpaste, shampoo, and sun screen. I observe piles of abandoned items in refugios, often extra shoes, with notes inviting anyone to please take them. The story of the Australian brothers who left behind a trail of fine wine in a desperate effort to lighten their load makes the rounds of the Camino grapevine.

As I go deeper into the Camino, these observations and my own experiences help me understand that leaving behind all the things that filled my life, literally as well as figuratively, is key to a successful pilgrimage. A heavy pack leads to a host of physical problems, including tendonitis, sprains, and blisters, not to mention pain and fatigue in all parts of the body. But it's more than just the weight. Being unencumbered makes life so much easier. Until going on this journey, I wasn't aware of how much of my time and energy were consumed by *things*—cars, home, wardrobe, yard, balky computers, for example—and all the while, I was working long hours at a demanding job and trying to be a good wife and mother.

I assumed that was just the way life was, had to be. So these first days on the Camino, I see the concept of leaving behind *things* as doing without, a deprivation that I must accept as part of a pilgrim's burden. But I get along just fine without these modern "conveniences," and gradually I understand that rather than being deprived, I am, in fact, being given the gift of time. Time and also space for my thoughts to wander at will. Time and space to savor the moment and head off into the unknown with nothing but myself. But I'm getting ahead of my story.

Juliette and I continue on our little path in the sun. The temperature is perfect for walking and the way is lovely, but now she's developed worrisome twinges in her right knee. By the time we get to the next village the pain in her knee has become unbearable. We have no choice but to stop in Zubiri. Luckily, we find a hotel room that is even better than last night's. After showering and washing out our clothes, we consider going to the refugio on the other side of town to get a stamp for our credentials but decide it's impossible to walk that far, so we head for the hotel bar instead. And that's where we learn that bars, hotels, restaurants, and even individuals, as well as refugios and churches, stamp credentials. If the stamp looks official and is signed and dated, it counts.

The next morning, Juliette is much better, a combination of resting her leg and a good night's sleep.

"My knee is fine," she declares after a few tentative steps. "*Allons-y!*" (Let's do it!)

The road out of town passes by a massive, unsightly cement factory, then becomes a pleasant path that meanders alternately through woods and across fields. The air is fragrant with the alluring scent of honeysuckle and wild roses. The sun's out, and the sky's a vivid blue.

But after just five kilometers, Juliette's knee pain returns with a vengeance. There is nothing to do but walk into the closest town to look for a taxi to the Trinidad de Arre refugio, where we plan to stop for the night. A few minutes later, we spot a church steeple visible above the trees, then a path that appears to head toward the church and, most likely, some form of civilization. We take the path, and soon we're standing in the middle of a little village. It shows no signs of life, even though it's now 10 a.m. Then opposite the refugio, which is locked up tight, a matronly lady with a bright red apron tied around her ample waist appears at the front door of a house and begins sweeping the steps. When she hears us approach, she looks up suspiciously. We wave.

"Please, señora. Is there a taxi here?" I ask, using my best Spanish. "My friend, she can't walk. Her knee, it hurts."

"*Aquí, no hay taxi,*" she replies brusquely.

Much to my surprise, she has understood me. I smile at the thought, realizing as I do that she must think I'm crazy for being happy that there are no taxis in this hamlet.

"Is there a taxi nearby?" I ask, wiping the inappropriate grin off my face. "Would you be kind enough to give us a phone number for a taxi, *por favor?*"

She looks at us. Then she turns around and yells into the house: "*Hé, Juan,* I've got some pilgrims here."

An elfish man peers down from an open second-floor window, takes one look at us, and yells back, "*Sí, ya voy. ¡Pronto!*" (OK, I'm coming, right away.)

In seconds, he's standing at the doorway and greets us with a quizzical smile.

"I'm the warden of the village refugio," he says in Spanish. "How can I help you?"

He listens patiently while I explain the problem.

"There are no taxis here, but I'm driving to Pamplona shortly on some errands. I'll drop off your friend at the Trinidad de Arre refugio," he offers. "It's a good place, and there's a pharmacy across the street where she can see about her knee."

Perfect, I think. *We need to take the plunge and try a refugio. This seals it.*

The man disappears briefly, then reappears carrying a bulging pack with a scallop shell that apparently belongs to another disabled pilgrim. He has a brief but spirited conversation with his wife, of which I understand nothing—well, maybe my Spanish isn't so good after all— then he takes Juliette's pack and puts it in the trunk with the other one.

"Come with me, Kate. Don't you want a ride?" asks Juliette plaintively.

I hesitate, reluctant to quit after just two days. "I would really like to walk," I say. "Let's meet at the refugio. I'll be there in a few hours, and we'll have plenty of time to see about your knee. You can sit in the sun and relax until I get there."

She looks disappointed but doesn't insist. The miniature car takes off in a cloud of dust, the señor waving cheerily out the window, and I walk out of town to rejoin the Camino, some five thousand miles from home, with not another human being in sight. I follow the path up a hill and into a pine forest.

Steps Out of Time

How could you ever hope to enter the
mystery of this place beyond places
unless you are silent, alone, open to the
secret voices?

Lee Hoinacki, *El Camino: Walking to Santiago de Compostela*

Chapter Four

Juliette's Bad Luck

May 31 – June 1, just outside of Larrasoaña to Puente la Reina via Trinidad de Arre (Pamplona).

The forest is magical. I'm surrounded by more shades of green than I ever imagined. Silvery ferns and emerald ivy carpet the forest floor; celadon tones of new growth pine contrast with the faded yellow of older needles; darker boxwood glistens against the soft shades of the pin oaks, whose canopy creates a dappled pattern on the undergrowth. Along sunny spots on the dirt trail, delicate pink roses add an occasional jolt of color. This is the first time I've walked alone on the Camino, and with no one to talk with, I am immersed in the forest. It is breathtaking.

After some time, the path becomes a narrow ribbon in the hot sun as it winds across cultivated fields and past little hamlets that consist of nothing but a handful of centuries-old stone houses. I'm captivated by the enormous roses in the front yard of one of the homes and can't resist taking a discreet whiff. They are less fragrant than their wild cousins, but their colors are dazzling—the jewel tones of rubies, pink tourmaline, and yellow sapphires.

I walk in absolute silence until mid-morning, when I pick up a noisy little stream. The path ducks into a forest, and I'm aware of the spicy scent of pine and the caress of a soft breeze. Birdsong becomes increasingly louder until I think I'm in the middle of an aviary. Other sounds converge—cowbells, sheep, and the rhythmic pounding of my staff hitting the ground. Wildflowers peek out from the undergrowth: forget-me-nots, bladder campion, shepherd's purse, and columbine.

The path is a ribbon in the hot sun.

The smells of wild mint, honeysuckle, sweat, and cow mix with the dominant scent of wild roses to create a surprisingly pleasant perfume: *Eau du Camino!*

I'm loving every minute, every sensation, down to the feeling of my feet connecting with the path. With each step, I feel the pull of the earth and its release as I lift my foot and move forward. Then I'm earthbound again when it touches the ground. I've been alone in the forest before and know the pleasure of solitude, but I've never experienced this intense awareness of beauty and place.

All my senses are engaged, save one, I think, *and I can fix that.* Heading for the stream bank, I find a shady spot, nestle up against a tree, and take a chocolate bar out of my pack. The day is not uncomfortably hot, but it's warm enough that the chocolate has melted. No problem. I lick it off the wrapper—it's like a hot fudge sundae without the ice cream, and who needs ice cream when you've got warm, gooey chocolate? I am amazed at the peaceful feeling that comes over me as I sit here. I'm minding my own business, thoughts wandering, and the next thing I know, I feel an overwhelming sense of . . . What *is* this sensation? Total contentment? Timelessness? Inclusiveness? Well, I like it, and that's enough for me. I sit by the stream for a long time, very much part of the physical world that surrounds me and intrigued by this new sensation. Time passes. Eventually, reluctantly, I know I must start walking again. I don't meet anyone on the trail until I arrive at the outskirts of Pamplona two and a half hours later.

The refugio where I will meet Juliette lies at the far end of a sturdy Romanesque bridge over the River Ulzama, at the entrance to the Pamplona suburb of Trinidad de Arre. Housed in a medieval monastery, this building has sheltered pilgrims for centuries. Juliette spots me as I approach the bridge and limps over to meet me, waving in slow motion with both arms. She's trying to smile, but when I see the listless look in her eyes, I'm hit with a wave of apprehension.

"*Bonjour,*" she says, forcing another smile. "How was your walk?"

"Good," I reply. "How was your morning?" I try not to sound too enthusiastic because I don't want to make her feel bad, but I suspect my beaming face gives me away.

She reports that the warden was very nice and dropped her off right in front of the refugio.

"And your knee?" I ask. "Shall we try to find a doctor who can take a look at it?"

Juliette is way ahead of me. She has already consulted the pharmacist, who took one look at her knee and arranged for her to see a doctor that very morning.

"The news is not good," Juliette says with a vexed look. "The doctor said I've got a bad case of tendonitis. I have to stop walking for five days, maybe longer. She gave me some pills and an ointment, but she says the only cure is rest."

"Maybe we could just walk slowly for the next few days," I suggest.

"I don't think so," she says, shaking her head firmly. "I called Jean [her doctor brother], and he said that if I continue walking before I'm free of pain, my knee will never heal and I could do permanent damage. Besides, it's impossible to walk through this kind of pain."

Now what? I can't argue with pain and the orders of two doctors, especially when it's someone else's knee. But my heart sinks. I can see it coming—Juliette will want me to stop walking, too. Yet if I lose five days, I won't be able to reach Santiago in time to make it back to Paris for my flight home.

We cross the bridge in silence; several minutes pass.

"Well, we wanted to stay here tonight anyway," I say, as we reach the refugio. "Let's see how you feel in the morning. At least we're near a big city. If worse comes to worst, you can take a few days off and hang out in Pamplona. Then when you're ready to walk again, we'll meet at a refugio a little farther on, one that you can get to by bus."

She shrugs her shoulders and nods. So for now, we sit on the cool stone patio in front of the refugio and wait for it to open. Jill and Lil (the Australian sisters with the shopping bag) are already there, as are a young German couple on their honeymoon and a friendly Norwegian man. Over the next hour, others join us in the shade and we trade stories, commiserate about our aches and pains, and share food. Eventually, the priest opens up for business. Short and chubby, he wears a cassock, and with his round face he looks like a white-haired cherub. Two by two, he welcomes us into his tiny office where he stamps our credentials and collects the fee.

When everybody has paid, he ushers us into the refugio vestibule and proceeds to give us a tour of the facilities, speaking in slow Spanish and pantomiming his words for the benefit of his international audience He shows us the cozy library, noting with pride its scattered assortment of books in several languages; the well-equipped kitchen; two large, spotless bathrooms, one for men and one for women; the sleeping room, with forty bunk beds lined up in neat rows; and finally a small walled garden with several clotheslines.

Then the priest gathers us around him again, wags his finger, and puts his hands behind his ears.

"*Escuchen bien. Una regla importante.* (Listen up. A very important rule.) "I turn off the lights and lock the door at 10 p.m.," he says, pointing to the

Steps Out of Time

door and turning an imaginary key. Then holding up ten fingers, he rests his folded hands against his cheek and closes his eyes.

"Tomorrow morning, you leave by eight," he continues, now holding up eight fingers, then making a shooing motion. "No exceptions. *Adiós.*"

And with a quick wave, he disappears.

I naively think it will be just this group tonight, but soon a steady stream of pilgrims begins to arrive, and by four the refugio is full and the priest is turning people away. Meanwhile, I'm busy with the refugio routine, which begins with a shower. Most pilgrims shower when they arrive rather than in the morning, both to wash away the accumulated grime of a day on the trail and to get an earlier start the next day. The water is hot, the showers have an opaque curtain, and somebody's radio is playing Miles Davis. All is well. I put on clean clothes, wash out the day's sweat-soaked items, and hang them to dry in the garden.

Juliette and I will prepare dinner at the refugio tonight, so after relaxing a bit in the garden, we visit a nearby supermarket, Juliette hobbling along as best she can. On the way back, we stop at a bakery to buy pastries for breakfast. I choose a luscious-looking *pain au raisin*, a pastry made of buttery croissant dough spread with a thick layer of *crème anglaise* and raisins and topped with a sugar glaze. The sight of it makes my mouth water.

When we get back to the refugio with our provisions, Robert, the Samaritan, waves to us from the bridge.

"Tea?" he offers, pointing to a spot halfway across the bridge where he has set up a tea service, complete with biscuits and napkins.

"Sure, why not?" I reply.

Juliette looks skeptical but acquiesces. I quickly put our groceries in the fridge, except for the bread and pastries, which Juliette sets on her bunk, and we join Robert on the bridge.

"You're limping," he remarks, looking at Juliette as he pours tea. "I hope it's not tendonitis."

She puts her napkin in her lap and nods. "I'm afraid so. I saw a doctor this morning."

"Well, you won't be walking for a bit," he comments, passing the milk and sugar.

"I have a solution," he proposes, edging closer to Juliette. "Why don't you come with me? I could use a pilgrim helper. I'll take both of you into the city tomorrow, your friend can walk from there, and you can help me minister to pilgrims. What do you say?"

She giggles, demurs, and giggles some more. He's charmed and takes her flirtations as agreement, but when he suggests a time to meet, her face turns dark and she says she can't go with him.

"OK," he says, "think about it. You can let me know tonight. I'll be in my camper, parked over there on the far side of the bridge. Come anytime. I'll be waiting for you." He smiles at her expectantly.

As soon as he's out of hearing, Juliette explodes: "There is no way I'm going with that man! You know what he's after. What is it with these Brits?" Her outburst catches me by surprise. I didn't pick up any insult or inappropriate innuendo. I suspect her reaction has more to do with being hit on regularly and the shenanigans of her British ex-husband than it does with Robert. But she doesn't want to tell him she won't go with him. Finally, we agree that I will go tell him Juliette doesn't want to be his helper. I think this is a lot of drama about nothing, but later, when I talk with Robert, he confides that she reminds him of a former lover—in short, it turns out Juliette's suspicions are correct. And when he learns she doesn't want to ride with him tomorrow, he rescinds his offer of a ride to Pamplona, declines my offer of dinner, and bids me a curt good-bye. I go back to the refugio and tell Juliette everything's taken care of, and that's when I discover that my *pain au raisin* is missing from Juliette's bunk.

"Who did this?" I cry out to the handful of pilgrims who are nearby. "I know it's only a pastry, but this is stealing!" Exasperated, I throw my arms in the air. "Isn't theft inconsistent with pilgrimage?"

Others, more experienced in the ways of refugios, are unfazed.

"Human nature," a French pilgrim tells me with a Gallic shrug. "Some things never change."

He's right. Crimes, large and small, against pilgrims on their way to Santiago are documented from the earliest days. The author of *The Pilgrim's Guide* bemoaned the ferrymen who intentionally overloaded their boats, causing them to capsize, and when the pilgrims drowned, "then the wicked boatmen [were] delighted and appropriate[d] the possessions of the dead. . . ." He railed against evil toll collectors who would beat a pilgrim who refused to pay improper fees, ". . . abusing him and rummaging into his very breeches," and warned that the Navarese and Basque people would kill a French pilgrim for nothing more than a penny. I try to put this petty theft of a pastry in perspective—at least modern-day pilgrims don't risk death (or so I believe at that moment). Maybe I'm idealizing the pilgrimage experience and need a reality check—but I don't get over the loss of my pastry until after dinner.

Juliette prepares a delicious meal—a salade niçoise followed by a slice of perfectly ripe Brie and succulent fresh figs. The bottle of Rioja she selected is very nice, with that distinctive blend of subtle fruit and oak. Later, the Australian sisters join us, and together we polish off the wine. All of a sudden it's 9:30, only half an hour until lights out. I hurry to get the dishes done while Juliette limps off to collect her laundry. Then I go over tomorrow's route, feeling both anxious and exhilarated. What will I do if she can't continue for the next few days? What will *she* do?

The priest returns and announces five minutes until lights out.

"*¡Venga! ¡Venga!*" he insists, poking his head in both the ladies' and men's bathrooms to hurry everyone along. "Quickly! Off to bed!"

He scurries around until everyone is in bed, turns off the lights, and leaves, locking the door behind him. After a few moments of whispered good nights, it grows very quiet, and I congratulate myself on recognizing the wisdom of staying in a refugio. The signs are good. I have a lower bunk, and it's near an open window. My new sleeping bag is just the right weight and quite comfortable. But before I can doze off, the Dutchman in the lower bunk to my left begins snoring. The noise is so loud and unexpected that I sit up in alarm, hitting my head on the bunk above. He sounds like a freight train. Inge, a young German woman who will become a treasured companion along the way, snarls at him in English. He stops for a few minutes—then starts up again, louder than ever. Others make comments in an array of languages with varying degrees of politeness. He rolls over, and the aural assault continues. I remember my earplugs, an item most pilgrim packing lists recommend as essential for exactly this situation, but they barely muffle the noise and I don't like having something stuck in my ears. I give up and remove them. The racket continues unabated.

Around midnight, the pilgrimage to the bathroom begins. One by one, all night long, middle-aged men get up, stumble into the bathroom, turn on the light, relieve themselves noisily, turn off the light, and go back to bed. The bathroom walls don't reach the ceiling, so when they switch on the light, it's three minutes of instant daylight in the sleeping room. Sometime in the night, I hear a piercing soprano scream—from Juliette. The person in the bunk above her stepped on her mattress when climbing down. Half asleep, she is convinced that someone is trying to get into her bed and panics. What with the racket from the snoring, nobody pays any attention.

When the first pilgrims get up at 5:30, it's a relief. The night from hell is finally over. An alarm squawks insistently. After a few minutes, the owner curses loudly and turns it off, just as a Spanish pilgrim switches on the overhead lights. Everybody—except the snorer—is exhausted. I lie in my bunk, trying to find the courage to move, when the snorer gets up. He sees me glare at him, looks right past me, takes off his briefs, and puts on his shorts, everything dangling right in my face. I close my eyes, but the odor is overwhelming, like a very ripe Munster. Burying my head in my sleeping bag, I breathe through my mouth and wait for him to go away. *What am I doing here?* I ask myself as I resist the urge to gag.

When I resurface, I wonder, as I have all night long, how it can be so stuffy right next to an open window. Examining the window in the daylight, I discover that the walls of this old convent are a good three-feet thick and, as a consequence, each window well houses two windows, one flush with the exterior wall and one flush with the interior wall. The Frenchman had opened the interior window, not realizing that no fresh air could get in unless he also opened the exterior window.

"Didn't you notice that the exterior windows are padlocked shut?" asks a German pilgrim in response to my grousing.

"How can we get fresh air?" I reply. "Don't they think about that?"

He laughs at me. "You don't know the half of it. When the priest leaves at night to go home, he locks the only door to the refugio with a key from the outside. It's not just the air that can't get in or out."

What? Doesn't it occur to the priest that we might need an escape in an emergency? I think of the hundreds who have died in nightclub fires because they couldn't escape. *Merde!* Is this an instance of having to accept a situation over which I have no control? If so, I'm not sure I'm up to the test.

A few minutes later, Juliette staggers over to my bed. Her knee is not any better, and now she is also doubled over with stomach pain, her face an unbecoming shade of yellow-green. She won't be going very far today. Jill is in bad shape, too, with painful oozing blisters. After a brief discussion, we decide to pool our resources and get a taxi to Pamplona, six kilometers away. Juliette will check into a hotel to rest and recover. Jill and Lil will see a doctor about Jill's blisters, mail home the contents of their shopping bag, and take a rest day. I will continue on alone for a few days, then Juliette and I will meet up at a location on the Camino that she can get to by bus.

We try to call for a taxi using Lil's cell phone, but when the taxi service does not answer its advertised 24/7 number, she and I go off on foot to find one. After a couple of false starts (a taxi stand with no taxis, taxis lined up at a stand but no drivers), we succeed in hailing a cab.

"*¿Peregrinas? ¿No?*" says the jovial Spaniard, peering out from behind the wheel. "I bet you want to go to Pamplona, hey? Hop in."

We go back to the refugio, pick up Jill and Juliette, and head for Pamplona, where we drop Jill and Lil off at the post office. Then our driver takes Juliette and me to a small hotel that he assures us is "pilgrim-friendly." Juliette's room is small, bland, and depressing—just a single bed up against the wall and a wooden, straight-back chair—but it has a private bath and an open window that looks out on a tree-lined street.

"By comparison to last night, it's fantastic," she says happily—and hurries to the bathroom.

Later, we go to the hotel coffee shop to get tea for Juliette and breakfast for me before I head out. We also need to decide where to meet up when Juliette has recovered enough to continue her pilgrimage. At least that's what I think we're going to talk about. Juliette has other ideas.

"Let's abandon the pilgrimage and go to a beach resort," she proposes. "I don't have enough time off to go all the way to Santiago anyway."

My jaw drops. She hasn't breathed a word of any possible issues with going all the way to Santiago, but before I can figure out how to respond, she's laying out her new plan.

"I'll be able to travel in a few days," she continues. "The Costa Brava is beautiful this time of year and not crowded yet. It's just a couple of hours from here by train. Why not?" she urges.

I want to be charitable about Juliette's physical problems, but I feel betrayed. I had no idea she wasn't planning to walk the entire distance when we discussed the trip. It might have been fine with me to do just a portion of the pilgrimage together, but I feel set up by this last-minute revelation. And I am increasingly certain that I *must* continue. The pilgrimage to Santiago has been rumbling around in the back of my mind for decades, and I have been planning this trip for most of a year. When else will I have the time to train, take a month off, and still be young enough to walk five hundred miles? (At this moment, I lack the perspective on aging that I'll gain from Theo, whom I'll meet in a few days.)

On the other hand, Juliette's eyes are pleading. My friend is sick and she's going through rough times personally. Despite her bravado, if she goes home now, I know she'll carry with her the burden of this defeat for a long time. And with one more thing to be depressed about, she'll be in even worse shape than if she had never started out on this so-called pilgrimage.

What kind of friend would go off and leave her? I know she invited herself at the last minute, even if she wasn't entirely forthcoming about her intentions. But I agreed, so now I've got an obligation to her.

I can't do it.

"I'm sure the Costa Brava would be terrific," I lie. (I'm not a beach person.) "But I need to keep going. I'm not sure why, but I have to continue on."

"It's OK, Kate," she assures me, patting my hand. "I understand." But her trembling lower lip and listless eyes tell a different story.

After some small talk about things to do in Pamplona while she recovers, I pay the bill and strap on my pack.

"I'll call you in a few days on your cell phone and we'll figure out a place to meet," I promise. "Follow the doctor's orders and you'll be ready to go in no time."

But even as I say the words, I sense she has reached a different conclusion.

Juliette nods and we exchange pathetic smiles. She looks completely defeated; I feel really low. We kiss on both cheeks, wish each other well, and I walk out of the hotel.

My route takes me through the heart of this bustling modern city, the largest on the Camino. Pamplona has been an important stop on the pilgrimage since the earliest days because of its many facilities. In 1086, for example, city records tell of a new fifty-bed hospice that provided lodging, food, and medical care to pilgrims—women only—on the way to Santiago.

Soon after leaving the city, still on sidewalks, the route goes past a field of giant sunflowers. Then it becomes a path that snakes through fields of golden barley, heading for the crest of a hill where a row of modern windmills—sleek, white wind turbines—stands guard. It's very windy, but the breeze feels good in the hot sun and makes soothing ripples across the knee-high barley. The fields of grain really do wave, I think, with a twinge of homesickness.

Pilgrimage is not just for guys.

Women have gone on pilgrimages to Santiago de Compostela since the earliest days of this tradition. They went for the usual reasons: to perform acts of devotion, do penance, seek a pardon or cure, give thanks, honor a bequest, or simply for the thrill of a great adventure at a time when pilgrimage was the only way ordinary women could hope to travel, much less travel alone. Sometimes, gender-specific motivations figured in, such as hoping to conceive a child or find (or flee) a husband.

The names of the majority of early pilgrims to Santiago, men as well as women, are not recorded, but we do have some examples of women pilgrims from that era. They include Saint Bridget of Sweden (1341); Margery of Kempe, an English mystic who bore fourteen children before she began a series of pilgrimages, including one to Santiago (1417); Queen Isabella of Spain (1486); and her daughter, Juana (1520). The Wife of Bath, Chaucer's fictional character in *The Canterbury Tales*, written in the late fourteenth century, also went to Santiago—twice. I think it's safe to assume that this lusty, headstrong woman, who was looking for her sixth husband, had a fine time. And of course, more recently, there's Shirley MacLaine . . . and me.

Thus women have always been a presence on the Camino, and though a minority, they have steadily increased in numbers. On June 30, 2002, the day I arrived in Santiago, 26.6 percent of Compostelas awarded that day went to women (64 of the total of 240). In June of 2013 (daily figures are not available), 43 percent of Compostelas awarded went to women (12,627 out of 29,374). Note that these statistics include only pilgrims who chose to wait in line for a Compostela.

Steps Out of Time

Up ahead, I see Jacques and Maïté, a French couple Juliette and I met in the refugio last night. They wave me over from their resting spot under the shade of a tree. Maïté has a round, owl-like face, Harry Potter glasses, and a long brown braid that hangs to her waist; she wears a jaunty white Panama hat. We are the same age, fifty-seven. Jacques has ruddy cheeks and sandy hair that's beginning to recede. His bright yellow T-shirt looks cheery against the brown fields. They both have welcoming smiles, though Maïté's is more reserved.

Neither she nor Jacques speaks any English, and as they have since we first met, they both address me in French using *tu,* the familiar form of "you." Initially, this linguistic familiarity among strangers makes me uncomfortable. In French, the proper way to address an adult you don't know is to use *vous,* the polite form of "you." But I soon realize that things are different on the Camino. Day after day pilgrims share bedrooms, bathrooms, hopes and fears, joys and sorrows with complete strangers, and a comfortable intimacy develops. Using *tu* acknowledges the camaraderie of the Camino at the outset by reminding us that we are all in the same boat. In no time, *tu* feels like a natural form of address on the trail.

"Où est ton amie?" (Where's your friend?), asks Maïté. When I tell them that Juliette may abandon her pilgrimage, Maïté's response surprises me.

"This is much better for you," she says unequivocally. "And for her. Your friend is not ready to make a pilgrimage yet. She's too needy, and you would spend your pilgrimage looking after her. That's not the point."

Apparently, Maïté's sentiments about Juliette's readiness to walk the Camino are correct. When I call Juliette several days later to arrange a meeting place, she is already back in her Paris apartment. I know we each did what we had to do, but I still feel deeply ambivalent about abandoning her in Pamplona, especially since her bad luck was my good fortune. Juliette was a great companion those first few days when everything was new and anxieties were high, and starting out with my friend plunged me immediately into the network of French pilgrims, which greatly enriched my experience. Yet once alone, I realized that while I loved the camaraderie of traveling with Juliette, I could enter the world of the Camino only through the times of solitude that I would have missed had I been traveling with a companion.

"Juliette will be fine," Maïté says, reading something—guilt, perhaps?—into my apparently serious expression. "Come. Join us."

So I take off my pack and go over to sit with them in the grass on this inviting hillside in northern Spain. Maïté tells me that they started out on foot from their home in a small village in Normandy a month ago and have already walked over five hundred miles. Both have recently retired,

Maïté from her job as an elementary school teacher and Jacques from his as an agricultural engineer.

"It was the perfect time for us to set out on a pilgrimage *pour faire le point*" (to see where we are and think about what's next), says Jacques.

We trade stories about our children with pleasure and longing, compare problems with our feet and shoulders, and discover that we share the same excitement tinged with uncertainty about what lies ahead on this trail that will, we hope, take us all the way to Santiago. And something clicks, perhaps because we are far from home in time and mental space as well as distance. Maïté's white Panama hat and Jacques' yellow T-shirt become familiar and welcome sights over the next month as we turn into a compatible threesome on several sections of the Camino.

After our break, the climb is unrelenting. It's that experience familiar to hikers when you think you're almost there, only to discover another crest ahead and that you're not even close to your destination. Then just when I think I can't go any farther, I hear the soft whirring of wind turbines. A few minutes later, we're standing on the Alto del Perdón, being greeted by other pilgrims—and by Robert, the spurned Samaritan, whose camper is parked on the far side of the ridge road. He chose well when he identified this summit as a spot where tired pilgrims would appreciate refreshments and encouragement. He asks about Juliette and is crestfallen when I tell him she had to stop walking, but soon he's once again the jovial host, serving coffee and biscuits to recently arrived pilgrims. A whimsical sculpture of a dozen pilgrims, including two on horseback, as well as a dog and two donkeys, dances along the summit like a parade of exuberant giant paper dolls, adding a lighthearted note to the scene at the top. (One of these figures is this book's cover girl!)

Standing on the ridge, I appreciate the spectacular view—ahead of me, to the west, lie successive mountain ranges as far as I can see, and behind me, tiny in the distance, Pamplona. But while the panorama is lovely, it is also a sobering reminder of what lies ahead. A lot of climbing stands between me and Santiago. Jacques and Maïté will stop tonight at a nearby village with a famous octagonal church. I feel energized by the break and decide to walk on to Puente de la Reina. It lies just over the first hill and past three villages that are already visible on the distant plain. The end is practically in sight.

Or so I think. I misjudge how long it will take me to cover the distance and how miserably hot it will be once I reach the plain below. When I finally drag into Puente de la Reina, I'm soaking wet down to my underwear. I have been on the trail for ten hours, the last three of them on a scorching hot path in full sun. Rivulets of sweat pour off my face and into my eyes; my shoulders feel like somebody is smashing them with a hammer. The refugio at the far end of town—my original destination—is out of the question. I stop at the first hotel I come to, an upscale place on the outskirts of town.

The receptionist takes one look at me and, before I utter a word, announces that the hotel is full, but pointing to a service staircase, offers me a bed in their refugio.

Uh oh, I think, remembering Robert the Samaritan's warning about "hotel rip-offs."

"It's a scam," he told me. "Hotels get greedy and try to make money off pilgrims by setting up refugios in unused basement space and charging twice the going rate. The karma's wrong."

Well, I'm too tired to go a step farther.

"*Fantástico,*" I say, handing the receptionist my credential and a ten-euro note.

I shouldn't have been so quick to judge. This refugio is new and spotless, with a spacious sitting area, a modern kitchen, and separate, if tiny, bathrooms for men and women. The sleeping rooms are parceled into compartments for four, with one pair of bunk beds stacked on either side of a miniscule center aisle. Although the walls of the sleeping rooms are nothing but straw shades, this simple separation makes for a quieter, more private space, and, as I will later discover, minimizes the harshness of the hallway lights when someone turns them on in the middle of the night. The refugio has no windows, but its ventilation system must surely work better than windows that don't open to the outside. Best of all, it's not crowded—I have a sleeping compartment to myself.

The pilgrims staying here are very friendly. I am particularly drawn to Catherine, who introduces herself as I am getting out of the shower. A Canadian, she is walking the Camino with her husband to mark their retirement. She smiles and chats away, buck naked and completely uninhibited. Meanwhile, I am ridiculous, trying to cover myself with my little sports towel and pretending to be nonchalant while we stand there, two naked strangers talking about the weather. She's my kind of sixty, I think. Maybe that birthday won't be so bad after all.

At seven sharp, the refugio crowd is ushered into the hotel dining room for a pilgrim menu. Restaurants all along the Camino offer pilgrims a special prix fixe dinner and, although details vary, the meal is always plentiful and cheaper than the regular offerings. Here, the pilgrim menu means three courses with limited choices, but all you can eat and drink, served family-style. This arrangement works well for everyone—pilgrims are starved and ready to eat at an early hour (for Spain), the restaurant staff can easily get us in and out before the restaurant opens to the public at nine, and the hotel makes a nice little profit from the additional seating. I have a huge plate of spaghetti Bolognese for my starter (twice what I would eat at home for a main course), followed by a perfectly cooked pan-fried trout, an endless supply of French fries, a chilled green salad, and crusty fresh bread. Dessert is yogurt. The red wine from Obaños is excellent, and each time we finish off a bottle, another one appears.

I sit next to Ian, an Australian corporate attorney and a new father. He doesn't have enough vacation time to do the entire Camino, so he's walking selected sections and taking the bus in between. This way, he reasons, he can at least sample its variety in the time he has. But he sees the trip as not just a vacation.

"Do you believe all these stories about the Camino?" Ian asks, pouring himself another glass of wine. "You know, how it's supposed to make you see things more clearly so you go home with answers. Something like that."

I tear off another piece of bread and reach for the wine. "I don't know, I'm reserving judgment," I say. "What kind of answers are you looking for?"

He sighs. "Life. How to cope. I like my work and I love my family. But my job is unrelenting. Before, I didn't have enough time for myself or my wife. Now, with a baby . . . well, it's hard to see how all the pieces fit together." He pulls out a photo of a smiling baby and his serious look turns into one of pure joy. This man is going to be a great father.

"That elusive balance, it's my litany," I say, oohing and ahhing over his adorable little child. "I've spent the last twenty years trying to figure it out. Welcome to parenthood."

Over another bottle of wine, I tell Ian about my experiences during those early years when we had demanding careers, two babies, and Philip's young son every other week. For example, the day I showed up for court in a stylish navy blue suit and pumps—one navy and the other black. In my sleep-deprived state, I had thought I was doing well to get out the door on schedule and prepared for the hearing—no time for fashion details, like matching shoes. Or how I was determined to carve out time from my law practice to volunteer as a parent-helper at kindergarten each week, inevitably returning to work with a souvenir on my clothes—a blob of red paint on my skirt, a smattering of glitter on my shoe—and a smile in my heart.

"Those were busy days," I tell this new parent, "but precious ones. I loved my family and my work. I hope I did a decent job of juggling professional and family needs, but there was never any *me* time—time to read a book or go for a walk."

"Or go to the bar with my mates," he adds wistfully.

"I know," I reply, "but I'm coming to believe that this is an inevitable trade-off, and what's more, it's OK. Those early years go by so fast."

I think to myself how hopeful it is to find men seeking to achieve a balance between work and family, self and others. Now, with more men caring for their young children, and more employers willing to make accommodations, it must be easier. Not easy, but better. I don't tell him about the guilt I still feel sometimes when I think about my efforts to balance the competing—and sometimes conflicting—needs and demands of my young family, my marriage, my job, and other responsibilities to family, friends, and community. Maybe he'll do a better job. We don't solve anything during our dinner conversation—I still wonder if the only answer is thirty-hour days—but by the third bottle of wine, we're feeling pretty good.

After dinner, I go outside to enjoy the evening air. It's Saturday night and there's a wedding party at the hotel. Elegantly dressed couples parade in and out, walking arm-in-arm. Some of them nod and wish me a ¡buen camino! I must be a pilgrim—who else would be dressed like this and sitting on the steps of a fancy hotel on a Saturday evening? Others look right past me. Their reaction reminds me of the old woman with wild gray hair and a loaded shopping cart who roams around Ann Arbor. I have a glimmer of what might go through her head when people look at her disparagingly or, worse yet, don't see her. Who is that woman and what life does she lead? How will I react the next time our paths cross?

I'm lost in thought about the experience of being invisible when I realize it's 10:15, fifteen minutes after the refugio closes. I push these uncomfortable musings out of my mind—the Camino will give me many more chances at them—and rush downstairs, hoping the door won't be locked. It's not, but the lights are off, so I fumble around in the darkness, trying to get ready for bed as silently as possible. An hour later, I'm awakened by a young Spaniard who comes in and turns on all the lights, happily whistling the Habañera from *Carmen*.

Refugios do have their ups and downs, I think, as I turn over and go back to sleep.

The peculiar fascination of the road to Santiago for the pilgrim today is that, in addition to its religious and historical significance, it seems also a continual reminder of the further ghostly journey towards *Ultima Thule*, the undiscovered land from which no traveler returns.

Walter Starkie, *The Road to Santiago*

Chapter Five

Death on the Camino

June 2, Puente la Reina to Estella.

The route the next morning begins by crossing the River Arga on the pedestrian-only medieval bridge, *el Puente la Reina* (the Queen's Bridge), for which the town is named. At the suggestion of Ian, the Australian lawyer, I take a detour on my way out of town to admire the old bridge from a vantage point on the new bridge. Following his directions, I walk past stone houses with their well-tended rose gardens, past the geranium-lined patios of several bars, and through a commercial center that's just waking up. The air is still and fragrant, the sky a melange of pastels.

When I reach the new bridge, I walk halfway across, and then, setting down my pack, I lean against the railing and gaze out over the River Arga in the direction of the old bridge. It's like looking at a life-size travel poster, but one that comes with the gentle sound of flowing water and the scents of summer. The bridge's arches are perfectly mirrored in the blue water and appear as giant orbs through which the Arga and the surrounding countryside can be viewed. Pilgrims stream across the Queen's Bridge, some in groups, some alone, body language hopeful, strolling or power walking as the spirit moves them. Their staffs bob up and down rhythmically, as if an invisible conductor were keeping the beat. When they reach the other side, they step onto a path that curves around to pass within a few steps of the new bridge.

It's tempting to continue across the new bridge, rejoin the path, and be on my way, but I decide not to take the shortcut. I want to be part of that stream of humanity crossing the old bridge as it has for centuries.

The medieval Puente la Reina over the River Arga.

It's not easy, however, to find my way back to the Queen's Bridge. For half an hour, I walk back and forth along the main road, repeatedly missing the well-marked entrance to the little lane that leads to the Queen's Bridge. I was too busy breathing the sweet morning air and admiring the roses to notice it.

When I finally step onto the Puente la Reina, I know it was worth the effort. The strength and beauty of the old bridge take my breath away. Every block of the ash-colored stone has been hand-hewn in perfect proportion, though with the most rudimentary of tools. I savor each step and love walking on these stones worn smooth by centuries of pilgrims. This act of respect for tradition is repaid with an infusion of strength and determination from my predecessors—I can actually *feel* their energy, like a sip of hot tea on a cold afternoon. Standing on the bridge, enveloped mentally and physically by the Camino, I am flooded with an extraordinary sensation of timeless calm.

Lovely, I think, *this existence removed from real life.*

I meet up with Jacques and Maïté a few minutes later, when I step off the old bridge and onto the path.

"*Tu prends le temps de vivre*" (You're taking the time to live), Jacques says, when I tell them how moved I was by first seeing and then walking across the old bridge.

I'm dumbfounded by his comment. *You mean this is real life, too?* I think. We walk together the rest of the morning, mostly in silence. I don't know their thoughts, but mine drift around this idea that real life might be more than duties, responsibilities, and accomplishments.

Around eleven, we stop for a brief rest. When Jacques and Maïté hear that I haven't had breakfast, they offer to make coffee for me on their little stove. But we decide to wait and see if there is an open bar in the next village, already visible on a distant hilltop. After four days on the Camino, the basic principle of how to site a village in the Middle Ages has

Steps Out of Time

become clear to me: put it on top of the tallest hill around. A main reason for doing this was to give villagers the advantage in case of an attack. And, of course, the church—the heart and soul of the village—had to stand at the very pinnacle, surrounded by the homes of the villagers who looked up to it for protection and guidance, then as today. These quite reasonable principles, however, have repercussions for pilgrims: the constant up and down is a major cause of the blisters and tendonitis from which many suffer. There is no question of using the flattest and most direct path from point A to point B and skipping the church. This is a pilgrimage after all.

Today follows the pattern. Shortly after leaving Puente la Reina, the Camino climbs a hilltop to the first village, goes past the church, and down the other side. It then passes through vineyards to the outskirts of the next village where the church reigns at the top of an even steeper hill. Maïté puts her head down and starts up the slope; she will go to church for the noon Mass. Jacques wanders off, and I look for a bar where I can have breakfast.

I find one just around the corner—a picturesque little place serving morning coffee on a patio that overlooks the municipal garden. Soothing sounds come from a graceful stone fountain, and in the bar's kitchen someone is browning meat with garlic and onions, the beginning of Sunday lunch. Since I am the only customer, I have my pick of tables. I choose a small round one with a blue mosaic top and two wrought-iron chairs that are positioned to face the garden. If I crane my neck and look straight up, I can see the church tower. Below it, stone houses cascade down the hillside, lush pots of purple and pink geraniums hanging off the balconies. Flocks of rambunctious swallows dart in and out of the spaces between the houses. A church bell chimes the quarter hour with a simple, tinny ring. The slight breeze feels wonderful, especially given how swelteringly hot the day has become. I sit there for over an hour, enjoying café con leche, eating yogurt and almonds, and writing in my journal.

I'm pulled out of my thoughts when Inge (the young German woman from the refugio at Trinidad de Arre) walks by on her way to fill her water bottle at the fountain.

"Look!" she says excitedly, waving a walking stick. It's well-used but beautifully carved and just the right height for her. "Providence! I found this yesterday, abandoned along the trail, waiting for me to come along. It's helping with my knee problems already. "

She has mentioned knee issues before, claiming she got them from running up and down the hills the first few days. "Running away from my troubles at home," is how she put it. Meanwhile, I tend a giant blister on my big toe. I invite Inge to share my table, but she is anxious to get to Estella, where she's heard beds are in short supply. She fills her water bottle and starts up the hill. Estella is my goal for the night, too, but it's only twelve kilometers from Puente la Reina, so I figure I have lots of time. Eventually, when the bell chimes the end of noon Mass, I feel ready to tackle the long, steep climb to the top of the village. Following the yellow arrows, I make my way up the narrow cobblestone lanes to the church. From there, the Camino descends abruptly into shadeless, uncultivated fields where it becomes a dirt path that soon merges with the ruins of a Roman road. The old road is barely distinguishable from the surrounding countryside—its large, irregularly shaped paving stones lie haphazardly on the cinnamon-colored earth. Thick patches of grass weave among them, a reminder that it's been centuries since Roman legions marched across Spain. I like the idea that the ancient path, once used by bellicose warriors bent on conquest, now serves simple pilgrims seeking their own personal—and peaceful—goals.

The air has the earthy smell of hot, dry fields; the sun beats down mercilessly. Traces of the Roman road become increasingly faint until it disappears altogether. I'm again on a dirt path that takes me through vineyards and olive groves, always with the hazy mountains in the distance. The cerulean sky is punctuated by a single white cumulus cloud, and it's *hot*. The only sounds are my footsteps, crickets, and the regular thump of my walking stick as it hits the packed dirt of the trail. When I'm lucky, a bit of wind rustles through the fields.

A village takes shape on the horizon. I hope it's Estella, where I plan to spend the night, but I can't be sure from my map. What I do know is that I'm once again soaking wet and tired beyond words, but there is nothing to do but keep plodding along. A few minutes later, the Camino heads into a tunnel under the main highway, and I am ecstatic. For a fleeting instant, I have second thoughts about going into the dark underpass alone, but my apprehension is quickly pushed aside by relief at finding some shade.

As my eyes adjust, I make out the figure of a man sitting on a ledge halfway through the tunnel. He is powerfully built with a don't-mess-with-me look, though later when he stands up to leave, I see that he's shorter than I am. Wearing a dark olive shirt and Bermuda shorts and a black beret cocked at just the right angle, he looks like a member of an elite army team. Heavy-duty black braces protect both knees. This Frenchman, named Paul, explains that he is a victim of tendonitis, developed from walking too fast and carrying too much weight. But his case isn't so serious.

"The doctor told me I could continue walking but only if I promised to go very, very slowly and get the weight of my pack down to five kilos," he tells me. "So, I sent home everything but a change of clothes, and I'm strolling through Spain."

"You sure can't have much in that tiny pack," I comment, noting that it looks ludicrous on his broad muscular back. "Do you even have a sleeping bag?"

"Nope," he confirms, "that went back, too. I stay in hotels now, and that solves the problem of bedding and towels."

He looks at his watch. "I take lots of breaks but never for very long," he explains. "If I want to make it to Estella tonight, I need to get going. It's quite a distance yet."

My heart sinks. "Isn't that Estella just ahead?"

Pulling out his map, he shows me where we are. I missed a stage when I added up the kilometers last night. The village in the distance is Lorca; it's another nine kilometers to Estella.

"Don't look so glum," he says, with a laugh and a pat on the back. "Just take your time and you'll get there."

As he stands to leave, he pulls a black tube out of his pack. I'm trying to imagine what in the world he's carrying when he snaps it open with the push of a button and an umbrella pops up.

"You should try it," he comments, seeing the surprised look on my face. "I have to walk long hours since I go very slowly. The umbrella makes it bearable to keep going in the middle of the day when the sun is so intense."

And with that, he straps on his pack, lifts his umbrella into position, and ambles off as if he were going for a walk in the Luxembourg Gardens.

"*Bonne route!*" he calls out. "I hope we'll meet again."

Sitting on a rough cement ledge in a dark, dank highway underpass that smells of diesel exhaust and shudders with each passing truck feels much nicer than it sounds. I amuse myself by looking out into the intense sunlight at the end of the tunnel and framing different canvases with my fingers—one with houses, one without; one highlighting the few trees in the distance; and another that is mostly sky. Anything to avoid having to go back out into the fierce sun.

Several minutes later, the woman I met in the shower at the refugio last night walks up with her husband. Catherine is beaming and full of energy; her husband is visibly, even worrisomely, tired. Half an hour ago, I watched them from a distance as they hesitated before a slight incline, looking for a way to avoid the climb. Eventually, they opted to walk on the shoulder of the highway instead of continuing on the path. *A dangerous place to walk,* I remember thinking.

They collapse on the ledge beside me, both drenched with sweat.

"Have some almonds," I offer. "The salt will be good for you."

I also give them a taste of my new favorite snack, a melted chocolate bar. Eating it is like licking the pan from a batch of freshly-made fudge at Christmastime. I try to hold that thought and imagine the feel of snowflakes on my face, hoping this will cool me off, but it doesn't. We chat briefly, about nothing really, then I gather up my courage and head out into the blinding light.

The last part of the day is awful. What possessed me to walk this pilgrimage? It is really hot, and Estella is really far. I can't get beyond the pain—the roiling ache of the blisters that cover my feet; the sharp, high-pitched pain in my shoulders; and the general malaise of being so hot and tired. The last hour especially is brutal, up and down on a narrow dirt trail in the blistering sun.

A kilometer or so before Estella, sopping wet and moving at a slow crawl, I flop down in the grass beside the trail to take a break. I am lying spread-eagle under a tree trying to decide if I will ever be able to move again when two Spanish pilgrims walk by.

One of them comes over, bows, and says: "*Los que van a morir, los saludan! Entiendes?*" (Those who are about to die, we salute them! Get it?)

When he starts to speak, he has a joking demeanor. Suddenly and without any warning, he looks into my eyes, and his expression turns deadly serious. *What does he see?* I wonder. His friendly manner evaporates, and he just stares at me somberly. The heat must be getting to me, I think.

"Do you need water?" his friend asks me.

"*No, gracias,*" I reply. "What I need is energy, and you can't give me that."

"*¡Ay, señora!* The fame and fortune I would have if I could give out energy on this old road," he says, with a hearty laugh and a bow.

This breaks the dark mood of the other man, who grins and nods in agreement. Then we wish each other a *¡buen camino!* and they walk on. A few minutes later, I struggle to my feet and continue on into town.

When I get to Estella, the refugio is full, but an Italian pilgrim tells me about a pensión (boarding house) on the other side of town with clean rooms and private baths for only twenty euros. It's hard to find, so he walks with me to the first intersection, then gives me careful directions to the bar where I must inquire about a room. I'm uncertain as I walk into the crowded room, but the young woman bartender catches my eye right away, smiles, and motions for me to come over. Minutes later, I have the key for a room in a modern, multi-story apartment building just across the street.

The room is a little threadbare but clean, and the hardwood floor glows. Best of all, the private bathroom looks incredibly inviting, as does the somewhat frayed but thick towel—the height of luxury after trying to dry off last night with my useless sports towel. At the thought of bathing in privacy and a real towel, my fatigue begins to dissipate. I'm just stepping out of the shower when a violent thunderstorm hits, the kind that sends your cat streaking off to her most secret hiding spot. The late-afternoon sky turns completely black. Thunder and lightning crash and flash, and rain pounding against the metal shutters sounds like a herd of galloping horses. I switch on the lights and tend to a golf-ball-size blister on the ball

Steps Out of Time

of my right foot while I wait for the storm to pass, thankful it did not hit until I was safely in my room.

After the weather clears, I walk to the refugio to have my credential stamped. Jacques and Maïté are sitting in the foyer, staring into space. Their faces are pale; they look awful.

"What happened to you?" I ask, expecting a tale of infected blisters or some other physical ailment.

"You didn't hear about the accident?" Jacques replies. "It was just a few hours ago on the main highway that you cross to get to Estella. You must have been there just about the time it happened."

Maïté picks up the story. "We were standing on a wide grassy area near the road when we heard squealing brakes and a dull thud. Then silence. I turned around and saw a car upside down in the grass and a young man wiggling out the window on the driver's side. He tried to run away, but Jacques wouldn't let him. We didn't know if he was OK, and he needed to be there when the police showed up to investigate. Another pilgrim was standing not too far from where the car landed, paralyzed and pale as a ghost. We went over to see if we could help, and he finally managed to get out that his wife was trapped under the car. But there was no sign of her. No sign of life." She hesitates. "The pilgrim under the car was Catherine."

I slump against the wall, stunned. The break we shared in the underpass couldn't have been more than half an hour before her death. I see Catherine so clearly in my mind's eye, vibrantly alive as she sat on the cement ledge laughing and relishing the chocolate I shared with her. The sight of her kind face and smile when I turned around to wave as I left the underpass is one of the images of the Camino that stays with me, even now, and it still sends a chill up my spine.

All of a sudden, a wave of mental nausea sweeps over me when I remember the words of the Spanish pilgrim outside Estella: "*Los que van a morir, los saludan!*" I somehow know—and I think he did, too—that the Catherine who died a couple of hours ago could have just as easily been this Katharine.

"Kate?" Maïté says. "Kate! Are you OK?"

"Yeah, sure," I say, struggling to comprehend what I'm hearing.

"They were standing in the grass, not even on the shoulder of the road," Jacques whispers in disbelief. "I have never felt so helpless. I didn't know if Catherine was dead or alive, but I couldn't do anything. Maybe we could have saved her. But I couldn't budge the car. I couldn't do anything," he repeats.

"I flagged down a car and went to the police station for help," Maïté says. "I was frantic by the time I got there, but the cops seemed annoyed at being bothered. When we finally got back to the scene, I figured it out. They were friends with the driver. They went right up to him and started joking around. Can you imagine? This young man had just killed someone because he got drunk at a soccer match then tried to drive home, and the police couldn't be bothered about getting the car off Catherine. Or tending to her husband, who was about to pass out from shock. Or talking to us.

"How could they not talk to us?" Maïté adds indignantly. "We practically witnessed the accident. Finally they agreed to come to the refugio by seven tonight to take our statements."

"But the warden told us not to hold our breath," says Jacques. "She's sure the police will never show up."

They never do. This region of Spain—Navarra—is autonomous and even has its own local police force instead of the *Guardia Civil*, which serves the rest of the country. Tales are rampant about police misconduct, cronyism, and abuse of foreigners here. This situation bears out the rumors. The whole thing is surreal. Then I learn that Catherine is the third pilgrim to die on the Camino so far this year, and it's only early June. The first was a man who died of a heart attack.

"It happens," says Jacques. "Pilgrims die just like everybody else."

Then there was the Brazilian pilgrim who got caught in a snow storm on the Route de Napoléon and never made it to Roncesvalles. And now, Catherine. The story goes that if you die in route, you benefit from all the indulgences you would have earned if you'd made it to Santiago and, what's more, you go straight to heaven. This is no consolation.

Numb, we decide to go to a tapas bar for a glass of wine and something to eat. The minute we walk in the door, we know it's the wrong place for us tonight, but there's no choice. Though it is almost 8:30, nothing else within walking distance is serving food for another hour, and we don't want to go to bed without eating. Everything about the place is glitzy and loud. The packed bar is brightly lit with sleek, white globes. Disco music blares. Couples and groups of friends hang out, laughing and munching from dozens of plates of appetizers, trying to hear and be heard over the music and the buzz of many conversations.

We find a table in the corner and sit there, dazed, morale in a puddle around our feet. Servers zip around, trays held high. They are laughing and friendly with the locals, abrupt and surly with us. It takes forever to get three glasses of wine, which the waiter slings our way, sloshing wine on the table and us. He throws some napkins our way and hurries off without a word. Eventually he returns with the tapas we ordered, but none of us has much appetite.

In the early days of the pilgrimage to Santiago, Estella got rave reviews: *The Pilgrim's Guide* declared it "fertile in good bread and excellent wine and meat and fish and full of all delights." Perhaps in recognition of its assets, King Sancho Ramirez chartered the town in 1090 for the express purpose of providing a welcoming safe haven for pilgrims on the long, barren stretch between Pamplona and Nájera. Over time, the town has forgotten its founding principles. Today, we experience no trace of friendliness, much less concern, from the police or anyone else.

I am so thankful for Jacques and Maïté's company this evening. Had I been by myself, I would have spent a very long, solitary, and unsettling night in my room. Instead, I sit with friends, and in the midst of the chaos, we quietly sip our wine and brood. Though drawn together by the shared experience of Catherine's brutal death, we mourn privately until, as if on some unspoken cue, we begin to talk about what we have experienced today. The partygoers and noise that surround us fade into a background blur. None of us has known Catherine for more than twenty-four hours, but we all feel profoundly affected by her fatal accident this afternoon. It was so completely unexpected—and avoidable, which makes it all the more shocking.

There is no question that the accident changes my feelings about the Camino. The energizing sense of adventure that was the defining feature until now is eclipsed by an overwhelming feeling of vulnerability. Not fear really, but an acute awareness of the fragility of human life. I suddenly appreciate the courage of my predecessors, who confronted mortal dangers daily—wild animals, bands of robbers, an unmarked route, harsh weather conditions—all of which they faced without waterproof clothing, plentiful accommodations, frequent bars, ready communications with family and friends back home, and most of the other conveniences today's pilgrims enjoy.

These early pilgrims were truly strangers in a strange land, which is the origin of the word "pilgrim," from the Latin *peregrinus*: one that comes from foreign parts. And that's exactly how I feel tonight—an outsider who must find her own way, if she is to reach her destination. I don't know about Jacques, but Maïté has found a renewed sense of purpose in today's events.

"I will ask the priests at Santiago to say a Mass for Catherine's soul," she vows.

We order more wine and are feeling slightly better when we look at our watches and realize that it's 9:50, ten minutes until the refugio locks its doors. We quickly pay the bill, then Jacques and Maïté take off at a fast trot, hoping to make it back to the refugio by closing time.

I walk briskly back to the bar across from my room. I am feeling an urgent need to hear Philip's voice, and I am sure the woman bartender will let me use the phone to make a collect call home. I haven't phoned since Saint-Jean-Pied-de-Port, five days ago, and Philip's probably wondering if I'm still alive.

My news won't be very reassuring.

*Il est même nécessaire d'apprendre à savourer
cette gratuité du passager, du fugitif,
comme Ronsard avec sa rose.*

You must even learn to savor that gratuitous
gift of the transitory, the ephemeral,
just like Ronsard with his rose.

Michel Bureau, S.J., *Pèlerin! Marcher vers Compostelle*

Chapter Six

A Pilgrim's Perspective on Time

June 3 – 4, Estella to Logroño via Los Arcos.

My alarm goes off at 5:45, but I can't will myself to get up or even turn on a light, though the room is pitch black. I lie very still, listening for signs of life. I hear none. The wind that was howling last night has worn itself out; no sounds come from the building or the street below. Only the hallucinatory images of a smiling Catherine weave in and out of my mind as I drift between degrees of wakefulness. *Still as a tomb,* I remember thinking uneasily.

I wake again at 7:30, thinking of my conversation with Philip last night. He was concerned when he heard about the accident and must have sensed my anxiety. Recalling his calm, reassuring words gives me the boost I need to get out of bed. Within minutes, I'm on my way to the bar to turn in my key and have a coffee. The friendly woman bartender of last night has been replaced by a brusque young man. He is not happy to see me, nor are the other patrons—men of all ages, from scrawny adolescents beginning to sprout facial hair to grizzled old men, bent over and toothless, with rheumy eyes. They glare at me for a long time before turning back to their coffee and conversations. The bartender ignores me.

"*Un café con leche, por favor,*" I finally say to the back of his head. Without acknowledging me, he goes to the espresso machine, prepares my coffee, and sets it down in front of me.

"*Un euro,*" he barks, staring at me defiantly.

I pay, look him straight in the eye—and am hit with an urge to laugh.

The rules of machismo are alive and well. Though I keep my mouth firm, the bartender sees the laughter in my eyes. A flicker of something approaching a smile crosses his face, but quickly disappears. His stature in the eyes of his buddies is on the line. It goes without saying that if I were young and cute, it would be a different matter. It might even be different if I didn't look quite so frumpy in my baggy, rumpled clothes that I've worn every day for a week now and my grimy walking shoes and stained white socks. A wide-brimmed Tilley hat completes my outfit. My niece calls it my "Little Bo Peep hat," which I suspect is not a compliment, but I love this hat that keeps the sun off my face and neck and also works reasonably well in the rain. The bar patrons do not care for the look, judging by their hostile stares. But they are not pilgrims. I gulp down my coffee in one swallow. I can't get out of this town fast enough.

The Camino climbs as it heads into the countryside, reaching the famous Irache wine fountain on the outskirts of town in about ten minutes. It's an elaborate affair with twin spigots, one offering red wine from the local vineyards and the other fresh water from a nearby spring. A statue of a medieval pilgrim stands in an alcove above the fountain, and on a nearby wall, a poem invites pilgrims to drink the wine if they want to arrive at Santiago full of strength and vitality. All of a sudden, a thunderous rumble announces the arrival of a group of youthful and energetic Italian cyclists. They quickly dismount, wildly excited about this fountain of free wine, each jostling to be the first to get his mouth under the wine spigot. Dressed in black and yellow skin-tight suits, yellow aerodynamically-designed helmets, and black gloves and shoes, they look like a swarm of juvenile bees fighting over a honey pot. I take a long drink of cool spring water and move on, leaving them to their boisterous pleasures.

The path makes its way across the eerily quiet grounds of the disused eleventh-century monastery of Santa María de la Real de Irache, then undulates gently through fields of grain and past prosperous-looking farms. Mid-morning, it begins to duck in and out of a scrub-oak forest. Although the little woods are crisscrossed with paths, yellow arrows clearly mark the way at each intersection, and the constant presence of pilgrims further confirms that I am going in the right direction. We exchange waves and greetings as we overtake each other on the trail—strangers, yet part of a community, bonded by our common destination.

"The birds are out in force this morning," I write in my journal, "and their singing and the presence of my fellow pilgrims begin to raise my sagging spirits." This little passage makes me smile when I reread it during a break that afternoon—I like the new perspective I am developing.

I arrive at my stop for the night, the Roman town of Los Arcos, during the siesta. It is deserted except for the occasional pilgrim, whose footsteps send up billowing clouds of dust. Dozens of minuscule shops—all closed—line the colorless main street, their grimy windows displaying an unappealing combination of practical items and American-influenced kitsch. This town is so dreary that I consider continuing on, but I'm just too hot and tired to walk any farther.

The municipal refugio that I pass on the way through town is full, so I opt for a hotel on the other side of the plaza. It's also closed when I arrive, but I rouse the bartender and get the last room, a second-floor single, bath down the hall. He hands me the key, and I go upstairs to discover a homey, comfortable little room. The twin bed is covered with a spotless white cotton spread and on the opposite wall, a white lace curtain flutters across an open window. Just right for one tired person hoping for a good night's sleep.

A couple of hours later, when siesta time is over, I go out and discover a transformed town. People of all ages are pouring into the street, chattering happily, and I quickly realize that Los Arcos is, in fact, pilgrim-friendly and charming in a small-town-in-the-middle-of-nowhere way. The villagers, even little kids, smile and wish pilgrims a *¡buen camino!* The bartenders are friendly and patient with my rudimentary Spanish. On the main square, I come across two local matrons who take issue with the practice of some shopkeepers, whom they insist charge pilgrims a higher price than villagers. These matrons, dressed all in black and looking formidable, stand guard outside the offending shops and warn unsuspecting pilgrims to go elsewhere, nodding happily when pilgrims take their advice.

That evening, I have dinner at a popular bar, then go to the Pilgrim Mass in the Church of Santa María. Built over a six-hundred-year period, beginning in the twelfth century, this massive stone structure is uninspiring from the outside, but the interior is quite simply dazzling. Elaborate and exquisitely crafted gold ornamentation decorates the church's many altar pieces, and in the low lighting, the metal glows warmly. A deep red alcove high above the central altar displays a thirteenth-century statue of Mary and the infant Jesus, their painfully expressive faces a tribute to the unknown artist who worked his magic centuries ago.

I am fascinated by the curlicue-festooned organ. The artist has painted larger-than-life human faces on several of the soaring vertical pipes, positioning them so that the openings of the pipes become mouths, complete with fierce-looking teeth. Above them, a row of magnificent horizontal pipes extend into the vast space of the sanctuary like a row of golden baroque trumpets. Carved figures of two bearded old men on either side of the organist's bench struggle mightily to support the weight of the instrument and appear so realistic that I expect to hear them groan, yet with their look of intense concentration, they are almost comical. They look right at me, reminding me that we all struggle at times, and, if we're lucky, something beautiful may result.

I sit quietly during the Mass, admiring this old church. The splendor, even opulence, of the church's interior is extraordinary—and all the more so in comparison with the austerity of its exterior and the rest of the town. I think I should be scandalized at this display of wealth in the face of the relative poverty of the villagers and the surrounding area. Instead, I see it as a metaphor for the contrast between the starkness of the exterior world and the richness of the spiritual world that continues to assert itself along the Camino.

When Mass is over, the priest asks the pilgrims to stay "*un minuto, por favor,*" and motions for us to approach the altar. We assemble around him in a ragged semicircle and he asks where we are from. Then he disappears behind the lectern, reappearing seconds later with several stacks of cards which he proceeds to distribute by language. When he calls out "English," I raise my hand. Only one other hand goes up, that of a tall, gray-haired woman with jet black eyes, who is standing next to me. "Not many of us," she whispers in her strong Scottish brogue. A photo of the church's statue of Saint James is on the front of the card. On the back, in the selected language, is the same benediction I received at Roncesvalles, the one that has sent pilgrims on their way since the eleventh century. I love this reminder that I am becoming part of an ages-old tradition.

When we all have cards, the priest invites us back to a large room that is as ornate as the sanctuary. There another priest stamps our credentials, taking the time to talk with each of us, always in our native language. By the time we've all been leisurely welcomed, it's late—the pilgrims staying in the refugio must hurry to get back before it closes, and the priests are ready to go to dinner.

"*¡Buen camino!*" says the multi-lingual priest as he gently shoos us out the door. "*May you go with God.*"

When I get back to my hotel, it's not yet dark, but exhausted, I quickly wash up and snuggle down into the blissfully clean sheets. Before taking off my glasses, I happen to look out my little window. I am awed by what I see. Layer after layer of mountains, surrounded by a soft pink haze, provide a majestic backdrop. Off to the side, remnants of a glorious sunset slice the sky with a deeper pink tinged with purple. I watch, fascinated, as a black mantle—not a clear nighttime black but the irregular black of storm clouds—silently envelopes the mountains, enclosing me in a space that feels safe and secure, in spite of the threatening weather. Against this velvety curtain, the outline of the tower of a distant church or monastery stands tall and imposing, stark yet serenely beautiful.

The perfectly tended garden of an old stone house fills the foreground of the picture. Pink and white rose bushes—so close I catch a whiff of their delicate fragrance—edge dozens of rows of carefully weeded vegetables. Unintimidated by the encroaching blackness, an old man stands in the garden, leaning on a hoe and watching the sky. He remains motionless, contemplating who knows what as I contemplate him and this living painting. I am entranced by the simple majesty of the scene—and overcome by my own inadequacies. I feel such a need to capture this moment, in words, on a canvas, through music, with a photograph. How else can the experience be preserved and shared except through a work of art? Yet I don't know where to begin.

Both mesmerized and disheartened, I continue staring out the window, and as I do, my discouragement fades, imperceptibly at first, as I am pulled into this moment. Startled, then intrigued by what's happening, I try to let go of my need to think consciously about what I am experiencing, to understand or capture it. And as I relax, I am absorbed into the scene and feel myself becoming a participant in the beauty of this moment. It's alluring and intoxicating. I am simply here, in this place, at this time, completely at peace. I savor the moment, sensing—later knowing—that I have received a precious gift. It is one that I will carry with me for a very long time.

Mortality, and thoughts of Catherine, re-assert themselves the next morning at the village cemetery, which I pass on my way out of town. It sits at the top of a small incline, and as is the custom in Spanish villages, it is surrounded by a tall stone wall with a locked, wrought-iron gate. A poem chiseled in the lintel catches my eye:

Yo que fui	I was once
Lo que tú eres,	What you are,
Tú serás	You will be
Lo que yo soy.	What I am.

I stop before the gate, struck by the blunt truth of these words. They're in such contrast to the mood many American cemeteries strive to create with their statues of benevolently smiling angels and messages about eternal life. The words on this cemetery gate strike me as a pithy version of a sonnet by the sixteenth-century French poet, Pierre de Ronsard. In very courtly and elegant language, he compares his beloved to a rose and laments the fleeting nature of beauty: "*Las! Voyez comme en peu d'espace / Mignonne, elle a dessus la place / Las, las! Ses beautés laissé choir . . .*"

(Ah, Mignonne, in how few hours / The petals of her purple flowers / All have faded, fallen, died . . .) Though the tone of the two poems is very different, both are poignant reminders of the precious fragility of life and the fleeting beauty of the present moment.

When I start walking again, I notice a tiny, wispy cylinder off in the distance. It appears to be reaching into the pale gray dawn but is so close in color to the sky that it's barely visible. Looking again, squinting this time, I see that it's the church spire in the next village. This morning will go quickly and easily. Within half an hour, I'll be in a little village bar, enjoying a freshly prepared café con leche and a pastry.

Fifteen minutes later, the spire is still only an inch high. Checking my map, I discover that it is seven-and-a-half kilometers away, a few minutes in a car. But at my pace—about four kilometers an hour, the speed of a moderate walk—it will take just short of two hours. My spirits sink. Two hours to reach a goal I can already see. How can I enjoy the moment if it takes so long to get anywhere? Will I *ever* arrive at Santiago? I can't process the idea that speed of achievement might not be the best measure. The endless path continues, and so do I, mechanically putting one foot in front of the other.

Half an hour later, still grousing to myself, I stop to pop a couple of pills for the pain in my shoulders. As I'm putting on my pack to start walking again, a pilgrim approaches. He pauses, and we exchange the usual greeting—¡buen camino!—said with enthusiasm no matter how you feel.

"*Soy Jorge, de Brasil,*" he says in Spanish. (I'm Jorge, from Brazil.)

I introduce myself, but that's as far as the conversation goes. The weather is gray, the landscape empty and lonely. Neither of us feels very talkative, though we're both happy to have company. We walk together in silence, through the first village where there is nothing but a few lifeless houses, and on to the next. This village also appears deserted, but we notice a small, inconspicuous sign for a bar on the side of a building. The door is open. We go in, down some stairs, and through another doorway. Without warning, we are in a warm and cozy space that is crammed with half a dozen long wooden tables and benches full of pilgrims caught up in animated conversation. I'm ready to start walking again as soon as I finish my coffee, but Jorge is starting in on politics with the bartender. I wave good-bye and head into the mist—better not tarry if I want to make Logroño tonight.

The bar is still in sight when the heavens open up. That expression takes on new meaning for me—it's as if someone is pouring bucket after bucket of ice water on my head. The narrow trail is cut into a steep hillside, but up ahead I see a wide level spot where I can set down my pack and put on my pèlerine. A woman about my age and two girls in their early twenties have also stopped there to put on rain gear. They speak to me in rapid-fire Spanish but slow it down when they realize I'm having trouble following the conversation.

We help each other get our pèlerines pulled down over our packs and set off together in the downpour. The woman, Suzette, is French, but will be moving to Mexico with her husband (also French) as soon as she finishes the Camino. The girls, Mariana and Sara, are art history majors from Mexico City. They explain that they are walking the Camino because of their interest in religious art, although they have been frustrated to find that churches along the way are almost always locked up tight. This threesome has been walking together for a couple of days now.

In the heavy rain, the smooth dirt of the path turns quickly into squishy, treacherous mud. We slide around, grabbing onto each other for support. Soon, we are all splattered with dripping brown goo; tenacious globs clump to the bottom of our shoes, making our feet so heavy we can hardly lift them. Suzette insists the problem is caused by our poor walking techniques, which she happily critiques for the next ten minutes. None of her ideas help—the suction created each time we put a foot down continues to turn every step into a struggle. I try to clean off our shoes with my walking stick, but—as Suzette warned—it's a wasted effort. Two steps and we are once again tottering along on a four-inch platform of mud.

Even in these miserable conditions, Mariana and Sara remain upbeat and walking with them is energizing and fun. They tell me about their boyfriends and their studies and want to know all about my children and my life. I am surprised that they are content to walk with Suzette and me. We are, after all, the age of their mothers, maybe even their grandmothers, but when I mention this to them, they look at me like I'm from Mars.

"We'd never dream of doing this with our own mothers! *¡Qué loca!*" (You're crazy!), they say.

"But why?" I ask. "I'm sure your mothers are very nice. They have to be to have raised you."

"Our mothers want to control us. They treat us like children," they explain.

Hearing these two young women verbalize their need to be respected as autonomous adults and realizing that they really *are* adults has the force of revelation. If I fall and break a leg tomorrow, the trip will be worth it if I can remember just this single conversation.

Though I know my children—who are the ages of these young women—are adults, I finally grasp that I haven't yet accepted this fact on a gut level. *No wonder,* I think defensively. How can I forget the experience of holding my newborn child, witnessing first steps, marking the childhood events and transitions in which I took such deep—and unexpected—pleasure? And it all happened in the blink of an eye. Though the changes seemed imperceptibly slow at the time, the cumulative effect kicked in. Before I knew it, my babies had moved from childhood to adulthood, from one plane of existence to another. I'd hoped they would, of course. But what wasn't so apparent to me was that the dynamics of the parent-child relationship also needed to evolve, and for that to happen, I, too, had to change.

I'll always be a parent to my children (and a child to my parents), but what I understand on this day on the Camino, walking beside these strong and competent young women, is that a parent must not only recognize but also respect the adult child's autonomy. This doesn't diminish the love, but it does change the nature of the relationship. Old patterns and habits (not all good ones) are well-established, and acknowledging and accommodating this shifting ground is not easy. Yet talking with these young women makes me vow to embrace the transition, and the more gracefully, the better. It's the implacable movement of time at work, once again.

Savor the moment, Ronsard says.

But accept that it will pass, the Camino replies.

The rain eventually stops, although the sky remains leaden and the path slippery. The vistas, however, are terrific, and the trail is often lined with bright red poppies and purple thistles whose colors glow in the gray of this day. About four kilometers from Viana, I stop for a snack and a break from Suzette's constant chattering, while she and my young friends continue on.

I've just started walking again when Jorge catches up with me. He's more talkative now.

"I'm here because I need to take time to think about the direction of my life and my priorities, and I know the Camino will help me," he says. "It was hard to get a month off. I'm an engineer and we're in the middle of a three-year project. But I told my boss that either I could have the time to make this pilgrimage, or I would quit. He gave me the time."

"I can't imagine a U.S. firm giving an employee a month off for a pilgrimage," I say.

"We're a Catholic country, and my boss is very faithful," Jorge offers by way of explanation.

"I have four reasons for making this pilgrimage," he continues, and engineer-like, he lists them. "One, I want to get in better physical condition. Two, I want to improve my self-esteem. Three, it is to reaffirm my religious faith, and four, I want to understand the mystery of death."

This last one catches me by surprise.

"Number four is the hardest," I say. "I think the best you can hope for is acceptance. It's that line from Manrique's poem: '*Nuestras vidas son ríos que van a dar en la mar que es el morir.*' (Our lives are rivers that flow into the sea which is death.) Do you know it? I used to think the image was pessimistic and frightening. Now, it strikes me as a realistic assessment of our human condition."

Jorge likes the line of poetry, which he hadn't heard, but is startled that I question his ability to understand death. He is confident that he will be able to reconcile his scientific understanding of death as the end of any physical, tangible sign of life with his belief in the Catholic faith and its teachings of eternal life. I am less certain he will find the understanding he seeks, though I hope he will.

At the outskirts of Viana, we catch up with Mariana, Sara, and Suzette. Jorge, who is a smart, good-looking, well-educated man in his mid-thirties, behaves like an awkward teenager around the young women. He's nervous, his comments are inappropriate, and his jokes are not funny. He wants desperately to impress them but is tripping all over his feet and his tongue. I see why he wants to work on his self-esteem. The girls are merciless, mocking and taunting Jorge every time he opens his mouth, though his Spanish is flawless. Perhaps Sara's knee has something to do with her attitude. It started hurting when we were battling the mud and got progressively worse to the point where now she can't walk without terrible pain. She's also exhausted.

"I didn't sleep even a second last night," she complains. "The man above me snored constantly. It was like the world's longest freight train rumbling past my ears."

There is no question of going any farther today for them. When we reach Viana, they go directly to the refugio. Jorge continues walking, and I stop for a sandwich at a bar that caters to pilgrims. Later, I'm filling my water bottle at the fountain in the cathedral square, preparing to head out, when Jacques and Maïté walk up and invite me to have lunch with them. Why not? We go back to the bar I just left, where the bartender greets me as if I am a regular. Forty-five minutes and a second lunch later, we start out together for Logroño. The sky is still dark and threatening, but at least we don't have to contend with the merciless sun, and it's cooler now, after the rain.

About an hour from the city center the rain starts up again. At first, it's a monotonous drizzle. Within twenty minutes, deafening thunder makes conversation impossible, lightning flashes all around us, and it's once again pouring. We arrive at the Logroño refugio in the late afternoon, exhausted from walking some thirty kilometers in mostly awful weather. Happily, the refugio still has beds and is well-kept. A fountain burbles away in the garden, oblivious to the downpour, while forlorn-looking white plastic chairs suggest sunnier days. Inside, the common area has comfortable reading chairs and sofas. One corner is set up as a computer station with two computers, both with Internet connections.

The sight of these machines is electrifying. E-mail! I get in line immediately, excited at the idea of a keyboard under my fingers, thinking of all the messages I'll send and anticipating all those that will be waiting for me. But wait, I can't access my e-mail account. I changed my password before I left for Europe and do not remember the new one. Elation turns to despair—and back to elation when I realize that it's only 11 a.m. in Ann Arbor. I can call my secretary to find out my new password. Then I remember my son's face when I showed him my packing list.

"You're really not taking your laptop?" he said. "Wow, Mom, you'll be away forty days. Are you sure? You've never gone more than a couple of days without checking your e-mail. How will you manage?" he asked with concern.

Second thoughts creep in. I am increasingly drawn to this difficult, weird, and wonderful place that is the Camino, but I think that the price of admission may be to set aside the activities, concerns, and pleasures that consume my time at home. Maybe logging on—catching up and reconnecting with all I left behind—would not be a good thing. I stand in line for some time, but when my turn approaches, I make my decision. Much as I want to touch base with my "real" life, I want even more to try to experience the Camino on its terms, not mine.

I turn my back on the machines and slowly the urge—and the afternoon—pass.

Je panse, donc je suis.

I bandage, therefore I am.

Luc Adrian, *Compostelle: Carnet de route d'un pèlerin*

6-06-02

Chapter Seven

Rain and Pain

June 5 – 6, Logroño to Santo Domingo via Nájera.

The next morning, the clatter of rain against the windows pulls me out of a nightmare in which I am slogging through waist-deep mud. Bleary-eyed, I look around and discover not a lake of mud, but a cavernous room crammed with bunk beds. It's only 7:15, but the sleeping room is empty except for Jacques and Maïté, who are just beginning to stir, and me. The kitchen is also deserted when we go downstairs fifteen minutes later. We eat in silence, three slumped figures lined up in a row at the long kitchen table with our backs to the window and the gloomy weather. Not one of us is ready to face a second day of walking in the rain.

Finally, Maïté breaks the silence. "*Alors, les amis?* " (Well, friends?)

We wash the dishes, put on our backpacks and pèlerines, and go out into the downpour. Yellow arrows lead us through town on a paved path, but when we reach the city limits, they appear to point away from the path and down a steep, muddy slope. Right into a pond-size puddle.

"*Merde*," says Jacques, "tell me that's not right."

"They can't mean for us to go down there," I agree. "Let's stay on the path."

We continue on, but after just a few steps, we notice a crew of construction workers in a field off to our right who are waving their arms wildly—at us. They call out in pidgin Spanish thick with the music of the west coast of Africa.

"*¡He! ¡Hola, peregrinos!* Look! Here, this way," they say, pointing down the slope we want desperately to avoid. "Please! No that way."

We wave an acknowledgment, backtrack, and look at the arrows again. Rivulets from the heavy rain race down the treeless hillside.

Maïté sighs. "I think they're right. The arrows point down there."

She takes a few steps and slips to her knees. Jacques tries to grab her, but his feet slide out from under him, and he ends up sitting in several inches of mud. I plant my walking stick, reach out my other hand to help them, and we try again, slipping and sliding all the way to the bottom, where Jacques wades into the standing water.

"Look," he says. "It's only up to my ankles. Just enough to wash off my boots."

Maïté and I roll our eyes.

The rain doesn't let up until a couple of hours later as we arrive at the first village. The first bar we come to is a nondescript place, but it turns out to have fantastic homemade food. We wolf down huge bowls of delicious soup, thick with whole cloves of soft roasted garlic, and a loaf of crusty country-style bread. Then, still hungry, we savor equally generous servings of tasty lentil soup, well-seasoned with big slices of chorizo, and another loaf of bread. This time we add a glass of Rioja, the local red wine, and finally, tea and cookies. The bartender watches us in amazement. I'm amazed myself at how much I can eat on the trail. (And in spite of eating all I want the entire time I'm on the trail—including generous quantities of chocolate, almonds, and beer—I lose eight pounds during the time I'm gone.)

After this "farmer's breakfast," as Jacques calls it, we're finally warm, dry, and full. It's pouring again so we're reluctant to leave our cozy little table, but eventually we bundle up, refill our water bottles at the town fountain, and hit the trail.

Then we walk.

And walk.

And walk.

In the mid-afternoon, the rain turns to hail. Jacques's leg hurts. Maïté aches all over, and the blister on my big toe is sending shooting pains up to my hip. The three of us are freezing our butts off, but there is nothing to do but keep walking. By the time we reach the eleventh-century monastery that houses the Nájera refugio, we are about to collapse.

The massive front door is open, revealing a very blond Spanish lady, fiftyish and stern, who stands before a small table with a cash box.

"*Credenciales*," she demands.

We hand them over.

"Three euros each, *por favor*."

We pay.

She points to a narrow staircase that leads to a landing with bunk beds. "That way," she says, without even the hint of a smile. "You have three bunks in the mezzanine, numbers four, five, and six, two lowers and an upper."

Bad luck on both counts, I think, a grumpy warden and beds in the overflow room. I turn out to be wrong about the bed assignments. The mezzanine has only ten beds and is relatively quiet, whereas the main sleeping room on the third floor has fifty beds, and we learn the next morning that they were filled mostly with snorers.

"I'll take the upper, *mesdames*," says Jacques.

He and I flop down on our bunks. The mattresses protest with a squishy sound. They are foam rubber and not new. Maïté heads for the shower while Jacques and I compare notes about tomorrow's route. It will be an easy day, we agree, only twenty-one kilometers. After eight days of walking, I know that I can do twenty-some kilometers without a problem. It's not until I approach thirty that I struggle.

"The water could be hotter," Maïté says, when she gets back.

I go down and give the shower a try. One push of the button, and I let out a howl.

"Madam, are you well?" asks the startled young Italian in the next shower stall, which is separated from mine by a shoulder-high wall.

"No! Well, yes. I guess I'm OK," I say. "This water's pretty cold."

Reassured, he goes happily back to his aria. "Take courage, madam."

In fact, the water is freezing, the shower drafty. I'm chilled to the bone and my blisters hurt. Washing my hair is out of the question; in fact, if I hadn't already soaped up, I'd forget about a shower today, in spite of the fact I'm covered with mud. Monastic conditions suck. I dry off as best I can with my pathetic sports towel and put on all of my clothing—both pairs of pants, all my shirts, my jacket, two pairs of socks, everything except my pèlerine—and go to the common area to assess the damage to my feet. The blond warden notices me sitting there with my foot in my face, comes over, takes one look at the impressive blister on my big toe, and says to me in Spanish, "Blister. Very bad. Me take care of it."

I sigh, wishing she didn't think she needed to use baby talk to communicate with me. Then I realize I'm focusing on the wrong thing. She is trying to help me, not insult me. I start to thank her, but she's already hurried off. She reappears a minute later with a large tray full of bottles of all sizes, tape, bandages, scissors, and needles.

"I've seen the refugio blister expert take care of bad feet many times. I know exactly what to do," she assures me.

I'm a little nervous—it isn't clear to me if she has any actual experience treating blisters. On the other hand, she's well-prepared, whereas I have only a small tube of first-aid cream. Besides, I can't get my toe in a position to see what I'm doing.

Tricks to avoid blisters

"It would be impossible to overstate how much your feet hurt when you walk the Camino de Santiago." — Hape Kerkeling, *I'm Off Then: Losing and Finding Myself on the Camino de Santiago*

It is also impossible to overstate the importance of footwear.

To avoid blisters:
- Wear good quality, well-fitting boots or shoes that you have tested on long walks over varied terrain.
- Wear good quality, well-fitting socks made of a durable fabric that wicks moisture, such as washable wool or a synthetic blend.
- Take off your boots every few hours, especially on hot days, to give your feet a break and air out your boots. If your socks are wet and sweaty, change them. Moisture is your enemy.
- Treat hot spots immediately. Do not wait for a blister to develop.

Here's another less-well-known tip that I learned from my Idaho friend, Bee, when we walked a section of the pilgrimage route in France to celebrate our sixtieth birthdays. Mid-way through the trip, I developed an excruciatingly painful infected blister. When it healed, I was ready to do anything to avoid more blisters, so I agreed to try something Bee had been urging me to do for years: I coated my toes with petroleum jelly in the morning before putting on my socks. To my surprise, this admittedly greasy remedy worked like a charm. I highly recommend it.

"*Vale,*" I tell her, "*gracias.*"

She pulls up a chair, sits down opposite me, and pulling on a pair of new rubber gloves, she sets my foot in her lap and cleans my toe with a vile-smelling brown gel. Then she takes out a large needle from a sterile packet and starts jabbing awkwardly at my toe, dabbing at it with a piece of cotton as it drains. (Fortunately the operation was painless.) After cleaning my toe again with the smelly stuff, she goes off to find some gauze. Meanwhile, other pilgrims begin to gather.

David and Christine, a young French couple, lean over and whisper in my ear, in French.

"That's not how to treat blisters, not like that," they insist. "You must run a needle and thread through the blister, in one end and out the other, being very careful not to pierce the area outside the blister, or the pain will be excruciating. Then you cut off the needle and leave the thread in place overnight so the blister can continue to drain. And don't cover it—blisters heal better if they are exposed to air overnight."

They show me their feet. White threads stick out of their heels and toes at wild angles. When the warden comes back, I try to tell her that I will use David and Christine's method on my other blisters, but my Spanish is not up to the job. She goes off and returns with a needle and thread, ready to experiment with their method—on my toe. I am trying to thank her and leave when The Blister Expert walks in. He takes one look at the needle and thread and says something I don't understand, but it can only be an emphatic "No Way." Motioning for me to put my foot back on the chair, he says something else I don't catch, but I get the gist.

The Blister Expert.

"*Sí, señor,*" I say with a salute, doing as he directs. It's clear I have no choice unless I want to go back out into the rainy night.

He puts on a pair of sterile gloves and carefully examines the blister.

"Do you mind if I take a photo?" I ask.

Surely this is as much a part of the Camino as the churches and landscapes. He gives me a funny look but nods, so I take a shot of my foot in his lap and the top of his balding head, bent in intense concentration. Other pilgrims watch him work, with looks that range from adoration to terror.

"You did a fine job," The Blister Expert tells his watching colleague. She beams.

Then he turns to me. "Leave the dressing in place tomorrow for walking, and let it come off naturally. Your foot will hurt tonight, but you'll be fine by morning."

I thank him very sincerely, realizing as I say the words that my foot has already stopped hurting.

By now, a long line of fellow sufferers has formed, and for over an hour, he meticulously treats each one. Meanwhile, my new French friends inspect his handiwork. They agree that he's done a good job, though they still insist that their method is superior. Later that evening, the blond warden comes over to check on my foot, and we discover we both speak French, which means we can have a conversation. When she learns I'm from the U.S., she's eager to tell me about her travels in Canada.

"It was a wonderful trip. I love North America. In fact, I've thought about going to the United States, too, but it's too foreign and too dangerous," she declares. "You know, the guns and all, it's just not safe. And drugs—they say anyone can buy them, no problem. Then there are all the foreign tourists who get murdered in Miami."

I try to counter her exaggerated views by talking about everyday life in Ann Arbor, but I do not succeed in changing her opinion or persuading her that the United States is no more dangerous than any European country, all things considered.

"Next time I travel," she says, "I will go to Mexico."

Now there's a safe place! I think in amazement.

She also tells me about her commitment to the Camino. This woman, whose name I never learn, travels to Nájera from her home one hundred kilometers away several times a year to run the municipal refugio. One of several volunteer wardens who staff the refugio year round, she is on duty 24/7 during her one-week stints. Her compensation? Whatever satisfaction she gets out of handling a different crowd of pilgrims each night, many of whom are tired and testy.

She's starting to tell me how she has recently completed the Camino by walking ten days each summer for four years, but our conversation is interrupted by the arrival of five Spanish cyclists, all women. They are wet and tired, and it's dark and raining again, but the refugio is full as are all other local accommodations. The warden takes pity on them and agrees to let them sleep on the floor in the common area. There's lots of commotion as pilgrims help the warden move tables out of the way and bring up tattered mattresses from storage. Then it's 10 p.m. and lights out.

The next morning, the warden starts patrolling at 6:30. Prompted by her insistent urging—"Get up! Get up! Pilgrims don't sleep all day!"—I manage to crawl out of my warm sleeping bag and face the morning chill. Jacques, Maïté, and I breakfast together, a feast of bread, butter, chocolate, herbal tea, yogurt, and luscious fresh peaches. When we leave the refugio around 7:45—once again the last ones to go—it's still raining, and the sky is a swirling pattern of dark and light. Our flapping pèlerines sound like tacking sails, which makes me think of a sailing trip with my dad several years ago. But try as I may, I can't remember what it feels like to be gently rocked by a warm breeze. We force ourselves to move briskly, even though we're feeling sluggish, because the minute we slow down we start to shiver. Our only break is a quick lunch stop of pooled resources, which we eat huddled against the wall of a deserted building that offers a little shelter from the frosty gale.

Tonight we will stay in Santo Domingo, a Camino town named after the eleventh-century hermit who cleared a road through the treacherous forest west of Nájera, hence the saint's name, Santo Domingo de la Calzada (Saint Sunday of the Causeway). He also built and tended a pilgrim hospice in this town, which the Spanish government transformed into a luxury hotel called a *parador* many centuries later.

"Of course, real pilgrims don't stay in luxury hotels," I explained to an Ann Arbor friend during a pre-pilgrimage lunch. "Too bad for me. I love nice surroundings and good food, but it's just inconsistent with the pilgrim way," I said with conviction, as if I knew what I was talking about.

"I think you've got this all wrong," she replied. "What about the kings and queens who went to Santiago on a pilgrimage? You better believe they didn't stay in refugios, not if they're as bad as you say. Just pretend you're from a noble family and experience the pilgrimage from that perspective for a night."

I hesitated. Her argument was very tempting.

"Besides," she continued, "didn't you tell me that three of the four paradores on the Camino are located in old pilgrim hospices? You'd be literally following in the steps of your predecessors. Surely there's nothing wrong with that."

In the end, I reserved at all four Camino paradores, making my best guess at arrival dates and tucking the hotel phone numbers in my passport, in case I didn't get there on time or changed my mind. The Santo Domingo parador is the first of the four, and I will stay there tonight, although I remain ambivalent—so much so that I don't tell Jacques and Maïté where I am staying, only that I'll go to a hotel. We part ways in the town center, where a sign takes them down a side street to the refugio, and arrange to meet later at the Pilgrim Mass.

The lobby of the Santo Domingo parador radiates elegance. Immense bouquets of fresh flowers decorate massive oak tables that shine like mirrors; classical music plays softly. All the men in the lobby are wearing suits and ties; the women are elegantly dressed and accompanied. Except me.

Paradores

The Spanish government established a chain of luxury hotels called *paradores* in the 1920s for the dual purposes of providing hospitality for travelers and rescuing historic buildings that were falling into disrepair. Most are in old castles, monasteries, convents, palaces, manor houses, or pilgrim hospices that have been updated to modern standards. Parador dining rooms typically feature local cuisine and wines. For more information, see the parador website at www.paradores-spain.com/

What am I doing here? I wonder. *Maybe I'd better leave before they ask me to go.* But my need for privacy and a hot shower prevails over principles and pride. Besides, the blond warden last night in Nájera told me to be sure to have coffee at the Santo Domingo parador, which she described as "special and very historic for pilgrims."

I walk up to the desk clerk, who wears a well-tailored black suit and has perfect teeth and sultry dark eyes.

"*Tengo una reserva*," I say in my most confident Spanish. "*Me llamo Kate Soper.*"

He doesn't bat an eyelash when he looks at me. In fact, he smiles. "*Buenos días, Señora Soper,* and welcome. We've been expecting you. We're glad you're staying with us."

I am amazed at his warm reception. They must be OK with pilgrim guests.

"Let's stamp your credential before we forget," he continues, motioning for me to hand him my pilgrim passport, which he stamps, dates, and initials with a flourish. Then he hands me a black and gold pen and asks me to sign the guest register while he studies his computer monitor.

"Perhaps this pilgrim would like a room with a view," he muses out loud.

Handing a brass key to the hovering uniformed bellman, he turns to me.

"I wish you a very pleasant stay, madam. Now Manuel will show you to your room."

What? My only luggage is my small pack on the floor beside me, and the elevator is just a few steps away.

"*Por favor, señora,*" says Manuel. He picks up my grubby backpack and motions for me to get in the mirrored elevator with its polished brass trim.

"*Un momento,* I need to take off my shoes," I tell him. He starts to object, but one look at my mud-caked, soggy shoes, and he nods discreetly.

"Perhaps it would be better," he says with a little bow, but he insists on carrying them.

When we get to my room, Manuel heads straight for the window, draws back the heavy gold curtains, and waits for my reaction. The Romanesque cathedral that fills the frame appears close enough to touch, its yellow bricks illuminated by beams of sunshine that pierce the storm clouds. The deep rich sound of its bells fills my room with music.

"*¡Es magnífica!*" I say, moved almost to tears by the combination of the kindness of the staff, the luxurious surroundings that are *mine* for the night, and the magnificent view.

Manuel nods in agreement, then shows me around the room, explaining its many luxurious features. I can't believe that he's treating me like a real guest, in spite of my grubby attire and dirty face and hands. Then it occurs to me that his respectful behavior may be *because* I am a trail-weary pilgrim. He's Spanish, after all, and the Camino is part of his national heritage. Whatever the reason, I am grateful and give him a good tip. He smiles, offers a snappy little salute, and disappears.

Within minutes, I'm soaking in the oversize bathtub, armed with a cold beer from the minibar and plenty of bubbles from hotel shampoo. *Which is the greatest luxury*, I wonder, *the privacy, the hot bath, the phone from which I can call home without waiting in line, the down pillow, the fresh-smelling towels?* I take another swallow of beer. Maybe I'm just not pilgrim material. Don't pilgrims scorn creature comforts? I am supposed to be in the refugio with Jacques and Maïté, taking a cold shower. I wonder if staying here will disqualify me from getting a Compostela. Not that I care. We aren't all cut out to be pilgrims, I decide philosophically, as I take another long sip of beer and sink back into the warm water and bubbles.

When I finally get out of the tub, one giant but happy prune, new blisters on my little toe have puffed up. I perform surgery using my French friends' string method, then I put on my clean set of clothes and go to the cathedral to meet Jacques and Maïté. They are not there, and nothing is happening. A priest tells me that the Pilgrim Mass is in a different church tonight and gives me explicit directions, but either the directions are incorrect or I misunderstood them. I can't find the church, even after several more sets of directions. Meanwhile the rain is getting heavy again, so I give up and go back to the cathedral to look around.

I do a double take when I hear cackling chickens behind me. High in the west wall of the south transept, a white hen and cockerel strut about in an elegant Renaissance chicken coop. This unlikely pair bears witness to a medieval legend (some would say miracle) of the Camino, the story of the *pendu dépendu*, the hanged man who was unhanged.

According to the local version of the story, a young man and his parents were on a pilgrimage to Santiago and stopped for the night at an inn in Santo Domingo. The innkeeper's daughter took a fancy to the young man, but because he was a devout pilgrim, he refused her advances. Furious, she hid some silver in his pack and cried thief when he left town the next morning. The silver was discovered and, without further ado, the young man was hanged. His heartbroken parents continued to Santiago, but when they passed through Santo Domingo on their way home, they were astonished to discover their son still hanging from the gibbet—and miraculously still alive.

"It was Saint James," he told his ecstatic parents. "He supported my weight and kept me from strangling until you could return and rescue me."

The parents cut their son down and rushed off to tell the town official about the miracle that had happened, arriving just as he was sitting down to a dinner of roasted chickens.

"Your son is no more alive than my dinner," he said mockingly, and at that moment the chickens on the platter sprouted feathers and flew away.

The pair of chickens that now live in the cathedral are said to be descendants of the twelfth-century official's botched dinner and a reminder of the miraculous power of Saint James. They used to be kept at eye level, but pilgrims insisted on yanking off feathers for good luck, so today's descendants are well out of reach, fully feathered, plump, and pampered.

My mouth watering, I return to the parador for my evening meal. The Gothic stone arches and coffered wooden ceiling of the dining room are bathed in soft light that shows off the skill of the medieval craftsmen. "[Entering the parador] is like stepping back in time when the church was the richest body and the rich and famous made their holy pilgrimages," proclaims the parador literature. Right on. The maître d' gives me a corner table and is very attentive. I wonder if he notices the white threads sticking out of my feet. If so, he pretends not to see them as he helps me select a menu of regional specialties—a perfectly seasoned casserole of snails, ham, and tomatoes followed by oxtail-stuffed peppers in an impossibly delicious red wine sauce, and a superb local wine, a *Ribera del Duerna*. For dessert, I take his suggestion and order a *tarta de Santiago*, a tasty almond cake with a powdered sugar scallop shell stenciled on top, followed by an infusion made from local herbs.

By the time I climb into bed, I feel pretty good, until I notice that my left foot is a brownish red and purple color. I start to panic at the thought of the Italian pilgrim who almost died from a blood infection that she picked up on the Camino, a combination of oozing blisters and unsanitary refugio conditions. But exhaustion trumps fear of death. I sink back into my soft down pillow, unable to make any other movement or even consider what else I might do (if I could get out of bed). A soothing breeze and the sound of a gentle rain float in through my open window.

Un véritable pèlerinage consiste à tout laisser. . . . Laisser ce qui rend notre vie de plus en plus rapide et élaborée. Mais aussi laisser— c'est peut-être le plus difficile—l'idée que nous nous faisons de nous-mêmes et des autres.

A true pilgrimage consists of leaving everything behind. . . . Setting aside that which makes our lives increasingly fast and complicated. But what is perhaps most difficult is leaving behind the perceptions that we have of ourselves and others.

Luc Adrian, *Compostelle: Carnet de route d'un pèlerin*

2-6-2009

Chapter Eight

A Pilgrim's Progress

June 7, Santo Domingo to Belorado.

I wake to a clear sky—the first in three days. Then I remember about my foot and, taking a deep breath, I pull it out from under the covers. I expect to find an oozing purple mess, but it's reassuringly pink, with just a few white threads hanging out. Relieved and thankful, I throw on my clothes and go downstairs for a simple breakfast of coffee and a roll before I start walking.

But a parador breakfast turns out to be anything but simple. When I arrive at the dining room, I discover a lavish buffet, spread out over three enormous, tiered tables. Draped with white linen cloths and decorated with fresh flowers and greens, they look like giant wedding cakes. One is crammed with platters of luscious fresh fruit, trays of sliced local cheeses, bowls of fresh goat cheese, and plate after plate of different kinds of sausages and hams. Another table features a dozen silver warming dishes, their contents hidden by gleaming covers; breads of all shapes and sizes; and a variety of spreads. The third table is loaded with cakes, cookies, pastries, and other sweets, pitchers of juice, and a big silver bowl of yogurts on ice. Black-suited waiters serve steaming, fragrant coffee from silver pots; people talk in quiet voices as silverware jingles against china.

Jorge, my Brazilian friend, is returning to his table after visiting the buffet. He juggles two large dinner plates, both overflowing, and has a kid-in-a-candy-store grin on his face.

"*¡Hola!*" he calls out with a nod. "*¡Muy buenos días!*"

I wave back. Jorge is certainly getting his money's worth. This feast costs only eight euros for all you can eat, and he has enough to tide him over until breakfast tomorrow. But I can't imagine eating such a big meal before starting an all-day walk.

"Is it possible to get something light?" I ask the head waiter when he arrives with a little bow to show me to a table. "A pastry and coffee, perhaps?"

His welcoming smile vanishes. "Certainly not, señora. You see before you what we offer for breakfast. I assure you that everything is fresh and delicious."

"You have a lovely spread," I agree, "but it's much more than I want this early. Can't I get just coffee and a roll? *¿Por favor?*"

Jorge overhears the conversation, sets his plates down, and jumps right in.

"Surely she can get just a snack," he interjects, rather authoritatively it seems to me.

"*¡Imposible!*" insists the waiter petulantly. "We only have a buffet at breakfast."

"The policy of all or nothing is ridiculous," Jorge proclaims, looking surprised at the waiter's refusal.

"A rule is a rule," responds the waiter firmly.

"All I really want is coffee and a pastry," I repeat meekly.

Jorge and the waiter lock eyes, and their voices rise as they stand there in the middle of the very chic dining room debating the merits of the parador breakfast policy. It becomes quickly apparent to me that this is a chauvinist *pas de deux*: Jorge—who is three times as big as the diminutive waiter—is determined to help me out, but his opponent is not budging an inch. Finally, Jorge throws up his arms in exasperation. The little waiter puffs out his chest, and with the smirk of a victor, he cranes his neck, dismisses Jorge with a withering look, and turns to me.

"There's a little bar around the corner where you can get something light, señora. Why don't you try it?" he murmurs, struggling not to gloat. "It's right on the Camino. You can't miss it, and it opens early."

"*Vale*" (sounds good), I tell him, relieved that this embarrassing scene is over. "*Gracias.*"

The waiter offers a perfunctory smile and goes off to seat his next clients. Jorge bows to me apologetically, we wish each other a *¡buen camino!,* and I turn to go.

As I leave the dining room, a middle-aged Englishman motions me over to his table. Dressed in a suit and tie and shiny black dress shoes, every hair in order, he is clearly not a pilgrim.

"What was that all about?" he asks sympathetically. "Were you being kicked out?"

Kicked out? Me? My jaw drops. The Englishman, who observed the scene from across the room, must have concluded that the head waiter refused to seat me. I briefly explain what happened and slink out of the dining room, feeling simultaneously annoyed and marginalized. The Englishman is right—the waiter didn't want me in his dining room.

It's those sexist standards at work, I mutter to myself. Standards that judge women, but not men, by appearance. I was pretty much fine with my decision to bring only functional clothes, and a bare minimum at that, until this little episode. Now, I can't help feeling that it's because of the way I am dressed that the waiter dismissed my request so summarily. There's no getting around the fact that I *do* look shabby in my scruffy shoes and baggy clothes that no longer come clean by hand-washing in cold-water. Yet Jorge's clothes are just as stained and rumpled as mine, and he hasn't even shaved, but nobody questions whether *he* belongs in the parador dining room.

But as I drink my coffee in exile at the little bar around the corner and replay the scene in my mind, I begin to wonder if maybe I'm the one who is jumping to conclusions. After all, the waiter was just doing his job. It's entirely possible he wouldn't have bent the rules for a well-dressed matron either. (Penelope Cruz is another matter . . .) As for the Englishman, his assumption wasn't unreasonable, given what he witnessed, and he seemed genuinely chagrined that I was turned away.

Another coffee and a pastry later, I think I can see the humor in the little exchange with the waiter, and I decide to treat this experience as a reminder that sexist motivations are not behind every unpleasant exchange I have with men. Just as important, I need to acknowledge my own buy-in to this particular point of view, the one I've heard all my life about the importance of a woman's appearance. A good haircut, staying trim, reasonably stylish clothes—these things do make me feel good about myself—and I am influenced by exterior trappings, others' as well as my own.

The Camino points to something more fundamental, to a way of thinking about self and others that looks inward past window-dressing and the usual social identifiers. Pilgrims leave behind professional and social tags when they enter the Camino. Here we're fellow human beings. Period. Often I know only the first name and nationality of people I meet on the trail, sometimes not even that, and with our standard pilgrim attire, we don't offer the usual visual cues to who we are and what we do in life. Yet we affect each other in profound ways. On this level playing field, we talk easily about whatever is on our minds, and the insights from strangers can be surprisingly perceptive.

The French pilgrim at Compostelle 2000 (the Paris pilgrim association) was on to something when she told me that the Camino is more than a physical place. It does present breathtaking encounters with the land itself, but it also pushes me to look beyond the physical world. My experience today offers me the chance to experience a self-image that is both richer and simpler than one that is constrained by appearance and possessions. When my time on the Camino comes to an end, I will inevitably return to a world where, like it or not, these things matter. I can't change that. But maybe I can change my perspective and try to transcend the superficial in ways that will keep me grounded, even after I return home.

These coffee shop musings lead me to another insight. Before I leave town, I go back to the hotel I have just left and ask the clerk to please cancel my reservations at the other paradores on the Camino.

"My room was wonderful," I tell the desk clerk, "and the dinner was terrific. But it just doesn't feel right to stay in luxury hotels. I am a pilgrim, you see."

In spite of my relapse last night, when I happily wallowed in creature comforts, I am becoming part of a long line of pilgrim seekers, and more so each day. It is true that hundreds of thousands of pilgrims stayed in the very spot this parador occupies. Many died here. But I can't feel their presence. The extensive renovations that added elegant marble bathrooms and fancy furnishings and brought the premises up to luxurious twenty-first-century standards have also removed all traces of the pilgrims the old hospice served. By comparison, the traditional pilgrim shelters, though humble, teem with life and place me squarely within the pilgrim tradition. The contrast between the luxury of the paradores and the humble simplicity of the refugios is too great.

The clerk is surprised but very gracious.

"As you like, Señora Soper, though we are always pleased to welcome pilgrims. If you reconsider, please give us a call. I hope you'll come back to see us another time." And he offers his hand as he wishes me a *¡buen camino!*

Another encounter this same morning reinforces the idea that the richness of my experiences does not depend on my appearance or professional and social identifiers. The route out of Santo Domingo parallels the main road initially but soon leaves behind all traces of civilization to become a path in the countryside. The sky is blue and cloudless, but it's very cold and fresh snow dusts the mountains to the west. I'm an hour out of town when I see a man rise out of the bushes, buckle his belt, and adjust his small pack. He looks my way. I wave, he returns my greeting, and I continue on, lost in thought.

A short while later, I become aware of shouting in the distance. Turning around, I see this same man waving his arms and yelling something I can't understand. I wave back and continue walking, but he becomes more agitated, shouting more and more loudly, now frantically motioning for me to come back. I hesitate. Maybe he's got a problem. In any event, he looks like he'll come after me if I don't go back, so I might as well find out what he wants.

As I approach, I see that he's pointing to a fork in the path where a yellow arrow directs pilgrims off to the right. I hadn't even noticed the intersection. Instead of following the yellow arrow, I had continued straight ahead, into the mountains. Who knows how long it would have been before I discovered my mistake? Or how dangerous my error could have been, given the cold and the snow? I thank the man, embarrassed at my carelessness.

"No te preocupes" (Don't worry about it), he says. "It's easy to miss an arrow. Fellow pilgrims need to look out for each other." And we start off together on the right path.

The next hour goes quickly as we settle into a brisk pace. He takes little steps in rapid succession, à la Roadrunner. Even with my long legs, I can barely keep up. It's hard to keep up with his Spanish, too, but he is patient with my efforts and tries to speak slowly. He's small and wiry, retired, and from Bilbao, in northern Spain. This is his fourth Camino, which probably explains his tiny pack—he's the only pilgrim I meet whose pack is smaller than mine. We never exchange names, but he is "Bilbao" to me, and I become for him "Meeetcheeegan" when he learns where I am from. He initiates a long and thoughtful conversation about the 9/11 attacks, which leads to exchanges on issues from gun control to national identity cards to climate change. Later in the day, rising temperatures warm the air, and the conversation lightens up. The flowers along the trail this morning are spectacular, and Bilbao knows them all by name.

"Have you noticed how poppies always grow alongside the wheat fields?" he asks, pointing to a vibrant red swatch of color.

"Of course, how could anyone miss them?" I say. "They shout energy and encouragement."

"There is an old Spanish song about the poppies. It's very beautiful," he says, and he begins to sing a flamenco-like melody in a heartfelt, if somewhat shaky, tenor. The music is poignant, and I understand just enough of the words to know it's a love story that ends badly.

Is this for real? I am walking across a carpet of wildflowers in the Spanish countryside, snow-covered peaks in the distance, blue sky above, and a man I have just met is serenading me with a medieval Spanish folksong. Aches and pains, the cold, the fatigue, the self-doubt all fade away. I feel alive down to my last molecule. Alive and acutely aware of how lucky I am to be here, in this place, at this moment. An image of Ronsard's rose comes to mind: this is an interlude to savor.

Later that morning, Bilbao and I stop for a break at a crowded bar in the village of Granon, and who should be there but Jacques and Maïté. I introduce them to Bilbao, and after a quick round of café con leche, Jacques, Maïté, and I head out; Bilbao will stay to watch a soccer match. As we leave, he warns us about the route ahead.

"The next two stages are problematic," he says shaking his head. "Not enough beds, and the refugios are in poor condition. Be sure you don't get to Belorado too late. I'll go to a hotel for the next two nights," he says knowingly. "Oh, and I've heard reports of dangerous dogs in the area ahead. Best not to travel alone today and tomorrow."

I'll heed his warning about wild dogs. Ever since reading about Shirley MacLaine's frightening encounter with them in her Camino memoir, I've been a little nervous about this possibility.

A frigid head wind picked up while we were in the bar, and by the time we start walking again, it's blowing hard and right in our face, chilling us to the bone. We're struggling to move forward when a group of Dutch pilgrims passes us, going at a very fast clip.

"There go the *PGV*," Jacques says.

I look puzzled. He taps his head with his index finger. "*Vas-y, Kate! Ce sont les pèlerins à grande vitesse.*"

Of course! The high-speed pilgrims, a word play on *TGV*, the French high-speed train, or *train à grande vitesse*. We decide we are the *train normal* and continue on at our usual pace, maybe even slower, as we struggle against the biting wind. When we finally arrive at the outskirts of Belorado, we're really dragging. Jacques has shooting pains that go all the way up his leg, and he's feverish. Maïté has a bad cough and her face is completely empty; she's somewhere beyond pain and exhaustion. My shoulders are screaming at me to STOP WALKING AND TAKE OFF MY PACK!

We push on.

The approach to Belorado goes past a small run-down warehouse and a pile of junk, then takes us right to the municipal refugio. When we see it, our hearts sink. It's a dilapidated building that has no windows and just one big door on a track, like a garage door. I can smell the dampness coming from the refugio's single dark and dirty room. The lady who runs it is standing outside. Our distress at the sight of this place must be obvious.

"There is a brand new three-star refugio just a few hundred meters farther on," she volunteers. "It opened for the season last week. I think you would prefer it, though it's expensive. Seven euros."

The warden raises her eyebrows at the price. This is the first we've heard of a three-star refugio, but it sounds good. We smile sheepishly and thank her.

Moments later, we're standing in front of the new refugio, which is located in a stately nineteenth-century building. The owner sits at a table just inside the front door, kids' toys surrounding him in a pile on the floor. We're too late—the sleeping rooms on the first floor are full, and all that's left are a few bunk beds and some mattresses on the floor in the attic. The owner offers this space to us at a special price of six euros each, one euro off the regular rate. That doesn't sound like much of a bargain for an attic room, but we are too tired to go any farther, and there may not be any rooms left in the next town by the time we could get there. Meanwhile, pilgrims keep arriving and snapping up beds. We pay our money and head up four long flights of stairs to claim our bunks.

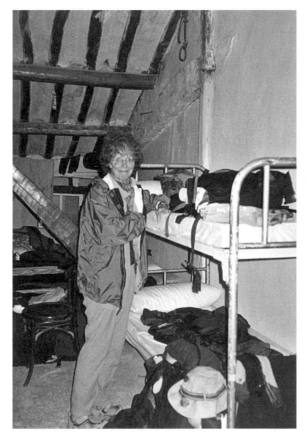

Attic of the three-star refugio in Belorado.

The overflow room is indeed an attic, complete with cobwebs and twenty-foot ceilings. A trapeze, parallel rings, and ropes hang randomly from the rafters, remnants of a gymnasium. Ragged, mismatched mattresses and old gym mats are interspersed with a dozen or so steel-framed bunk beds. The only bathroom is on the ground floor—we groan at the thought. But someone swept the floor not too long ago, and open windows at one end of the room provide natural light and fresh air. On a night like this——it's now raining again—we're glad to have a roof over our heads, and this is surely better than the municipal refugio. I end up with a top bunk for the first time—it's either that or a filthy mattress on the floor in a dark corner that screams "spiders!" But these bunk beds are tall and the top bed seems much higher off the floor than usual.

"How will I get up without pulling this flimsy thing over on me and my bunkmate?" I ask Jacques.

"Use a chair," he reasons, "you'll be fine."

Just then, Inge (my young German friend) swings up on her top bunk with one graceful leap of her thirty-year-younger legs. She sees us and waves.

"The water in the shower is just a trickle of ice water," she says, rolling her eyes dramatically. "Last night, I stayed in the most wonderful private refugio. We slept in an old tower, there was a fire in the fireplace, and dinner was included. Is this the price I pay for such a nice night?"

Maybe.

Jacques immediately crashes and takes a siesta. Maïté and I are shivering uncontrollably and can't face cold showers, so we decide to look for a place to get some hot tea. We put our pèlerines back on and go to the closest bar, where we spend the next three and a half hours sipping hot tea, writing in our journals, and waiting for the restaurant to start serving dinner. I also review the route for tomorrow. It will be a steady uphill climb most of the day but, except for a little stretch at the end, it shouldn't be too bad. Later, Jacques joins us for a pilgrim menu in the adjoining restaurant.

Jacques and Maïté go to bed right after dinner, but I'm not ready to sleep yet, so I wander into the refugio kitchen, hoping to find someone to talk with and a place to warm up before I turn in. It's deserted and drafty now that the stove is off. I sit there staring out the window into the night, wishing for a cup of hot tea. Shoving my icy hands into my pockets, I feel a piece of paper, pull it out, and discover the card with the eleventh-century pilgrim's blessing that the Los Arcos priest distributed after the Pilgrim Mass. When I first heard this blessing in Roncesvalles, I thought it was quaint but didn't speak to the modern-day pilgrim. Not so now. Reading the centuries-old text tonight, especially the part about fatigue, danger, heat, darkness, and dejection, I am reminded that these struggles are both universal and timeless—and just part of the deal. For over a thousand years, my fellow pilgrims have found the strength to continue. Of course I can do this.

The owner pops his head into the kitchen.

"Bedtime," he says. "You'll need your energy tomorrow," and he disappears before I can ask why.

I climb the four flights of stairs to the overflow sleeping room, find a chair, and manage to get up onto my top bunk without causing the entire rickety set-up to topple over. *Progress,* I think with a smile. But I go to sleep wondering if someone will move the chair before morning.

[The priest at San Juan de Ortega] admitted . . .
that some people could walk the whole way
to Santiago without ever knowing the meaning
of pilgrimage, while others could be true
pilgrims even traveling there by bus. It was all
"in the heart."

Bettina Selby, *Pilgrim's Road: A Journey to Santiago de Compostela*

Chapter Nine

Hearts and Minds

June 8, Belorado to San Juan de Ortega.

The next morning, the chair is still there, nestled up against the foot of my bunk, but I'm so exhausted it hardly matters. First, there were the bugs. Just as I was dozing off, I saw little black spots crawling around on my mattress. Dad's tales of nibbling bed bugs when he was stationed in Italy during World War II leapt to mind, stories that seemed hilarious to me as a child. Faced with the prospect of creepy creatures in my bed, I couldn't imagine what I had found so funny. I dug out my headlamp and searched up and down my mattress twice, but they had disappeared.

Then there was the snorer. I've gotten used to my earplugs by now, and they usually do the trick. Not last night—even with them firmly in place, the noise was loud enough to cause hearing loss. Inge tells me later that she'd been in the same room with this man before and knew what we were in for. In fact, she had bought an anti-snoring strip for him at the *farmacia* earlier in the day, but she was afraid to give it to him. Other pilgrims yelled at him in half a dozen languages all night long; he seemed completely unresponsive to this verbal abuse. However, the snorer was gone before dawn, perhaps because he knew the grief he'd have to endure if he was around when we got up. I discover that the church bells in this town ring on the quarter hour, all night.

Others leave between 5:30 and 6, then it's silence at last and I fall into a deep sleep. The next thing I know it's 7 a.m., and Jacques, Maïté, and I are once again the only ones left. Bleary-eyed and shaky, we pack up and tramp downstairs to the kitchen where a battered red kettle boils away on the old iron stove. It contains just enough hot water to fill three mugs. After a quick breakfast, we prepare to face the day. The owners are ready for us to leave so they can get their lives back for a few hours, until the next group arrives. They help us with our coats and packs, practically sweeping us out the door with their brooms.

Fresh snow blankets the mountain tops again today, and it's so cold that we can see our breath. I walk with a lurch on knees that refuse to bend, swinging my arms like a robot, in an attempt to get warm and loosen up. It starts to drizzle. We put on our pèlerines and walk in silence, heads down against the weather, trying to ignore the pain our bodies are causing us as we slog through the mud.

My mind is in neutral when I realize that the same four notes keep going through my head, more mantra than music. At first, it's distracting and annoying. Then I realize that the rhythm imposed by the notes is taking my mind off the cold and boredom and is actually pulling me forward. I let it happen and just keep going. I will have this experience several times on my pilgrimage when the going is tough. I cannot reproduce the tune at will, but when I need it, the notes simply appear and play over and over, like the hypnotic repetition of a music box, until I realize they have stopped—and I've arrived.

Around eleven, we come to an attractive-looking bar-restaurant on the outskirts of Villafranca Monte de Ocas. In spite of the hour, every chair is taken, and the gloriously warm room vibrates with conversations. Most of the customers are local workers on a mid-morning break, but there's a handful of pilgrims. The minute we walk through the door, our spirits rise and our mouths start to water. A constantly humming espresso machine exudes the aroma of dark roast coffee, and whole hams hang from the ceiling, giving off the robust scent of smoked meat. A fragrant soup that smells of basil and tomatoes simmers in a large black pot.

Some men wearing the blue jumpsuits typical of Spanish workers are leaving and offer us their table. We gratefully accept, shed our wet pèlerines, and go to the bar to order the restaurant's specialty: a sandwich made of smoked ham, a locally produced white cheese, and luscious tomatoes layered on a fresh baguette and drizzled with a fragrant, peppery olive oil. Jacques is ecstatic at the thought of good food. Me, too. The waiter places our sandwiches in front of us just as Suzette, the French woman who had been walking with the Mexican girls, comes up to our table.

"Sara got a terrible case of tendonitis," she announces glumly. "It's so bad that she had to abandon her pilgrimage. Mariana stayed with her, so now I have no one to walk with. It's too sad and lonely. I don't think I can keep going."

"Walk with us," offers Jacques.

"No, I can't go on. *C'est impossible!*" she says dramatically. "I will stay here tonight. Who knows about tomorrow?" And with that, she gives a half-hearted wave and drags herself out the door.

"She needs someone to boss around," sniffs Maïté, after Suzette leaves.

"Sergeant Suzette!" says Jacques, with a grin and a little salute.

It's noon before we leave the bustling warmth of the café. According to the bartender, it will take us two hours to walk to San Juan de Ortega, our goal for the night. Jacques laughs on hearing this.

"If it's two hours for him, it's at least three for us," he says, correctly as it turns out.

The path out of Villafranca climbs steeply and steadily for fifteen minutes, up to a clearing with a breathtaking view of the town below and the mountains ahead. Just beyond the clearing, we enter a scrub-oak forest that shimmers from the recent rain. Lush emerald ivy grows up the jet-black trunks; silvery moss intertwines with ivy on the forest floor in sensuous chaos. The glistening colors vibrate, a handful of attention-grabbing greens set off by the blackest of blacks, making the forest—and me—feel intensely alive. There is nothing, I think to myself, quite like being warm, dry, well-fed, with friends, and surrounded by beauty, especially after hours of tromping through the rain and cold.

Later, the path opens onto a high moorland cloaked with soft purple heather and deep yellow broom. Their heady fragrances, one spicy, the other sweet, permeate the air. We walk on top of the world for about a kilometer, distant snow-covered peaks at eye level, and then the trail carries us back into a stand of trees, this one a pine forest. Tall yellow flowers grow along the wide path. I reach for my camera, but, before I can take a photo, the rain starts up again, quickly becoming a downpour that pricks our skin through our clothes. Minutes later, the rain turns to hail, and we head for the shelter of the pines to wait out the worst of the storm. We must wade through a ditch of ankle-deep water to get there, but even with wet feet, we are struck by the beauty that surrounds us. Little white flowers—*stellaires*, Jacques says—are so abundant that we feel like we've been planted in the middle of a medieval tapestry.

When the hail turns to a drizzle we begin walking again, alternating the rest of the afternoon between oak forests, heather and broom moorlands, and stands of pine. As we walk across the land, the color of the earth also changes, from a soft brown to sweet potato red—just as it did on childhood visits to my adored South Carolina grandmother. We'd drive from our home in Illinois to see her every summer. My two sisters and I, packed in the back seat of the car, waited eagerly for the earth to turn color, a sure sign that we were almost there. Decades later, seeing red dirt still makes me happy.

Finally, about six kilometers from San Juan de Ortega, the rain stops and we take a break.

"Shall I make tea?" Jacques offers. "It will give us courage to go the distance."

He digs out three assorted containers—a cup, a small bowl, and a mug—and with great fanfare prepares tea for us on his propane stove, using water from each of our supplies. The brew that results is bitter, weak, and tastes like rust.

"Mmmm, this may be the most welcome cup of tea I've ever had. It's better than tea at the Ritz," I tell him, with a laugh and an awkward, seated curtsy.

Jacques sticks his little finger in the air and affects what he considers a proper English pose. We are giggling and drinking our tea when we notice a dark cloud rolling down the path, heading straight toward us. As the cloud gets closer, we realize it's a mob of people, at least fifty strong, and it's moving fast. We stare in disbelief. We haven't seen another soul all day, and the area's too remote for a casual stroll. We grow nervous as the mob gets closer. Then we see that it's a group of German tourists,

Jacques taking "tea at the Ritz."

Steps Out of Time

who are our age and immaculately dressed. In spite of the rain, even their boots are spotless. They wear *lederhosen* and hats cocked at jaunty angles, many with feathers.

We are filthy and bedraggled, hair matted and boots caked with dirt, as we sit by our mud puddle. Maïté has taken off her boots and socks, revealing impressive bandages. A matron breaks rank and comes up to us, clucking sympathetically. One man asks in German if he can get tea at this café, or at least we think that's what he says. Most of them get out their cameras and take our picture.

"*Ultreia, ultreia,*" they call out, with friendly waves as they parade past.

This ancient Galician word means "onward" or "go beyond your limits." It is the traditional word of encouragement to pilgrims on the way to Santiago but is no longer in fashion. In fact, the only time I hear it is from this group. After ten days on the trail, however, I think it is more appropriate than the current greeting of *¡buen camino!* which now feels like the uninspiring equivalent of "have a nice day."

The leader of the well-dressed Germans brings up the rear.

"Are they pilgrims?" we ask him in Spanish, hoping this will be a common language. It is.

He detects the smug disbelief in our voices and smiles indulgently.

"Sure," he says as he hurries off to catch up with his group, "but a different kind of pilgrim."

I'm considering what he might mean when he turns back to us and calls out, "But you know, we are all pilgrims on this earth."

The sky begins to clear as we near the monastery of San Juan de Ortega. We even catch glimpses of the sun and crave the warmth of those rays. Cuckoos are singing, and the air smells fresh after the rain. Then we crest a hill and the monastery emerges from the mist. Once again I think of my medieval predecessors, who must have felt the same relief and wonder I do now at the sight of this miraculous, hulking refuge after hours of walking, often in miserable conditions. The medieval stone buildings are dazzlingly white, so clean they look like they've been sand-blasted. More likely, this isolated spot has not been exposed to car exhaust and other pollutants in any significant degree over the centuries. Even today, only one small road leads to the little settlement consisting of a monastery and church, a bar, and a couple of houses.

San Juan de Ortega—Saint John of the Nettles—earned his name because he lived and worked in the midst of this desolate, overgrown forest. (*Ortega* is a corruption of the Spanish *ortiga*.) Born in 1080, San Juan was a disciple of Santo Domingo de la Calzada. He helped his mentor build a much-needed infrastructure for pilgrims along this section of the Camino, including roads, bridges, churches, and pilgrim hospices, some of which are still in use. Later, San Juan dedicated himself to helping pilgrims cross the dangerous wilderness between Villafranca and Burgos, then one of the most feared stretches of the Camino because of the steepness of the route, the harsh weather, and, especially, bandits who robbed and murdered defenseless pilgrims. In the second half of the twelfth century, he established this monastery and pilgrim hospice (now a refugio) where we will sleep tonight.

A sign points to the entrance, but although the door's open, there's no warden in sight. We're wondering what to do when Bilbao (the Spaniard who serenaded me) walks up.

"¡Hola, amigos! How's the walking? A little cold today, no?"

I nod in agreement, happy to see his friendly face after a hard afternoon. He explains that a priest and his sister run this refugio and that it's operated on a donation-only basis because they want everyone to be able to stay here, regardless of financial situation. Bilbao urges us to make a generous contribution. These donations are the refugio's only source of income, but many pilgrims think "donation" means "free" and give nothing. As a result, the refugio is always strapped for cash. We put some bills in the wooden box marked "donativo," then head off to the second story sleeping room to claim beds.

Inside, the monastery shows its age, especially the stairs where the footsteps of monks and pilgrims over the ages have hollowed out troughs in the stone. The facilities are basic, although with some homey touches: end tables by the bunks, ragged wool blankets on some of the beds, and even a few rickety chairs, so there's a place to sit beside your mattress. The bathroom, however, is in disrepair and dirty, and there's no toilet paper. The faucets have only cold water spigots—not even the pretense of hot water—and a sign forbids washing clothes in the sink. Well, that's a relief. I don't have to choose between wearing dirty clothes tomorrow or washing them in ice water. The building, which has no heating system, feels like a refrigerator. What must it be like in winter?

"This will be a monastic experience," an English woman comments cheerily. "But not much choice for tonight, is there?" she adds, rubbing her arms vigorously in an attempt to warm up.

No, but we can put off the inevitable. We head for the cozy and welcoming bar, the only warm public space in this little hamlet. Needless to say, they're doing a booming business. We find a table near a window, then go to the bar to order. I ask for cola cao, a drink I've discovered recently that consists of a mug of hot foamy milk that you mix with a packet of chocolaty powder to make a fabulous concoction. I go back for seconds, then thirds.

Around seven, Maïté announces that it's time to leave the warmth of this wonderful bar to go to the dark, dank, unheated church for a Pilgrim Mass that we won't understand because it will be in fast Spanish or Latin. ("I've heard there is a very good Pilgrim Mass here," is what she really says, but my version is more accurate.) Reluctantly, I put on my jacket and go with them into the frigid, unwelcoming night.

The priest arrives at the church about the same time we do. Wearing a hooded cassock, he looks like he has stepped out of the Middle Ages as he rattles an enormous key that opens the wrought iron gate to the chapel where he will say Mass. He beckons us to come in and sit down while he lights the candles, then he rushes through the service, never once making eye contact with his congregation. When Mass is over and we start to leave, he looks directly at us for the first time.

"No, wait a minute, don't go yet, please," he says in Spanish, motioning for us to sit down. "*Por favor,*" he repeats. "*Un momento,*" and he disappears behind the altar.

When he returns a few minutes later, now wearing a dark suit, he descends from the altar to stand directly in front of the first row of seats.

"Let's talk about the Camino and our journey," he says, addressing us in the first person plural. We are in this together, it seems. Here is his message:

> We are walking the Camino, but we don't know why. People who see us think we are mad. We must listen to what the Camino has to tell us. Is it an act of faith? Of belief? Of reaffirmation? We don't know. . . . The important thing is to remember that this is a Camino of contemplation. It leads to a life that is more intimate, more true, and more honest. Open your eyes and spirits to the discovery that awaits you.

He's so right. This old road is indeed a way of contemplation, but what it offers to each of us we must discover for ourselves. I, for one, am blown away by what I see when I slow down and look.

"Enough," the priest declares abruptly. "Time for garlic soup. Come with me to the monastery kitchen."

We follow him down a hallway, through a heavy wooden door, and into a large dining hall with a table that runs almost the length of the room. The priest takes his place at one end, in front of a covered black caldron that is surrounded by earthenware bowls.

"Please, sit," he says, motioning to the benches on either side of the table.

Though we are almost forty, there is room for everyone. The priest removes the cover from the huge pot and takes an appreciative whiff. Then he ladles fragrant garlic soup into the generous bowls, which the pilgrims closest to him distribute. Someone says his sister made the soup and that it's the world's best.

When everyone is served, the priest says a brief prayer and invites us to begin. He goes around the table while we eat and asks each person where he or she is from, counting the countries as he goes. There is one other American, a young man from California, as well as pilgrims from Spain, France, Italy, Austria, Brazil, New Zealand, Canada, Hungary, Portugal, and Japan.

"Only eleven countries are represented tonight," the priest notes. "Often, there are fifteen or more. So many nationalities doing the Camino together. Think about it. Our garlic soup is famous not because it is delicious—though it is—but because of what it has come to symbolize in this monastery. The garlic soup is an act of community. *Es una sopa de amor*" (it's a soup of love), he says thoughtfully.

He continues to talk about community and fraternity, international understanding, and being open to the Camino. I look around the table, struck by the mix of ages and nationalities and how comfortable everyone seems. He's onto something. We find a common language and talk to each other easily, though we were strangers half an hour ago.

When the priest announces that it's time to leave, we get up reluctantly. I think everyone in the room feels the same sense of camaraderie that I do. We have more to say to each other, yet once we leave this room, the conversations will end. Those freezing dormitories and icy bathrooms are just not conducive to talking. Rather, we'll dive into our sleeping bags as quickly as possible, pulling on every extra blanket we can find. Tonight, it's going to be chattering teeth that keep us awake.

Still, I am grateful that I learned about this monastery from my guidebook, and I am glad that I looked beyond cautionary words about the refugio being dirty and basic (both of which are true). This evening, I was touched again by the spirit of the Camino. The allure of this historic site, the fellowship of the garlic soup, the sound of the centuries-old church bells ringing against the silence of such an isolated spot—these experiences gain purchase in my consciousness.

Marchent ainsi ceux qu'il faudra soutenir et ceux qui soutiendront, ceux de la foi et ceux du doute, ceux du partage et ceux de l'indifférence, les bavards et les réservés . . .

And so they walk. Those who need help and those who help, the believers and the doubters, those who share and those who are indifferent, the talkative and the reserved . . .

Jean-Claude Bourlès, *Le Grand Chemin de Compostelle*

Chapter Ten

Camino Characters

June 9 – 10, San Juan de Ortega to Rabé via Burgos.

I wake at dawn. My nose, exposed in the tiny opening left after tightening the drawstring on my mummy sleeping bag, is an ice cube. I expand the opening slightly and look around. All I see are white clouds of exhaled breath, dozens of giant polka dots dancing around the monastery dormitory. Still, it was a good night. I found a tattered wool blanket, which I threw over my sleeping bag, and bundled up in three shirts, my lined vest, one pair of pants, two pairs of socks, and a scarf around my neck. I was almost warm. The Italian snorer next to me wasn't too loud—and besides, he was sitting across from me at the garlic-soup dinner last night and was nice, which probably made me more tolerant.

Jacques opens the shutters to a blue sky. "Maybe at least we won't be both cold and wet today," he remarks, though he looks unconvinced as he stands there shivering. According to a thermometer on the bathroom wall, the inside temperature is nine degrees Celsius (about forty-eight degrees Fahrenheit).

I pull on my second pair of pants and add my jacket. As I wash up in the frigid water, I think about the monks who lived here over the centuries, devoted to a life of the spirit and rejecting worldly pursuits, pleasures, or even some pretty basic comforts (like heat). They must have really been into the set-aside-creature-comfort program. We aren't, and move quickly this morning, eager to start walking so we can warm up.

There are three routes out of San Juan de Ortega: one follows the road and two are paths through the countryside. The road route is a direct shot to Burgos, and it is the most level and quickest of the options. Better yet, if we take the road, it would be virtually impossible to get lost. That sounds like a no-brainer, yet we hesitate. None of us can shake the feeling of vulnerability after Catherine's fatal accident, especially Jacques, who still hesitates each time he has to cross a highway. We're trying to decide what to do when Bilbao appears. I'm bemused and grateful to see him again—his habit of popping up just when I need help is very convenient.

"*Ay, peregrinos,*" he says, "you must take the middle way. It's only a little longer and will be easier on your feet and legs than road walking. Safer, too, and better for your spirits to walk in the countryside. Come, I'll show you the way."

Motioning for us to follow, he leads us to the start of the trail and waves us on our way. We've been walking about five minutes—the monastery is still in sight—when I realize that my ankle really hurts. Out of the blue, just like that.

"*J'ai mal,*" I say tentatively.

Jacques grouses at my unexpected announcement, but he insists we stop, takes off his pack, and rummages around for supplies.

"Here, this is what you need." He hands me a tube of a vile smelling gel, then produces a little red tablet that he holds to me out insistently. "It's an anti-inflammatory drug I got from a French doctor. You'll see. It works like a charm."

I'm a little nervous about taking somebody else's prescription medicine, but I have to somehow get to Burgos under my own power. I swallow one of his pills and smear the ointment all over my ankle. Maïté is convinced my pain is from tendonitis which, according to her, I'm developing because I'm not drinking enough water. As a matter of fact, I haven't been drinking much water recently, and, in my opinion, for good reason. It's been too miserably cold to stop and pee in the rain, so I've been avoiding the problem by not drinking liquids while on the trail. Peeing outside is not particularly convenient for the ladies, even in good weather—but forget it in an icy downpour. Nevertheless, I decide to start drinking more liquids right now if there is even a chance that this will help me avoid tendonitis.

I look at Maïté and take a long swig of water. We soldier on.

A short time later, the little dirt path passes through a pine forest filled with energetic and noisy birds. It then leaves the woods and begins to climb on an exposed rocky track that takes us to a high plateau with a 360-degree view of expansive golden plains and hazy blue mountains. Way off in the distance, in miniature, we see Burgos, our goal for the day. But we have learned that seeing is not being there, so we buckle down for a long haul.

A couple hours of breathtaking scenery later, we wind down off the plateau and into an area of vast fields of ripening grain that glow and sway in the sun. Sun! The azure sky is a perfect foil for the fire-engine-red poppies that grow profusely along the edge of the fields. I'm surrounded by beauty—immersed in it—but this morning that's not enough to get me beyond the pain. My feet, my legs, my shoulders, my spirits—everything hurts. Judging by their body language, Jacques and Maïté feel the same way. We trudge along in silence.

Eventually, the path leads us onto an isolated country lane that cuts across the seemingly endless fields. Maïté and I stop to heed the call of nature while Jacques walks ahead and is quickly out of sight behind a curve in the road. She and I have just started plodding along again when a beat-up old car comes rattling up from behind, slowing to a crawl as it pulls up beside us. The creepy guy in the passenger seat hangs out the window and leers. He's in his early twenties, has stringy dark hair and bad teeth, and we can smell the alcohol on his breath from several yards away. Another scruffy young Spaniard waves a large open bottle unsteadily from the back seat. The driver, who looks equally seedy, guzzles beer.

"¡Hola!" yells the driver. "Get in. We'll take you to the cathedral."

I barely register what's happening, but Maïté stiffens up and grabs my arm. Dragging me with her, she quickens our pace. Her face turns so steely that she scares me, too. No way would I mess with her.

"Certainly not," Maïté replies sternly, without turning around to look at him. "We're pilgrims, we go on foot."

"Don't stop walking and don't turn around," she says under her breath.

Eyes straight ahead, we force ourselves to walk at a more or less normal pace and pretend to ignore them. I hope they can't hear our pounding hearts. They talk loudly among themselves, but their speech is too garbled to understand. Several very long minutes later, they decide to take no for an answer, and as the car lurches past, I feel Maïté go limp. For the first time in hours, I'm relieved to discover that I can feel something besides pain, even if it is fear.

As the car rounds the curve, we hear it speed up, probably when these sleazy characters see Jacques. I'm glad I'm not alone and wonder what would have happened if I had been. A few days later, I hear about a German pilgrim who wasn't so lucky. He was jumped and badly beaten by a group of local men when he left the grounds of an isolated refugio to go for an after-dinner stroll.

About 11:30, we come to a standing-room-only-bar, miles from anywhere but with a full parking lot. This is obviously the place to have an aperitif on Sunday. We sit down at a patio table in full sun next to several pots of crimson geraniums and take stock. Jacques is feeling good, but he's the only one. Maïté's cough has returned with a vengeance, and now she's feverish, too. My ankle pain has spread up my leg to my hip, in spite of the remedies Jacques gave me earlier and in spite of all the water I've been guzzling.

Jacques looks us over and shakes his head. "I think we'd better see about a bus to Burgos. You ladies need a rest. Either you take it easy now or we risk not making it to Santiago. Besides, we only have to walk the last one hundred kilometers to get our Compostelas."

He gets no argument from us. Maïté asks the bartender—a dark-haired young man who introduces himself as Pedro—about buses. He tells us there is limited service on Sunday, and we've missed the last bus of the day.

"Can you call us a taxi?" she asks.

Pedro shakes his head. "No taxis today." He looks at Maïté; she coughs from somewhere deep in her chest. "But I'm going to Burgos when the bar closes. You can ride with me, if you don't mind waiting a *momentito*."

We thank him for his kind offer, accept, and go back to our table in the sun where we pass the time drinking—first beer to quench our thirst, then hot tea to warm up, and finally wine to put us out of our misery. The "little minute" has grown to three long hours by the time we finally pile into Pedro's car along with his shaggy, lumbering, toffee-colored dog and a matching suitcase. He puts on aviator sunglasses, smoothes down his hair, fastens his seat belt, and we roar out of the parking lot onto a tiny narrow road that has one blind curve after another. I flash to dying in a fiery crash, but Pedro turns out to be an excellent driver. As he approaches each curve, he honks several times.

"These roads are very dangerous," he says. "You have to anticipate problems and make sure that if anyone is coming in the other direction, he knows you're there. Spanish drivers!" he adds with a wink. "I drive a tractor-trailer during the week. I've seen enough accidents to know that you have to watch out for yourself."

I don't ask how many of them were fatal accidents, but I think of Catherine and wonder.

On the way to Burgos, Pedro points out all the old churches and relates the stories of the saints whose remains they guard. He also tells great jokes, often puns. We reach the city center in about fifteen minutes, a trip that would have taken us at least three hours on foot (and probably longer at today's pace). En route, we pass dozens of pilgrims, all of whom look miserable. *I'm glad that's not me,* I think happily from the back seat of the car, a drooling but very affectionate dog in my lap. Well, OK, I feel a little guilty, too. Then I turn to look at Maïté's flushed face, and this slight movement triggers a searing pain from my ankle to my knee.

Steps Out of Time

I don't think either of us could have walked anymore today, so I decide to feel grateful to Pedro and forget the guilt.

Minutes later, when Pedro pulls up to the curb to drop us off, he shakes hands with Jacques, ignoring Maïté and me, and my gratitude turns to annoyance. Jacques, who was sitting in the front seat (of course), doesn't speak any Spanish, so he and Pedro haven't exchanged a direct word the whole trip. But it's hard to stay mad at our knight in a shining auto. In retrospect, I wish I had extended my hand first, which is probably what a Spanish man would expect.

"I'll be in my rig, back on the road next week," Pedro says before he drives off. "I'll keep an eye out for you, and if I see you, I'll honk."

I'm going to be walking on the highway alongside trucks?

At Jacques' insistence, he and Maïté head directly for a military hospital in Burgos that he's heard treats ailing pilgrims. Maïté's fever has spiked again and she needs to see a doctor. Most likely, she also needs to rest a day or two. For a moment, I consider going with them to the hospital but decide instead to see how my ankle feels in the morning. We part with kisses all around and wishes for speedy recoveries from our various ailments.

"*A bientôt,*" we say, replacing the more final *au revoir* or *adieu* with "see you soon." It feels right.

But I won't see them tonight in the refugio. The urgent need for a good night's sleep and the burning desire to soak my aching body in a hot tub lead me to rethink my decision not to stay in hotels. I take a single room in a modest place just opposite the thirteenth-century cathedral, which means I can visit it by simply walking across the square. After a big dose of ibuprofen and a short rest in my *private* room with a *private* bath, I feel decent for the first time all day. I change into my sandals and my relatively clean shirt and go back out into the sunshine.

The sight of the cathedral takes my breath away. The white calcareous stone sparkles, and every detail of this masterpiece of Spanish Gothic architecture is visible, from its lacy spires to the gracefully carved statues and friezes of the façade's three arches. The interior is equally splendid. It offers priceless treasures crafted centuries ago: stone statuary, carved wooden choir stalls, altar pieces, side chapels, a rose window, and even the tomb of El Cid, Spain's national hero. I spend a couple of hours visiting its treasures—and running into pilgrim friends. I'm admiring the fine carvings of the Constables' chapel when David and Christine (the French blister experts) walk up. I show them my left foot, full of bits of white string, and thank them for the tip; they smile approvingly, and we compare notes on our experiences since we last saw each other in Nájera. My young French friends are no sooner out of view when Sara and Mariana (the Mexican girls) rush up and give me a hug.

"I have a bad case of tendonitis, and the doctor made me promise to stop walking," Sara announces. "He told me the Camino would be here for many more centuries, but if I didn't stop now, I wouldn't be able to come back to try again. He really scared me, so Mariana and I are doing the Camino by bus. But it's OK. We'll have another chance to be pilgrims, I'm sure of it."

She starts to tell me about the art treasures they have seen, but, as I listen to her, I am distracted by the weird sensation that something is out of sync.

"You're speaking perfect English," I finally blurt out.

She looks at me sheepishly. "You spoke to us in Spanish when we first met on the trail to Viana. We didn't want to offend you by switching languages."

"*Ay, ¡diós mío!*" I reply, instinctively switching to Spanish, then back to English. "How could you stand listening to me struggle in Spanish?"

They giggle. "Your Spanish isn't *that* bad," says Mariana. But I think she's just being nice—those first few times I tried to speak Spanish after not using it for many years, all I could get out was baby talk. What an unexpected kindness, this gift of patience from two young strangers. Their tolerance of my painstaking efforts gave me the confidence to continue using Spanish on the Camino, which in turn opened many doors. I will be forever grateful to them for giving me the courage to speak Spanish, as well as for their insights about adult children.

"We'll see you around," they say as they leave. "Kiss Suzette for us if you see her."

Half an hour later, while I'm admiring the rose window, Suzette herself bustles up. She is thrilled to know that Sara and Mariana are in Burgos and rushes off to look for them, instructing me to tell them that she's staying at the municipal refugio if I see them again.

That evening, I run into Jill and Lil, the Australian sisters. We go for a glass of wine and happily trade pilgrim stories until the sky has turned the deepest blue I've ever seen. The Camino, we agree, is much more beautiful and much more difficult than we expected. Walking back to my hotel, I realize that I'll probably be on my own tomorrow and start to feel lonely. I'm also a little anxious. The experience this morning with the car full of young drunkards has made me realize that however safe I may feel, no one ever knows what's around the corner. That's especially true now, as I'm about to begin crossing the desolate stretch known as the meseta. I push these thoughts away. I'll just have to believe in the power of the Camino.

I call home as soon as I get back to my room. My son, who is visiting for a few days, picks up the phone, and hearing his voice, then Philip's, brings a big lump to my throat. We talk for a long time, catching up on family news and what's happening in the world. They're amazed that I am unaware of any of the big news stories of the past two weeks, and I am bemused that they have so little idea of what my life is like on the Camino. But then how could they? It takes more than a few phone conversations to convey a sense of this place.

I tell my son about my leg pains and my uncertainty about whether I should continue walking.

"Don't worry, Mom," he encourages me. "Get a good night's sleep, and if it only hurts a little tomorrow, buy an elastic bandage and keep on truckin'. If it hurts a lot, lie low for a few days. But it doesn't sound like anything too serious. You'll be fine."

Reassured, I ring off, but I hang onto the receiver for several minutes before tucking it back in the cradle. They sound the same as ever, and that constancy is both a comfort and an anchor. Yet talking with them is also a disquieting reminder of what different spaces we inhabit right now. They live in the familiar world of cell phones, computers, constant access to the media, cars—a world of speed, convenience, competition, and material things. I'm in a very different place, one that is removed from those accoutrements and concerns, and I rather like my pared-down existence. I go to sleep not quite worrying, but certainly wondering how I'll put these two worlds together when I return home. My family and friends will likely be unchanged, but I'm not so sure I can say the same thing about myself. I'm not sure I want to.

The next morning, I'm relieved to discover that my leg is OK. In fact, nothing hurts, though I usually feel fine until I start walking. Nevertheless, I take my time and don't leave Burgos until 11:30. I walk alone for over an hour before stopping for water at a shaded rest area. As I'm leaving, a small, wiry man comes charging up, and we start off together. He has a ruddy complexion, thin gray hair, piercing gray eyes, and an eager smile. His bucket-style sun hat and plaid Bermuda shorts seem to place him on a golf course, but the scallop shell around his neck identifies him as a pilgrim. He speaks in a strong Scottish brogue.

"Do you know how I came to do the Camino?" he asks without any introduction. "I was hiking on a beach in New Zealand four years ago when I noticed a shell." He points proudly to the scallop shell he wears like an oversized necklace.

"'Pick me up,' this shell says to me."

He's dead serious.

"At first, I kept on walking," he continues, "but it called to me again. 'Pick me up, pick me up.' It was *quite* insistent. '*Well, fine,*' I thought, so I picked it up, put it in my pack, took it home, and forgot about it."

He bounces along energetically as he talks.

I am walking with Tigger, I think.

He shrugs his shoulders with a quick jerky motion and continues his story without stopping for breath.

"A year or so later, I was in the library doing some research, minding my own business, thank you very much, when I noticed a book, way down on the bottom shelf. 'Pick me up,' it said. I tried to ignore it, but it insisted, so finally I picked it up, and it was a book of stories about the Camino. I'd never heard of this Camino before, but when I looked through the book, I saw a picture of my shell, and suddenly it came to me that I was supposed to do the Saint James pilgrimage. So when I retired from the military at age sixty-five, I started walking. From London. I'm Rupert, by the way."

He holds out his hand.

"Why do you think you're supposed to walk the Camino?" I ask him, intrigued by his story. "What do you expect to find?"

"Me, of course!" he answers, without missing a beat.

And he launches into his medical history: a serious leg and back condition he overcame as a young man and, more recently, two heart attacks and arterial fibrosis.

"I'm lucky," he says. "My cardiologist wants to walk the Camino, too, and I think this made her more sympathetic to my plan. Anyone else would have probably told me no, not even negotiable. This one was willing to talk about it. She made me do extensive tests, but eventually she cleared me to go.

"Of course I have to be careful," he continues. "She warned me to stop and rest on any uphill stretches and to pay attention to how I feel. She says I'll faint if I exercise too much."

Some people might find walking one thousand miles across England and Spain rather a lot of exercise, I think, but can't say, because Rupert still hasn't stopped for a breath.

By the time we get to Tardajos, my ears are about to explode and my head aches from listening to Rupert's endless stories about his adventures. When I spot a park bench in the shade, I grab the chance for a respite.

"I need to take a little break," I say, repeating it twice before he realizes that I'm talking.

"Sure. Cheerio then!" he chirps, as he bounces off.

Rupert. Guileless, energetic, and completely uninhibited, he's not without charm—yet he doesn't wear well. At least not to me, and not here.

I'm sitting on the bench tending my feet when a large tour bus drives up—it's the immaculately dressed Germans that Jacques, Maïté, and I met on the path to San Juan de Ortega. As they pile out, I get the same looks of sympathy and amusement and am again surrounded by camera lenses.

"*Ultreia, ultreia,*" they call out as they head off to walk another section of the Camino.

From my park bench, I can see the church tower of the little village of Rabé, about two kilometers away, where there is a private refugio that is a possibility for tonight. Forty-five minutes later, as I'm leaving Tardajos, I spot Rupert standing in the shade of some trees, banging on a large green rubber rectangle.

"Mission control sent me a mat," he says, pointing to the air mattress he's now jumping on to deflate. "Makes it possible to nap."

"Mission control?" I say.

"My wife," he explains. "We've been married forty-one years. Made it so long because of my trips. I go away every year for two months. My Christmas present to my wife, don't you see. Saves on wrapping paper, too," he adds with a chuckle.

I suspect there is probably nothing she'd rather have.

By now, he's ready to go, so we start off together. Thankfully, it's a short distance to Rabé, and at least he tells different stories rather than repeating the same ones. We arrive at the small private refugio in Rabé around 2:45. Strains of Debussy's *La Mer* float through an open window. But in spite of the music and the open, unscreened window, nobody answers the doorbell of the attractive two-story stone house.

"That's why," says Rupert, pointing to a sign on the door. "Doesn't open until three o'clock."

In good time, the refugio owner arrives—a very friendly young woman in her mid-thirties with dark, curly hair and warm brown eyes.

"I'm Marivi," she says in Spanish, holding out her hand. "Welcome. I offer bed and dinner for five euros each."

Rupert feels refreshed after the break and decides to continue on. I'm trying to take care of my leg, so I will call this a rest day and stop here for the night. It's a bit early, but the next refugio is eight kilometers away, and they would be hard ones at the end of the day. Besides, I like the feel of this place. This refugio is charming and spotless, with a sunlit dormitory that has only four two-bed bunks—each with a clean white sheet, and even a pillow (a rarity). Marivi checks me in, then sends me off to claim a bed. After showering and doing my laundry, I go back to the sitting room where she is working at her make-shift desk. This cozy, quiet space is such a welcome change from the chaos of larger refugios.

Marivi has placed a large bouquet of yellow roses from her garden on the coffee table, along with several copies of a Spanish periodical about the pilgrimage to Santiago. One issue catches my eye because of a cover story about how to approach the Camino. The main point of the article is simply this:

> Don't complain about the accommodations. Instead, be thankful that you have a roof over your head and be grateful to the people through whose efforts you are offered inexpensive shelter during your pilgrimage. Remember that a pilgrimage is fundamentally a journey of the spirit. You must let go of the material world.

It's timely advice, though not so easy to implement for people who, like most Americans and Europeans, are used to a high standard of creature comfort. The refugio system pushes to a new level the idea of relaxing the primacy of the material world and its comforts. Refugios vary widely, from clean and welcoming safe havens that are a high point of the Camino to filthy health hazards that make your skin crawl, and this lovely home in Rabé, at least in my experience, is the exception, not the rule.

Not surprisingly, pilgrims have strong opinions about why—or even whether—to stay in refugios. One widely held view is that real pilgrims stay in refugios because these humble shelters serve as a constant reminder of the need to pare down to the essentials. Actually, they force pilgrims to confront, sometimes brutally, what it means to do without many privileges we take for granted, including privacy. The experience isn't necessarily fun, but maybe that's the point. Moreover, refugio life offers the opportunity to meet fellow pilgrims and engage in conversations that are central to the pilgrim experience. On a good night and in a good refugio, the camaraderie really *is* extraordinary, and let's face it, suffering together creates a powerful bond. A minister from West Virginia, with whom I walked one afternoon, told me that staying in refugios was essential to his pilgrimage because it put him in the place of others who are less fortunate. "It is a humbling experience that's a key part of the Camino for me," he explained.

On the other hand, some insist that nobody in his or her right mind would stay in a refugio and choose to be subjected to such primitive (or worse) conditions. One man told me that refugios are immoral and that it's too much temptation for men and women—strangers at that—to sleep in the same room and share the same bathroom. Then there is the attitude of the infamous "Parador Princess," a pilgrim from New York City who is supposed to have said: "If you can afford it, go for the best!"

What's a pilgrim to do? I struggled during my entire journey with the decision of where to stay, usually feeling guilty if I stayed in a hotel and sometimes miserable if I slept in a refugio. In retrospect, I believe that this is not an either-or situation. For me, a combination of refugios, modest hotels and pensiones, and the occasional parador was just right. I loved the uninhibited and carefree camaraderie of the refugios, and I was profoundly affected by the experience of doing without so many things I previously believed essential to my happiness and well-being. But the occasional night in a hotel allowed me to take time out and digest what was happening in ways that would not have been possible in the typical crowded refugio. And as a practical matter, after several rough nights in a refugio, I needed some sleep and privacy to avoid a meltdown.

But my bottom line on where to stay is this: there's no right or wrong answer. If you want to enter into the world of the Camino as a pilgrim, you might consider staying in refugios, at least a few times. The absence of creature comforts and privacy forces most of us out of our comfort zone, opening the way to broader understandings. But there are many ways to make a pilgrimage. Each of us starts from a different place, and your Camino will be shaped by your own personal needs and goals. Trust your instincts.

I sit for some time in the lounge, thoughts wandering, until I start to feel chilled. These old stone buildings can be amazingly cool, even without air conditioning and even in the extreme midday heat.

"Go sit in the sun on the plaza," says Marivi when she sees me shivering, "I'll call you when it's time for dinner."

So I go outside and settle in on a bench next to a bed of roses to wait three long hours until dinner. A short, portly Spaniard with well-cut salt-and-pepper hair and twinkly eyes occupies the other bench. He introduces himself as "Maxi," and soon we're busy trading stories about our pilgrimages, our travels, our philosophies of living (that sounds pretentious, I know, but this is the Camino)—and recipes. If this is what it means to kick back and relax, I'm starting to get the hang of it. It's not unusual for me to start up conversations with strangers, but the idea of sitting for several hours without some specific goal or task—and enjoying it—now that's a novel experience.

Around 8:30, Marivi calls us in for a simple supper, just the three of us sitting around the kitchen table for a meal of hearty, homemade vegetable soup, farm-fresh fried eggs, lots of good bread, and a salad of lettuce and succulent tomatoes from her garden, dressed with wonderfully fragrant olive oil and balsamic vinegar. We're just finishing dinner when a French pilgrim with a pack the size of a small refrigerator shows up. Marivi registers him and he goes up to bed while Maxi and I help Marivi clear off the table and do the dishes. Later that evening, when we say good night, Marivi takes me aside.

"Here, take this," she says, handing me a tiny scrap of paper. "It's my phone number. Call me if you need help during your pilgrimage—*cualquiera cosa* (any little thing). If you should have a problem, it could help to have someone who knows the language and the system. One never knows."

Then she embraces me and wishes me a *¡buen camino!* I thank her and tuck the little piece of paper into the secret pocket of my hat. And I think again about the role of the people who run the refugios. English-speakers call them wardens, but to the Spanish they are *hospitaleros/hospitaleras,* hosts and hostesses. Why did I ever see them as wardens, with all that word conjures of prisons and harsh discipline? I had a lot to learn.

*"Pèlerin, prépare-toi à souffrir: si tu dois mériter
ton pèlerinage, c'est ici le lieu!"*

Pilgrim, prepare to suffer: this [the meseta]
is the place where you'll find out if you're
worthy of your pilgrimage!

Jean-Claude Bourlès, *Le Grand Chemin de Compostelle.*

Chapter Eleven

Pilgrims' Proving Ground

June 11, Rabé to Castrojeríz.

Today, I will begin to cross the infamous meseta, a vast, bleak, and sparsely populated plateau that stretches across the center of the Iberian Peninsula at an average altitude of 650 meters, or 2,133 feet. The Camino traverses the meseta from around Burgos to Astorga—about a ten-day walk—but the landscape doesn't become desert-like until after the trail leaves the village of Rabé, that is to say, until this morning. Though the elevation chart for this section shows an essentially flat terrain, the meseta is reputedly the hardest stretch of the Camino. As far as I can tell, the problem seems to be monotony. Frankly, I look forward to the meseta as a welcome relief from the constant up and down of the past two weeks.

Everyone except me leaves Marivi's refugio when it's still pitch black outside. My bunkmates may be eager to start walking, but I think it's ridiculous to start out before I can see where I'm going. I roll over and go back to sleep, not waking again until first light. Fifteen minutes later, the village church chimes the hour, sending me on my way to the ringing of bells. The still morning air feels so cool that I stop to put on my vest. Though barren, the landscape has spots of green, and the path is well-marked and level. This is lovely, I think. I can't imagine why the meseta gets a bad rap.

By the time I reach the village of Hornillas about two hours later, the answer is becoming clear. It's only 8:50, but already the air has become heavy and deathly still. Heat waves shimmer above the town's dusty main street, which stretches as far as I can see like a scene out of a spaghetti

Western. The landscape is stark and monochromatic now—path, earth, horizon, and sky all a brownish gray. In the midst of this tedium, the village bar is irresistible. Within minutes I'm sipping a freshly made café con leche that comes with a caramel and a purr from the resident cat, who is the same color as the candy.

"*Se llama Peregrino*" (His name is Pilgrim), the bartender tells me, pointing to the cat. "He's named in your honor."

Peregrino deigns to accept my kinship—he rubs up against my legs, eager for the strokes to which he has become accustomed from homesick pilgrims missing their pets. Soon, I have my shoes off and am massaging my feet while I play with Peregrino and savor the coffee. Morning coffee on the Camino is a combination of therapy and a good party. In the business of everyday life, a coffee break is so insignificant that it doesn't merit even a passing reference when recalling the day's events. But here, after hours of walking, often with only one's thoughts for company, morning coffee provides a welcome reprieve from the weather and drudgery of the trail. By some miracle of the Camino, the bars that serve it are cool or toasty, depending on what would feel good given the outside temperature, and they seem to offer whatever a pilgrim needs in the way of comfort—conversation, companionable solitude, even a friendly cat. And the coffee really *is* delicious.

Life is looking decidedly less burdensome by the time I start off again, half an hour later. I take regular breaks all day because of the exhausting heat. On one, I leave the path and climb the hillside to sprawl out and take in the endless expanse of fields and sky. An old shepherd and his two dogs pass by me with a noisy, smelly flock of sheep that bleat and bob, kicking up clouds of dust. Later, a sturdy, young blond woman wearing lederhosen strides by, unencumbered by a pack, which no doubt explains why she's moving so quickly. Before long, a broad-shouldered young man with strong, tanned legs—also blond and also wearing lederhosen— shows up, puffing like a steam engine as he labors to keep up with his companion. I stare in disbelief—well, OK, disgust—when I realize why he's struggling. In addition to the huge pack he wears on his back, he carries another giant pack across his chest. *Hers, no doubt,* I think. But the scene is so comical that I can't help laughing as I gather up my courage and hit the trail.

In the distance, a bright red line runs parallel to the path and extends to the horizon, like a long, fire-engine-red pipeline. As I get closer, I see that it's not a pipeline at all but a vast field of brilliantly red poppies. They pulsate in the sun, transferring some of their energy and enthusiasm to my weary body and reminding me of Bilbao's impromptu serenade outside of Santo Domingo. What a contrast with the scene described by

Domenico Laffi, an Italian pilgrim who walked to Santiago from Italy in the seventeenth century. Then, instead of thousands of dazzling poppies, this landscape was barren and scorched by swarms of locusts so thick they obscured the sky. Packs of wolves roamed the area day and night, devouring fallen pilgrims and making it impossible to cross the plain safely except in mid-day when the shepherds were out with their big dogs. I wonder if I would have had the courage to keep going under those conditions.

The next village, Hontanas, has also changed over the past four hundred years. Laffi described it as a "wretched place." To me, it feels like an oasis in the desert. The little village is immaculate, and even the dirt streets have been freshly swept. An inviting stone fountain bubbles away in the plaza; roses grow profusely around the doors of the old stone homes. I fill my water bottles and then sit in the shade to eat a banana and some almonds and chocolate. As usual in these little villages, unless it's the hour of the *paseo*, when everyone takes a pre-dinner stroll, the streets are deserted. But this time, the quiet doesn't last. A band of paunchy, middle-aged Italian cyclists roars into town, coming to a noisy stop at the fountain. These men wear tight neon-colored Lycra outfits that are not flattering. I am amazed at their total lack of self-consciousness. Leaping off their bikes, they rush around, gesticulating madly. Their leader, barely five feet tall and balding, sings opera arias in a decent tenor voice while the others laugh and talk non-stop. As quickly as they arrived, they ride off in a tightly formed pack that looks like a single, many-wheeled bicycle. Watching them go, I am struck by the urge to giggle and, looking around, I see that others have the same reaction. The easy camaraderie and upbeat behavior of these high-energy cyclists is contagious. *They are poster children for how to stop worrying about appearances and have a great time*, I think. *I could learn something from them.*

The church bell chimes the half hour and just as that sound fades away, a miniature yellow bread delivery truck comes sputtering up to the square, horn blasting. Within seconds, a dozen old ladies and a few old men appear in doorways, money in hand. They all know the driver and each other and chatter happily while they buy their bread. The driver is charming and solicitous with the old ladies, tipping his hat and listening attentively while each picks the loaf she wants. His elderly customers are amazingly agile as they beam and scurry around, even the ones who walk with canes. They've probably been neighbors longer than I've been alive.

Two Spanish pilgrims walk through the village, waving at everyone in sight. Minutes later the blond, lederhosen-clad couple arrives. (They apparently took even more breaks than I did.) He shrugs off his enormous packs, they settle in for a snack in the shade—and I become acutely aware that today everybody seems to come in couples or groups. Then there's me, a solitary traveler, as dusty, drab, and listless as the land I'm crossing. I know that I have, in fact, had company for much of my journey, and that with just a little effort, I could find someone to walk with me this afternoon. I also know in my head that many pilgrims prefer to travel alone, and with good reason, for pilgrimage, according to some, is a solitary endeavor.

This knowledge makes no difference right now. My solitude weighs heavily, and the desolate landscape feels overwhelming and ominous. I don't sense any of the excitement I experienced that day when I headed into the forest to walk alone for the first time, none of the wonder I felt when I stood in the rain on a tapestry of flowers. For the first time since leaving home, I feel profoundly alone, as if I have become the bleakness of the meseta itself. Later, I will understand that these times of solitude and loneliness were a chance to get to know myself, just like the lady at the Confraternity Practical Pilgrim's Day had said. But I can't see this while I'm here, suffocating on the meseta.

From the square, the Camino leaves Hontanas on a dirt road that heads steeply up and into the barren landscape. Dispirited and weary, I creep up the hill, back onto the plateau. There is no shade in sight. In fact, every step for the next two hours and fifteen minutes is in full sun. The chalk-colored soil looks like snow when it's visible through the scraggly vegetation, a delusional vision in this heat. The air reminds me of the American Midwest in August, earthy and thick. New sounds greet me on this stark hillside, ones I haven't heard before on the Camino—swarms of bees, energetic crickets, and frogs. What's most astonishing about this section of the pilgrimage, however, are the butterflies. For most of an hour, I am surrounded by fluttering bits of silent color as I trudge along, leaden and earthbound. The butterflies are orange with black edges, black with royal blue markings, snowy white, pale yellow, deep yellow with incandescent blue touches. With this last one, the University of Michigan battle cry comes into my head—*Go Blue!*—and it is my first happy thought in some time. Pulled ahead by the butterflies' energy, I concentrate on the need to keep going, conscious that I've entered a new stretch of the pilgrimage, one that is harsher, less friendly, and oh, so solitary.

An eternity later, moving at a slow crawl, I spot Castrojeríz, still four and a half kilometers away. As usual, it takes forever to get there and just as long again to walk through the sprawling Roman town. It's siesta time and the streets are empty. I see no yellow arrows, but there's only one main road, so I continue walking straight ahead, looking for a hotel where I can get a good night's sleep. I reach the far side of town without having found any refuge. When I realize that I'm about to head back onto the meseta, which is the last place I want to be, I turn around and retrace my steps. It's boiling hot, even in the shade. Pedro, the truck driver who gave us a ride to Burgos, described the climate on the meseta as "*nueve meses de invierno y tres de inferno*" (nine months of winter and three of hell). He nailed the part about hell.

I walk and walk, find myself back on the other side of town, turn around, and walk some more. I'm aware that I'm disorientated, but can't figure out what to do about it. Then, through the fog that has enveloped my brain, I am conscious of movement. A man is running after me. He is repeating the same thing over and over, but the words don't register.

"*¿Quieres el sello? ¿Quieres el sello?*"

Finally, I understand that he's asking if I want him to stamp my credential. I just stare at him as he takes my arm and leads me into a cool, dark space that I eventually realize is the reception area of a refugio. I must have walked past it three times without noticing.

"Rest a minute, you'll feel better," he says as he sits me down on a bench. "The heat is terrible today."

It's gloriously cool inside and, finally, my head clears. Maybe I'll stay here tonight. The hospitalero tells me with pride that they separate the men and women in this refugio, and that clinches it—I wouldn't have to contend with the loudest snorers.

"*Quiero una cama*" (I'd like a bed), I say.

"*¡Muy bien!*" he says. "Come over here and let's get you registered, then I'll give you a tour."

I look at him incredulously from the comfort of my bench deep in the cool vestibule.

"Do you mean you want me to move?" I ask him.

He laughs. "*¡No te preocupes!* (No worries!) You can sit on the bench as long as you like. Just let me know when you're ready."

Half an hour later, when my legs will again support me, we take care of the formalities. Then the hospitalero shows me to a sleeping room with twenty-four beds, stacked two high and grouped four to a cubicle. He assigns me a top bunk, but this time access isn't a problem because ladders are built into the side of each pair of beds. The room and its tiny bathroom are clean, and boots are stored in the hallway—all good signs. I shower, wash out my clothes, and go to the garden to write in my journal and rest.

That evening, when I walk back into the center of town to find a restaurant recommended by the hospitalero, I discover that Castrojeríz is a pretty town when it's cooler and I'm not delirious. The place he recommends is not much from the outside, but beyond the façade, I discover an inviting dining room run by a middle-aged couple. They greet me warmly.

"*¡Bienvenida!* Please, have a seat," says the señor, pulling out a chair. "We'll take good care of you."

I am so ready to be taken care of tonight, I think, as I dissolve into the cushioned chair.

He serves me an excellent pilgrim menu, prepared by his wife, that consists of *patata* (a hearty pork and potato stew), fresh pan-fried sardines, a crispy green salad, and *natas* (a custard-like desert). The Rioja that accompanies the meal is superb. Before I leave, I ask to take their photo. They agree but insist that I join them and ask a Frenchman at the next table to take the picture. I am turning to go when the Frenchman who took the photo invites me to have a glass of wine with him and his companions. Why not? At second glance, I recognize him as the man with the refrigerator-size pack from the private refugio in Rabé. He holds out a chair for me, and as I sit down he says something about our sleeping together last night.

"Not in your wildest dreams," I reply, without thinking.

The other Frenchmen at the table laugh uproariously—it seems my response was the right one. We settle quickly into a comfortable conversation and spend an hilarious couple of hours drinking together. These men are astounded that I am doing the Camino alone, especially since I am married. Their wives are at home, which, they explain, is exactly where they belong.

"That's where my husband is," I deadpan, "home taking care of the house and kids."

The Frenchmen erupt in laughter and start banging on the table.

"That's *so* American," they tell me, when they stop for breath.

I feel bad about this little lie, but I couldn't resist. In fact, our children are grown and no longer live at home; Philip is working on a book and preparing classes for the fall. I don't think he'd mind.

When I return to the refugio a little before ten, everyone else in my sleeping room is already in bed, exhausted after a day on the meseta. I soon join them, but when I climb up to my top bunk, I notice a problem with the head room. The lower bunks are a good three feet off the ground and provide enough space to sit up in bed, but as a result, the uppers are nosebleed height and have essentially no head room. I can barely raise up on my elbows before hitting my head on the ceiling. Then I notice that an eighteen-inch cement wall separates my bunk from the upper bunk of the adjacent men's cubicle, providing some privacy, and a few inches of open space between the top of the wall and the ceiling allow the air to circulate. This will be OK, I think, snuggling into my sleeping bag. The señor arrives minutes later, closes and locks the shutters, turns out the lights, and with a whispered "*buenas noches,*" he slips out.

The man on the other side of the wall starts snoring almost immediately. In spite of the cement separation, our heads are only inches apart, and it feels like he's snoring right in my ear. The racket builds and builds, continuing at a high decibel level for several minutes until he wakes himself up with the noise. It's quiet for a few minutes, then the cycle starts again. Finally, his travel companion, who managed to be assigned to his cubby in spite of the same-gender policy, starts yelling at him in German.

"Franz!" she screams, then bellows something about *schlaffen* (sleep).

Though I know only a few words of German, I can tell that she's really letting him have it, and for the rest of the night, he's silent. Well mostly— he continues to toss about, though he stops snoring. I think poor Franz is afraid to go to sleep because he knows he'll start to snore again, and she'll yell at him. I feel some sympathy for the stranger lying next to me when I realize it's the same young man who carried his companion's enormous pack across the meseta in the blazing sun, as well as his own. He's probably making so much noise from exhaustion, pure and simple. The Spanish woman in the lower bunk across from me buzzes away softly, somebody farther off sounds like an elephant trumpeting—and I am now wide awake.

I lie still in my bed, but I'm becoming acutely aware of a desperate need to sit up and get some air. Yet I can't move in this restricted space, except to roll from side to side. It takes every ounce of will power not to climb down and rush outside. Then I remember this is not an option—the doors and windows are locked shut. No red emergency exit lights indicate an escape route, and with the shutters closed, there's no moonlight to temper the darkness. I try to relax and shut my eyes, hoping this will keep me from panicking in the absolute darkness. Neither helps.

I've never experienced claustrophobia before, and the growing sensation of entrapment is terrible. My confined space is no worse than an MRI tube, I remind myself, and I essentially dozed through that test. I just closed my eyes, took deep breaths, and thought about an upcoming trip to France. Was it easy because I knew there was a sympathetic technician on the other side of the wall, with the power to rescue me at a moment's notice? Now I wish I could apologize to the man I had met in the MRI waiting room whose panic I treated so cavalierly.

I'm not a patient, I'm a pilgrim, I remind myself, and pilgrimage is about accepting the fundamental solitude and vulnerability of being human. About learning to be so focused on the interior voyage that exterior surroundings don't matter. About learning to *be*, as fully and completely as possible, in whatever space you are given, even if entombed in a refugio. I know all this, but on this night, at this moment, I can't do it. That this, too, shall pass doesn't even enter my mind.

I go into full mind-over-matter mode. It's ridiculous to have a meltdown over something as innocuous as being in a confined space in a pitch-black room with twenty-three other people. I'm not alone. I'm not going to be eaten by wolves. I'm not suffering from heat stroke. Philip loves me. I try to visualize skiing with him down the Big Burn run at Snowmass Mountain in Colorado.

The night passes.

Everyone eventually gets to the point of
bursting into tears somewhere along this route.
You just stand there and cry. You'll see!

Hape Kerkeling, *I'm Off Then: Losing and Finding Myself
on the Camino de Santiago*

Chapter Twelve

The Meseta Dries Tears

June 12, Castrojeríz to Frómista.

At 6 a.m., Gregorian chant by the monks of Santo Domingo de Silos fills our sleeping room, a recording from the hospitalero's boom box that he has turned up full blast. A few minutes later, he waltzes in and opens the shutters to the fresh morning air. Did I dream the agonies of last night?

"*¡Muy buenos días!*" he announces. "My wife will be serving coffee in the second-floor dining room in ten minutes."

Twenty-three pilgrims take turns splashing water on their faces at the single sink, pack up quickly, and go to breakfast ready to start walking. After my rough night, I need time to get going, so I throw on my clothes and head for the coffee without even the pretense of washing up or organizing my gear. I know I'll be sorry that I didn't take full advantage of the cool morning hours, but I'm just not ready to face this day. The other pilgrims are all long gone when I finally leave around seven, fortified with several cups of strong coffee and armed with a warm embrace and an enthusiastic *¡buen camino!* from the hospitalero. Maybe this day will be OK, I think. It's getting off to such a good start.

The minute I walk out the door, I know better. In that hour between my first glance out the window and stepping outside, the light has changed from glowing to harsh and the morning air has taken on a foreboding heaviness. The Mule Killers Hill, today's first challenge, is a thigh-burning climb on a rock-hard, deeply rutted dirt path. But I'm in luck. The musical mantra I experienced outside of Belorado comes into my head as I begin the ascent, and once again, these few notes replay over and over in my head and get me up the hill.

After the summit, the path descends to cross an immense cultivated plain, and the terrain is relatively flat the rest of the morning. Everyone else is ahead of me, so I'm alone on the trail, ambling along at a comfortable pace. For a time, my mind is in neutral, then my thoughts drift toward my father. How he would have relished this pilgrimage. The profusion of wildflowers; the challenge of hiking all day, day after day; many new friends just there for the making; good food and wine; the funny, odd, moving situations around every bend—all things he embraced with great enthusiasm. Though he died five years ago, I still feel his loss acutely.

The next thing I know, I am walking across the meseta with tears streaming down my face, tears of loss and remorse. I have so many wonderful memories of my father, happy memories of good times. Yet these memories continue to be overwhelmed by a deep sorrow over his death and lingering regrets over my lost opportunities. How does one exorcise painful memories so the good ones can take front and center stage? How do you get beyond regrets that can't be fixed? How easy it is to put off hard conversations, to forget that the only time you can count on with certainty is the present moment. The irony is that my father understood that you should not avoid difficult subjects and showed me by example the power and value of difficult, but necessary, conversations (my adolescence offered many opportunities).

"Don't duck, take it on the chin like a man," he would tell me when I tried to squirm out of a situation that needed to be addressed. Yet when it came to helping him with his own death, I ducked. Our last lucid conversation was in mid-July 1997, the night before we were both leaving for trips. He and my mother were going to Cape Cod with my youngest sister and her family; I was going to Idaho with Philip and our children for a raft trip down the Middle Fork of the Salmon River. When I called to wish my parents a safe journey, I detected an uncertainty in my father's voice that I had never heard before.

Twenty years earlier, at the relatively young age of sixty-three, Dad had been diagnosed with prostate cancer and given months to live. With characteristic optimism and determination, he refused to accept his prognosis, sought alternate treatments, and eventually the cancer went into remission and he got on with his life. Then, during our phone call that July evening, Dad told me some worrisome news—a routine blood test appeared to indicate that the cancer was back and spreading. His doctor wanted to do a procedure to assess the situation, but he reassured my father that it could wait until after his vacation. Later, I learned the blood test indicated that the cancer had spread throughout my father's body and that he was dying. Later, I learned that the follow-up procedure the doctor had ordered carried a high risk of stroke and blood clots. But during that July conversation, it was business as usual and cheery surface conversations prevailed until the very end.

"It doesn't look so good," Dad said, then paused.

It was the kind of hesitation that invited—no, let's be honest, cried out for—an acknowledgment. I know now that this had been my cue to tell him I was ready to listen and to be there for him, as he had been for me so many times during our fifty-two-year relationship.

"Hang in there, Dad," I said. "We'll talk when we get back."

It was late. Our flight left early the next morning, and we hadn't finished packing. There is always tomorrow. But there wasn't. The next time I saw him, three weeks later, he was lying semi-conscious in a hospital bed in Chicago. The follow-up procedure had revealed that the cancer had returned with a vengeance and caused Dad to suffer a neurological incident that left him drifting in and out of consciousness. We never had that conversation about his bad news—or any other conversation, for that matter. Dad was of a generation when men were supposed to be strong and silent. But had I reached out, I suspect he would have welcomed a willing ear and that our conversation would have brought comfort to both of us.

My other deep regret is that I didn't know how to ease his last days. In a life marked by much good fortune, his luck ran out at the end. His doctor, a caring and skilled practitioner who had always dealt with my parents with sensitivity and professionalism, was out of town when Dad returned early from his vacation and was immediately hospitalized. The young attending in charge was the polar opposite. Brash and arrogant, his hair in gelled spikes and wearing Gucci loafers (sans socks), he strutted around with his little following of residents. I can still see the look of incredulity on his face when my mother asked when Dad could go home.

"He's got cancer through his whole body," he snapped. "Haven't you seen the X-rays?"

Well, no, she hadn't, and neither had Dad, for that matter. I don't know what they had been told, but I know with certainty that they had neither understood nor accepted the gravity of his condition. Perhaps, in a misguided attempt at kindness, his long-time doctor had not been very direct about the prognosis. Or perhaps the news was so overwhelming that they needed more time to process it. And now, at the end, instead of being able to rely on the kindness and compassion of their seasoned practitioner, they had to suffer the brutal arrogance of this young doctor. It was a terrible blow that left us all defenseless and devastated. I was beside myself at the young doctor's unwillingness to engage with us on

The meseta near Frómista.

any level, saddened beyond words by the look in my mother's eyes, and terrified at the thought that I was failing my father again, this time by not ensuring he got the care he needed, emotionally as well as physically, as he lay dying.

Over the next few days, my mother, my middle sister, and I sat for hours at Dad's bedside. We would arrive in the morning to wait for the doctor's always short, abrupt, and unpredictable visits, which provided few answers to our questions about Dad's condition and treatment options. "He's putting up a fight; this is going to be a while" was the most I could get out of the doctor. His response felt unimaginably insensitive. Each night, we'd go home drained, try to get some sleep, and start the cycle again the next morning. Finally one day there was talk about taking him home.

"He'll be more comfortable," the nurse said.

We sensed we were taking him home to die, though this remained unspoken, and no one discussed with us what help we might need in caring for him. But bringing Dad home had to be better for him and for us. That night, as we got ready to leave, Dad, who was by then unable to speak, wouldn't let go of my hand. His eyes were pleading: *Don't go, please don't go. Don't leave me alone tonight.*

"We'll be back in the morning to take you home," I told him. "I love you, Dad, I love you."

But his grasp didn't loosen. I pulled his hand off mine and gave it to my sister to say goodnight. I couldn't bear to be the last one to break away.

Steps Out of Time

I so wish that either my sister or I had stayed with him that night. But bone-weary and worrying about what we thought lay ahead, we went home with Mother. Early the next morning the nurse called.

"You'd better come in," she said. "He's having trouble breathing."

Dad died twenty-five hours later.

I re-play so many scenes from his life as I trudge across the meseta— painful ones from those last days in the hospital; fun ones, like the great arguments we used to have, many of which lasted for years (gender-free language, for example); happy ones, like the look of pure delight on his face when his grandchildren ran up to him to offer big hugs. Half a century of family stories, a history that goes on, of course, but now without Dad. The steaming, oppressive meseta intensifies my feelings of loss. With no shade, no breeze, no sound, even the birds have abandoned me.

When I arrive at Boadilla three hours later, I am beyond exhausted. My face is streaked with a mixture of sweat and tears and my shirt sleeves are more brown than blue from wiping my brow. I try to compose myself, cleaning off my sunglasses and pulling my hat further down over my eyes as I approach the village square. Drained, I sit on top of the massive stone wall that surrounds an elaborate tiered fountain and take several drinks of the cool, sweet water. When I am feeling better, I have a quick lunch of cheese, bread, and chocolate, bathe my feet in the lower part of the fountain, and prepare to face the unrelenting sun. I need to get as far as Frómista today, another five kilometers along a flat path that follows a canal. Red poppies, blue morning glories, white daisies, and purple thistles appear sporadically along the trail, but what dominates is the vastness of the perfectly still wheat fields. And the ruthless heat. Only two days of the meseta down and about eight to go.

When I arrive in Frómista, there is no question where I will stay. I desperately need a good night's sleep and the privacy that only a hotel can offer. I soak for a very long time in my private bath, which alleviates the soreness in my shoulders and feet. Later that afternoon, I go out to buy fruit and cookies for breakfast, and on the way back to my hotel, stop at the eleventh-century Church of San Martín, which is the only cool place in this town without air conditioning. It is also a welcome refuge. Within minutes of sitting quietly on a pew and taking deep, cool breaths, I feel myself relaxing. I admire the splendid corbels and capitals carved with all manner of animals, plants, and mythological creatures and watch the filtered light play off the stonework. The only other person in the church is a middle-aged man several rows in front of me who is on his knees praying and fingering a gold cross. Exuding a feeling of tranquility, he adds to the peaceful aura of this little church.

That evening, unable to make any unnecessary effort, I eat in the hotel dining room. I am sitting at a window table for two, contemplating the menu, when a thin, angular man with a beak-like nose comes up to my table—the same man who had been praying in the church a few hours earlier. Tonight, as then, he wears hiking pants, a T-shirt, and the gold cross.

"May I join you?" he asks in French. "I find it sad to eat alone."

"*D'accord, pourquoi pas?*" (Sure, why not?) I say, although I'm not sure I want the company of this stranger who now appears very serious.

I misjudged. He turns out to be a great dinner companion and a Benedictine monk whose gentle manners and way of listening attentively to me (and the waiter and anyone else who passes by) immediately put me at ease. He tells me that he started his pilgrimage in north-central France and has already walked 1,514 kilometers (941 miles)—almost twice as far as I expect to walk in total—and he's got over four hundred kilometers to go. *As do I*, I think, with a sigh.

"I am between assignments," he volunteers, "and am taking this time to reflect on my new position. I hope the Camino will help me find my course."

I look at him, surprised. "I thought reflection was an essential part of a monk's way of life. How is it that you need to take time off from the monastery to be thoughtful?"

"People are people," he replies, with a shrug. "I have a supervisory role in the monastery and face the usual challenges of human nature.

My new assignment won't be any easier, so I am seeking guidance and strength from Saint James before undertaking it."

He tells me about some Americans from California who are traveling with a guitar and are always singing. "Walking with them is so gay and energizing," he says, with his first smile. He has also met a group of German students who are doing the Camino by singing in all the churches, which he thinks is a wonderful way to make a pilgrimage. On the other hand, he strongly disapproves of pilgrims who take the bus across the meseta.

"You need to experience it all," he insists, shaking his head, "the joy and the struggles. Life is about many different experiences. You must not try to select only the best. The difficulties are important. Even if we fail today, we learn something, and somehow we find the strength to try again tomorrow. How else can we be fully human?"

He smiles again, but smiling doesn't fit his face very well. I have the sense that he's weary of his responsibilities and shoulders more than his fair share of worries, yet he has a quiet strength and confidence that I can't help envying. Dinner flies by and all of a sudden it's almost 10 p.m., and he must hurry back to the refugio, or he'll be locked out.

"We won't see each other again," he says, "because I leave very early and walk fast. That's part of what's so extraordinary about the Camino— the people who come into your life, ever so briefly, yet mark you in some way. *Adieu, bon camino.*"

We shake hands, and he disappears.

A couple of weeks later, Inge, my young German friend, tells me about her encounter with this same monk, at a time when she couldn't get beyond her anger at Catherine's sudden and brutal death. She and Catherine had spent time together in the days immediately preceding the accident, and this shockingly violent loss of a new but already dear friend hit her hard. Discouraged and depressed, she was ready to abandon her pilgrimage and return to Berlin.

"No," he told her, "you can't quit now. You must continue. The meseta will dry your tears. You must go on," he repeated. "Later, you will understand."

"He was so earnest that I decided to take his advice. But how did he know?" she asks, her voice conveying both astonishment and gratitude. "After the meseta, the sadness was still there, but the despair I felt had lifted."

This was my experience, too, with my feelings about my father's death. It didn't happen right away, but little by little, after those difficult days on the meseta, I began to see things differently. The sadness and loss I felt when I thought of Dad remained, but affection and gratitude were claiming the foreground, and that made all the difference.

Solitude vécue, fraternité expérimentée,
souvent les deux en même temps.

Living in solitude, experimenting with
companionship, often both at the same time.

Michel Bureau, *Pèlerin! Marcher vers Compostelle*

Chapter Thirteen

Kindnesses

June 13, Frómista to Carrión de los Condes.

The next morning, I have a quick breakfast in my room that includes the peaches and cookies I picked up yesterday and my own special Camino tea. The peaches are sweet and juicy and may be the best ones since the Georgia Belles that I remember from childhood visits to my grandmother. Camino tea is my recipe for a hot breakfast drink when no stove is available to heat water: mix equal parts of hot water from the tap with room temperature juice from a juice box (the mixed tropical fruit flavor is especially nice); stir with a spoon, or, in a pinch, use your finger. One box makes two glasses. This tastes better than it sounds when you're on the road to Santiago.

I walk this morning on a wide, flat gravel path that runs alongside the highway all the way from Frómista to Carrión de los Condes, where I hope to sleep tonight. I've been on the road about an hour when I spot an old church at the top of a small hill. I walk over, hoping to visit it, but as usual, the door is locked. A German pilgrim named Rainer stands in the churchyard, staring solemnly at the crumbling gravestones. They lie at crazy angles in the tall, unmowed grass, most of them in pieces, any inscriptions long since effaced by time and weather.

"Pilgrim graves," he says in broken Spanish, "twelfth and thirteenth century. Very old."

"How do you know they are pilgrims?" I ask in Spanish.

He pulls out his German Camino guide and points to a page with a photo of the graves and some text I can't read. The sun is vicious now,

:trating my shirt and baking my shoulders and back. The air
/ grasses and is completely still. The silence is absolute; I can't
even hea⌐ ᴜur breathing. The place looks more like an abandoned rock
quarry than a cemetery, yet it is strangely affecting.

We stand there for some time in silent tribute to our predecessors.
They came from all over Europe hundreds of years ago to walk to Santiago
for reasons known only to them and died far from home, alone or among
strangers. Nothing here but a pile of rocks bears witness to their lives or
their journeys; not even a name on a tombstone remains. Yet wherever
they came from, they participated in the life of a community. They had
parents and siblings, spouses and children, friends and neighbors—
people who probably never even learned the fate of their loved ones.

But these crumbling remnants of lives lived centuries ago elicit
more than sadness. The presence of these nameless pilgrims who died
so long ago—even if represented only by fragments of tombstones
in an old cemetery in the middle of nowhere—is a reminder of the
continuity of the human spirit, and by their presence they encourage
us, their spiritual descendants. They had their time, did their best,
and moved on, destination unknown. Now it's our turn. Those of us
who come later bear witness to their struggles and validate their lives
by our efforts. It's the monk's message again: we must embrace the
hardships of life as well as the joys, because it is the struggles that
make us fully human. Both are integral parts of life, but how we deal
with adversity defines us. I wander back to the trail, alone with my
thoughts. Rainer is nowhere in sight.

Around lunchtime, I approach the hilltop town of Villacazar de Sirga,
home of the *Virgen Blanca,* the White Virgin, who became famous in the
thirteenth century because of a collection of then-popular songs praising
her. The renown of these songs led to an influx of pilgrims eager to
seek her protection and guidance, with the result that the pilgrimage to
Santiago was rerouted to pass through Villacazar. This is surely a testament
to the power of music. I like the idea that the Camino was shaped not just
by religious, economic, and political forces but also by abstract universal
human needs.

"Meeetcheeegan!" I hear, when I walk into the bar on the town square.
Bilbao is there drinking a coffee and talking with some locals.

"*¿Cómo estás?*" (How are you doing?), he asks, a big grin on his face.
"What's the condition of your feet?"

"*Bien,*" I reply. "*¿Y tú?*"

He mops his face with a napkin. "I'm making good time but this heat
is a killer. The food here is good; take advantage of it."

I order a *tortilla francesa* and a fresh-squeezed orange juice and take my lunch outside to enjoy it in the shade of the patio. All the outdoor tables are occupied, but a man who's sitting alone motions me over to join him. As I approach, I see that it's Rainer, the German pilgrim, and this time we discover a common language in French. Soon, we're trading stories about our lives, our families, and our experiences on the Camino, as if we were long-lost friends. He tells me, for example, about his fear of aging and about his hopes for a productive retirement, and we happily commiserate about our aches and pains.

I'm struck again by the irony of the situation—another personal conversation with a total stranger whom I will never see again when my time on the Camino is over. Who is this engaging German, really? Maybe he's a tyrant back home. But that's strangely irrelevant here on the Camino. Our common goal creates a bond that encourages us to reach out to strangers with kindness and makes these conversations seem like the most natural thing in the world. What's more, the anonymity is like a safety net. With nothing at stake, my guard is way down. I can listen to their ideas without being influenced (or threatened) by who they are and, as a result, my learning curve is way up. I love these random conversations.

When we get around to refugios—an inevitable topic among pilgrims—Rainer asks me if I know about the monastery in Carrión de los Condes that is run by the nuns of Saint Clare. It is reputed to be one of the best in Spain and is also one of the few Spanish refugios where it's possible to reserve ahead. In fact, I had learned about it from other pilgrims last night, but was too tired after dinner to face trying to call for a bed. Phones on the Camino are a constant challenge. They are scarce, may or may not work, and the payment system is random and unreliable. Case in point: the bar phone here works and there's no line to use it, but it only takes prepaid phone cards—something I don't have and can't purchase in this town.

"Please, use mine. It would be my pleasure," offers Rainer. "This phone card is my compromise with my wife. I left my cell phone at home because it didn't seem consistent with the spirit of pilgrimage."

I agree with him about cell phones. In an emergency, my family could always reach me through the Spanish police, and if I needed to make a call, someone would probably help me out. The one unsolvable problem might be if I were injured while walking alone and needed help. That's a chance I'm willing to take. Not being tethered to a cell phone has been one of the most freeing aspects of this journey. Finally, with help from Bilbao, the call goes through. The monastery refugio is fully booked tonight, but they still have one private room in the guest-room wing of the monastery, which I accept on the spot.

After the lunch break, I continue to make good time on the level gravel path, although I am experiencing some twinges in my right knee. When I reach Carrión de los Condes two hours later, the pain has become a steady ache and I'm happy to stop walking. The surrounding stone walls of the monastery look stern and unwelcoming from the street, but following arrows through a small stone doorway, I discover a lovely courtyard. Small windows dot the interior walls at regular intervals, looking like so many eyes watching over me; pots of white flowers perfume the air. The massive hand-hewn wooden cross in the center of the courtyard seems to extend its arms in welcome, like a loving parent. A smiling young man comes forward to greet me and, in no time, he registers me and accompanies me to the guest-room wing. We walk down a long, second-story hallway with numbered doors on each side, and when we get to the end, he pushes open a heavy oak door.

"Will this do?" he asks.

Will it ever. My immediate impression is one of perfect simplicity and order. A single window on the far wall frames the courtyard, and beyond, I see the walls of the monastery, the tile rooftops of the city, the treetops, and finally, two church steeples. A crucifix hangs on the wall between twin beds that are separated by a mission-style oak table with a small lamp. The terra cotta tile floor is worn smooth by centuries of pilgrim feet. In the small private bath, hot water comes out of the faucet on demand, and there is a thick, immaculate white bath towel—a pair of luxuries that leave me unspeakably happy.

Looking around, I feel the presence of the nun who carefully prepared this room for my arrival, adjusting the lamp shade, fluffing the pillow, and genuflecting before the crucifix on the way out, leaving a bit of her devotion behind. How else can I explain the restful feeling of this room? Even the bars on the window don't bother me. At least it opens so I can get fresh air, and stone walls won't catch fire.

I rest for some time in this wonderful space with my leg elevated, but the pain in my knee won't be ignored, in spite of a large dose of ibuprofen. Finally I decide to be on the safe side and visit the clinic that I had learned about from the hospitalero in Castrojeríz. On my way out, I stop by the office for directions. The young receptionist is getting ready to close for lunch and siesta, but he takes time to draw me a map and walks with me to the first intersection.

"I'm sure you'll be fine," he says, "but you're smart to see about your knee. *Buena suerte.*" (Good luck.)

I find the clinic without difficulty and explain to the receptionist that I would like to see someone about my knee.

"*Claro,*" she says. "It will just be a *momentito.*"

Steps Out of Time

A *momentito,* I now know, can be anywhere from a few minutes to a few hours, so I sit on a bench to wait. Half an hour later, she ushers me in to see the doctor, a friendly woman about my age. After examining me carefully, the doctor announces, to my relief, that I don't have tendonitis.

"Not yet. But you need to take it easy," she cautions, "or you're sure to develop it. And then you will have to stop walking, which you will not like, but you will have no choice. You must do small stages. Take your time, and rest often."

She also tells me to get a *rodillero* (a knee brace), explaining with her hands what this new word means. She insists that it must be made of neoprene and calls around until she locates a pharmacy with the right kind of brace. Finally, she prescribes a gel that I must use twice a day and an anti-inflammatory drug, which I am instructed to take with lots of food.

"Don't worry," I tell her with a laugh, "I eat like a horse."

From the startled look on the doctor's face, I understand that this expression loses something in translation. Or maybe I got it wrong and said something like "I eat horses"? Thanking her for her good care, I get out my wallet to pay.

"No, no, it's free," she says cheerfully, patting me on the arm and wishing me a *¡buen camino!* "We have to take good care of our pilgrims."

By the time I find the pharmacy, it's closed for siesta. I don't want to hang around outside until it re-opens, but the pain in my knee makes walking back to the monastery, only to return three hours later, even less appealing. I spot a bar across the street and realize I have another option. I hobble into the bar and order a beer. Those first few days on the trail, I ordered a bottled beer, usually a Heineken. Soon, however, I discovered that draft beer in these local bars is exquisite, cold, and about half the price of the imported bottles. So now I just order a draft, without even asking what it is.

I take my mouth-wateringly cold beer to the patio and away from the smoke and TV noise of the crowded bar. A Norwegian pilgrim whom I met yesterday is the only other person sitting outside on this fine summer day. He looks up and pulls out a chair.

"Why are you walking the Camino?" he asks as I settle in. When I hesitate, he volunteers that he hopes to gain perspective on his work with teens who have drug problems.

"The odds are against them," he says. "I learned that much pretty quickly. If I can help a few each year it's the best I can hope for, but it breaks my heart to see so many wasted young lives and destroyed families. I knew I needed to take a break when I couldn't stop thinking about the ones I couldn't help."

"What makes this trip a pilgrimage for you, instead of a vacation or R and R?" I ask.

"If you go in a spirit of meditation and reflection, it is a pilgrimage— otherwise, it is tourism," he says. "Which are you, a tourist or a pilgrim?"

"I think I am a pilgrim, but I'm just a beginner."

He laughs. "Don't worry, you will come to a better understanding as you go deeper into the Camino."

The time passes quickly as we trade stories and take turns buying beers. Around five, someone flips the sign in the window of the *farmacia* from "*cerrada*" to "*abierta*." I say goodbye and head across the street, thankful for another chance encounter.

The pharmacist is a young man, not much older than my son. He remembers the doctor's phone call and confirms that they have neoprene braces. After measuring my knee, he goes behind the counter and comes back with a weird-looking piece of navy blue elastic.

"Let's see how this fits," he says, as he hands me the brace, holding it open so I can put it on.

This sucker is heavy, and it's a struggle to pull it into place.

"Well," he says, "I have others that are less heavy and just as good as neoprene."

He hands me a lighter-weight brace that slips on like a fine leather glove and is almost gauze-like compared to the neoprene version.

"I wish my son could see me now," I tell the young man. "I am so un-athletic, he wouldn't believe that I'm trying on knee braces."

We have a good time joking about old ladies and sports, and he wants to know about my son, who loves sports, especially basketball. I am so happy to talk about him, but this brings on a wave of homesickness, and for a fleeting moment I question again what I am doing here. This young man, who is in no hurry, keeps me firmly anchored in the present. He launches into a discussion of the knee problems of basketball players and, in particular, the risk to young girls. Then he has me try on both braces again.

"What do you think?" he asks. "Which will it be?"

I hesitate, weighing comfort against doctor's orders.

"I'll be prudent and take this one," I say reaching for the neoprene brace. "It's going to be hot, but it will give more support."

"Yes, better to be prudent. And be sure not to wash your brace," he cautions me. "It won't dry overnight, even in this heat. If you wear it while it's wet, it will stretch out and won't give you any support. It may start to smell bad, but don't worry about it. It's more important to finish your pilgrimage than to smell sweet."

Languages on the Camino

I love languages, so for me being able to talk with French- and Spanish-speaking pilgrims was great fun and enriched my journey. Also, since English is not widely spoken in the little villages along the Camino, a basic knowledge of Spanish made it easier to take care of daily needs such as ordering food and asking for directions. In fact, an ability to speak any European language is an asset on the Camino, so if you have language skills, brush up on them before you leave on your pilgrimage and don't be afraid to use your knowledge en route. Even minimal skills are helpful. Often it's the *attempt* to communicate in someone else's language that leads to conversations and fascinating encounters. You may end up speaking some bizarre combination of languages intelligible to only the two of you, but you'd be surprised at how well this approach can work.

However, the ability to speak Spanish (or any language besides English) is not a requirement to have a successful journey on the Camino. Thousands of pilgrims each year come from English-speaking countries, and others you will meet along the way will be from all over the world and speak some English. If you seek company, you will find people to talk with. And it is not hard to find a translator when necessary, for example, for medical needs and pilgrim Masses. More important than language skills is your ability to *listen* to the Camino. The Camino speaks no language and every language, because it talks to your heart. Just listen.

As I leave, he offers his hand and wishes me a *¡buen camino!*

"I hope your knee's fine," he adds, with a big smile and a wave.

This young man is typical of pharmacists all along the Camino. As much nurse practitioner as pharmacist, they are often the first resource to consult in case of an injury or illness. Helpful, encouraging, and ever so patient with pilgrims—even those who speak no Spanish—the pharmacists are a Spanish national treasure.

When I get back to the monastery, the receptionist has returned from his lunch and siesta.

"*¡Hola!*" he greets me. "How did things go at the *clínica?*" I am surprised he remembers me, given the hustle and bustle of this large refugio-hotel—and even more surprised by his seemingly genuine concern.

"*Bien,*" I tell him. "The doctor and the pharmacist were very helpful. I'm all fixed up and ready to keep walking."

He smiles when I pull up my pant leg to show him my new brace.

"I'm sure it will do the trick. Now you'll get to Santiago for sure."

That night, when I get ready for bed, I think back about the kindnesses I have received today: from Rainer and Bilbao at the bar, the young receptionist at the monastery, the nun who prepared my room, the doctor, and the pharmacist. I'm used to being the caregiver, the one who fixes problems. But this day, others—and strangers at that—have cared about and for me. It's not easy or natural for me to accept help from others. I would rather offer assistance than be in the vulnerable position of needing it. Today's events help me see that accepting kindness is another way of letting go, not just of things and habits, but also of control. And perhaps others take pleasure in helping me, as I do in helping others when the tables are turned.

Feeling mellow, I go to the window for one last look before getting into bed. The sweet fragrance of the courtyard flowers drifts in through the open window. Floodlights illuminate the majestic wooden cross, its open arms offering protection from the surrounding darkness. The footsteps of pilgrims returning from dinner create a dull echo off the cobblestones that blends with the murmur of their voices. Distant church towers, poised like anachronistic rocket ships against the timeless night sky, merge past, present, and future. A few sparkling stars and the golden crescent moon make me think of my husband and children, thousands of miles away but under the same sky. I am blessed.

Il ne faut pas fuir ces temps morts . . .

You must not flee these empty moments . . .

Luc Adrian, *Compostelle: Carnet de route d'un pèlerin*

Chapter Fourteen

Are We There Yet?

June 14 – 16, Carrión de los Condes to just short of Reliegos via Calzadilla and Sahagún.

Mornings on the meseta begin with a difficult decision: whether to start early and take advantage of the fresh morning air—or sleep in and put off the inevitable as long as possible. Dawns are peaceful and cool, with soft pink sunrises. They last a heartbeat. The rest of the day offers nothing but the vast plain and an endless path. The heat is a wall that I smash into with each step. The sun blazes down, and my feet sweat and swell. Old blisters begin oozing again; new ones develop. There is no shade, no water, no distractions. The occasional dust devil whirls past. Now and then I pass a stone cross marking the spot where a pilgrim died en route to Santiago.

I decide to stop over-thinking this and just get moving. Leaving the refugio at first light, I walk slowly, as the doctor ordered. Yellow arrows lead me out of town and onto a pleasant country lane that follows the gentle curves of the land. I catch glimpses of a distant auto route, but it's far enough away not to intrude on the morning calm. The eighteen-wheelers flying down the highway look like toy trucks and, if I hear them at all, they sound like mosquitoes.

After an hour, the Camino veers off the road and onto a dirt track that weaves through wheat fields. In the distance, I see two figures, one wearing a white Panama hat, the other a yellow T-shirt, and instantly recognize Jacques and Maïté. Pilgrims on the Camino have so few possessions that each item is unique and defining. We know each other by details that wouldn't warrant a second glance back home—a gnarled, hand-carved walking stick tells me Inge is nearby, for example; a dented metal water bottle signals the presence of Rainer. Then there's Maïté's hat and Jacques' T-shirt. These memories are hard-wired. Years after I return home, a bright yellow T-shirt still makes me think of Jacques and his remarkably cheerful nature, while a white panama hat brings to mind Maïté and her coolly astute observations about people, and for a brief moment I'm back on the Camino with them, marching down the trail.

Jacques and Maïté spot me at the same time and wait for me to catch up. Maïté reports that the doctor in Burgos told her to rest for a week, but she felt much better after only twenty-four hours on antibiotics so they continued walking the next day, which is how they caught up with me so quickly. She wears gloves to protect her badly sunburned hands, but is otherwise fine. Jacques is his usual cheerful self. *Doesn't this man ever have a bad day?* I wonder. I tell them about my knee problem and the doctor's orders to go slowly.

"Not a problem for this gang!" replies Jacques, and we start off together at our usual amble.

It's barely eight, but already the heat is overwhelming. The Camino is a desolate and dusty path that stretches as far as my eye can see across the colorless plain, with nothing to break the mind-numbing tedium but a few spindly trees. We labor on for almost four hours before we spot Calzadilla down in a hollow—about another ten to fifteen minutes away. The church bells chime noon as we straggle into this singularly unattractive, one-street town plopped down in the middle of brown fields that spread out in all directions until they finally merge with the horizon.

We head for the village bar, where half a dozen boisterous Spanish bikers are amusing the standing-room-only crowd of pilgrims with their multilingual banter. Row after row of empty beer glasses stand on the bar in front of them. They down a final draft and totter over to their bikes, reeking of beer and sweat. We cozy up to the bar and order *"tres cervezas, por favor."*

A retired plumber from New Jersey named Mark is there, too, drinking a beer with the bartender. They appear to be buddies, though they speak only a few words of each other's language.

"We bonded, man, we bonded," says Mark. "Went off this morning without my passport, and Juan here drove me back to Carrión de los Condes to get it. We covered the whole distance in five minutes. Five freaking minutes! It took me the whole damn morning to get here the first time."

The bartender gives Mark a high five and they both laugh. Mark takes another swig of his beer and then removes his shoes to reveal feet covered with bandages.

"Let me tell you about being a tenderfoot," he says shaking his head. "I really get what that means now. Basically, it sucks," and he turns his attention to his blisters, which look like they're getting infected.

About 1 p.m., most of the pilgrims drift out the door, ready to continue on. Jacques, Maïté, and I are among the quitters. It's early to stop for the day, but we can't go any farther, though we've managed only seventeen and a half kilometers. My new brace has helped my knee problem—I didn't have any shooting pains today—but both legs feel like they're about to suffer an all-systems failure and the pain in my shoulders is bad. Jacques and Maïté are catatonic after just one beer. The bartender brings over a pitcher of water and three glasses and motions for us to drink. Eventually, Jacques and Maïté muster the energy to walk back to the refugio, where they will claim beds and take a nap. I opt for a single room above the bar, shared bath down the hall.

My tiny room is quiet, but with its single small window and no breeze, it's suffocatingly hot. As soon as I shower and do my laundry, I go back to the now-empty bar where a ceiling fan keeps it somewhat cooler. I order bottle after bottle of water and face the prospect of waiting seven and a half hours until it's time to meet Jacques and Maïté for dinner. The thought of that much time with nothing to do is daunting. I'm desperate for a good book or a newspaper, but that's impossible—the only store in town is a tiny grocery store and it's closed anyway. *The Simpsons* blares forth in Spanish on a TV mounted above the bar. I don't understand a word they're saying, and this just increases my feelings of isolation and discouragement. I think about calling home, but I can't because a general strike has knocked out all the services, including the phones.

I go back upstairs and flop down on my bed. At my wits' end for something to do, I re-calculate the remaining kilometers, and, to my surprise, discover that today I have reached the halfway point of my journey. Halfway. I know I should be elated that I have come this far and grateful for all the journey has given me. All I feel are acute loneliness and crushing fatigue. An eternity stands between me and dinner, the *only* event in my day, the *only* thing I have to look forward to. The irony is that I'm not even hungry—it's too hot to eat. But I'm desperate for something, anything, to happen. The first three days on the meseta were brutal, but today was the worst. Will the rest of the Camino be so desolate?

What has happened to the life force that is supposed to flow under the trail and inspire pilgrims? I have walked more than four hundred kilometers. Do I have anything to show for it besides giant blisters, sore shoulders, and a bum knee? The pleasures of yesterday are but the dimmest of memories. All I can think about are regrets—missing my family and friends, wishing I had been a better daughter, reliving failures as a parent—the list of shortcomings is as long as the hours stretching before me. Let's face it, I'm a fair-weather pilgrim.

Well, what's so terrible about that? When it's beautiful walking and people are kind, I feel inspired and full of life and energy; when I'm in a godforsaken place with sore feet and a collapsed body, my spirits sink and I want out. My friend the monk would not approve of my attitude, but it all seems pretty understandable to me. I try to get a grip, try to feel myself simply being in time and space. The problem is, I don't like anything about the place I'm in right now. There's just a blank wall and a miniscule window with a view of monotonous rooftops, a stark sky, and sun-baked fields. I am bored out of my mind, I'm dripping big blobs of sweat, and it's six hours and forty-seven minutes until dinner. I lie on my bed, propped up by a lumpy, foam-rubber pillow, and stare at the empty wall, waiting for the time to pass.

As I lie there, I recall a medieval poem one of the speakers recited the previous spring at the Confraternity of Saint James Practical Pilgrim's Day. The lines I remember went like this:

Go, pilgrim, pursue thy quest;
Go on the path, may nothing stop thee!
Take your share of the sun and your share of the dust;
Your heart aroused for the ephemeral!

At the time, I naively thought the message was: "You'll have good days and bad days, so take heart." After experiencing several days on the meseta, I interpret these lines differently. A more accurate summary would be: "This is going to be rough however you slice it, so suck it up and persevere." I repeat the lines several times out loud. Hearing a human voice, even my own, seems to anchor me in this dreadful space, and another interpretation of the poem dawns on me. Why not focus on the journey and on experiencing *this* moment, *this* ephemeral moment, which is my present—like it or not—and which, by definition, will pass? Maybe I can even find something redeeming about this miserable afternoon.

Just keep breathing and you'll get through this, I tell myself. As soon as I've formulated the thought, I realize that I've said these exact words time and again to others who were in stressful situations. I've always thought this was sound advice, so maybe I should try it. I draw in a long, deep breath, then exhale slowly, making an effort to feel myself alive here on the Camino. I do it again, then again, breathing in and breathing out, taking my sweet time, doing nothing more than the simple act of breathing. And gradually, ever so slowly, the frustration and boredom start to waft away, like little tendrils of dissipating smoke. The evening air becomes cooler. The sky softens, and as it does, the scene from my window becomes reassuringly timeless. *Patience and perspective,* I think. It's about learning to accept, maybe even appreciate, the good *and* the bad that make me human.

I leave the hotel at dawn the next morning, feeling somewhat recovered. For the first half hour, I am treated to a concert of birdsong; then the choir flies off for a siesta, leaving only the sound of my footsteps. The Camino climbs gently, following the abandoned roadbed of the old N 120. Expansive fields that had been drained of life yesterday by the glaring sun take on a friendly, welcoming look in the soft morning light. I see a yellow T-shirt and white Panama hat up ahead, but I'm content to go solo for now, as I ease into the day. This time, I don't try to catch up, and soon Jacques and Maïté are out of sight. They might also welcome some time away from me.

Shortly before I arrive at the first village, I pass an elegant lady of a certain age wearing a silk scarf, tied just so. She has to be French, I think, a judgment that is confirmed when I catch the furtive scent of bergamot and other spicy tones of my favorite French perfume. She also carries a backpack and wears a scallop shell around her neck so I know she is a pilgrim, but she seems out of place on this path in the middle of nowhere. Still we greet each other in Spanish, the usual *¡buen camino!* But though she greets me with a smile, her face radiates pain. She walks with a limp and a rolling gait, leaning heavily on her staff. Infected blisters? Tendonitis? I wonder if I should offer almonds or a word of encouragement, but she looks away quickly as soon as she has greeted me. My gesture would not be welcome, I decide, and continue walking.

A few minutes later, the Camino descends into a village, and I notice a man leaning against a wall, glaring at me.

"Have you seen my wife?" he barks out in French, using the familiar "*tu.*" I've never seen this man before, but he's definitely got an attitude about women. And how does he know I speak French? Probably the arrogant assumption, usually attributed to Americans, that everyone speaks their language. But of course! The elegant woman I saw a few minutes ago has to be his wife—they look alike in the way long-married couples often do. Now I really feel sorry for her.

"Yes, I passed her not too long ago. She'll be along soon," I tell him. He continues to glare at me, without another word.

"*Au revoir, bonne route,*" I say. You big jerk. This last bit comes out in a bubble, the way comic book characters "talk." It's a little trick that helped me keep my sanity when I was practicing law. When opposing counsel— or the judge or a witness or anyone who was causing me grief but with the bubble in my mind

whom I had to get along—said something particularly offensive, I would give my official, good-old-boy response, then add in a little bubble in my head what I really wanted to say. I can't tell you how much better that made me feel. It does this time, too.

About two hours later, I arrive at Terradillos, where there is supposed to be a refugio that serves breakfast. I am starved so keep a careful watch for signs for it or any other establishment that might serve food, or even just coffee, but the town offers only closed-up houses and empty streets. *Looks like all I'll get today is water and almonds*, I think glumly as I continue walking through the desolate village.

A few minutes later, just as I am about to head back onto the vastness of the meseta, the notes of Hildegard von Bingen's *De l'estase* float past. I pick up the scent of roses, hear the quiet humming of voices, and the refugio appears, looking like nothing short of a miracle. A dozen pilgrims sip coffee at white plastic tables on a stone patio shaded by large trees. Lush pink roses grow everywhere. Behind the patio, a verdant garden is crisscrossed with clotheslines hung with white sheets, a pair of pants, and a few random socks. The sight of the clotheslines triggers a childhood memory of playing on the backyard swing while my mother hung out the laundry. Why did I ever think clotheslines were unsightly? Here in this luxuriant garden they are the personification of home and family.

Jacques and Maïté wave me over to their table and make a place for me. Suzette is there, too, trying to hold court, but nobody pays her much attention. (Apparently she found the strength to continue after all.) Several Spaniards at another table are having a very good time, while some Germans study their maps and play with cameras. I linger for over an hour, trying to draw out the pleasures of this cool and welcoming spot, but when pilgrims begin to gather up their things and leave, I know it's time to move on. I start out alone because Jacques and Maïté are engrossed in conversation with the other French pilgrims.

"Wait for us," calls out Jacques, as I'm walking through the gate. "We're ready to go, too."

"We are destined to walk together," says Maïté. "Our paths keep crossing, and our paces are perfectly matched."

"You're right," I agree, "and it's lucky for me."

The casual way in which groups form, break up, and re-form is a fact of life on the Camino. We're all headed for the same destination and have the same limited options for where to stop for refreshments and a bed. While there is some variation in speed and distance traveled, most pilgrims cover between twenty and thirty kilometers a day, making it inevitable that paths will continue to cross. The three of us walk together the rest of the morning, all the way to Sahagún. It feels like a very long haul, though in fact, we walk only a total of six hours and fifteen minutes today. It's all we can stand in the unrelenting sun.

The scene that greets us when we arrive at Sahagún jolts us out of our lethargy. Throngs of gaily dressed people of all ages sashay down the street, swaying to bullfight music that blares from loudspeakers. Red-and-yellow Spanish flags and streamers hang from all the storefronts; the heavenly smell of grilling sausages permeates the air. Signs announce a bullfight at 5 p.m. in the *plaza de toros* and a party in the town square with bands and dancing, *starting* at 12:30 a.m. and lasting until dawn. We have arrived during the town's annual fiesta.

After a delicious sausage and a cold beer, we go to the municipal refugio—just in time to get three of the few remaining beds. Located in the attic of a de-sanctified brick church, the refugio is blissfully cool. Natural light streaming in from a bank of windows high above my head makes the enormous space feel light and airy. Best of all, this refugio has *six* showers.

Later that afternoon, we venture back outside. The party mood has continued to build and the streets are now almost impassable. We let ourselves be pulled along by the crowd and end up in front of the hotel where the bullfighters are staying just as the *picadores* emerge from the heavily guarded main door. A tinny trumpet blares. Little kids frantically wave flags. The cheers of the crowd are deafening. Then the stars of the show, the *matadores,* come swaggering out, swinging their capes and adjusting their black winged hats. The crowd goes berserk. I am surprised that the matadores are such small men, but with their flashing dark eyes and air of unwavering confidence, they appear to loom over the adoring crowd. The fluorescent colors of their *trajes de luces* (suits of light) are electrifying, right down to the hot-pink stockings one of them wears. I am taking photos when the matador with the pink stockings motions me over.

"*¡Venga!* Let's have a picture together," he proposes.

"*¡Sí!*" I reply, handing my camera to Jacques.

"Me too, me too!" Maïté squeals enthusiastically.

So up we go to this graying but dapper little matador, who puts an arm around me and flashes a toothy smile. For an instant, I feel like I'm sixteen years old and have just been asked to dance. Then the matadores and picadores get into formation at the head of the parade to the *plaza de toros,* waving grandly at the crowd. Behind them band after band marches by, each playing thunderous, energetic music, each a different tune. The sounds collide randomly; it's like sitting in a room with surround-sound, but with every speaker playing a different CD. People line the streets and cheer, adding their voices to the collective energy of the scene.

Maïté and me with the matador.

Jacques and Maïté follow the crowd to the bull ring, but it's too hot for me. I find an outdoor table at a bar, which is possible now that everyone else is headed to the bullfight, and after another cold beer, I scout out the route for the next morning. That evening, when we meet for dinner, Jacques and Maïté report that they had a great time, although they mostly watched the exuberant crowd. We briefly consider going to the *fiesta* with a group of French and Dutch pilgrims—even the refugio is celebrating tonight and won't lock the doors until 2 a.m.—but we're too wiped out, so we go back to the refugio.

I am about to climb into bed when I notice a woman lying on a sleeping bag on the floor behind the bunks, crying quietly. A man crouches over her, talking animatedly in French and shoving a fistful of pills in her face. It's the woman with the silk scarf whom I'd passed on the trail.

"I talked with her this afternoon when you were in the shower," Maïté whispers, pointing to the weeping woman. "She's in really bad shape. She's got tendonitis in both knees, she's overweight, and you should see her twisted, swollen foot. She's not ready for this, not at all, but her husband won't let her quit. He's a doctor, you'd think he'd recognize her limits. And wouldn't you think he'd let her take the last bunk instead of claiming it for himself! *Ça alors!*"

The doctor shakes his head dismissively at his wife, gives up on the pills, glares threateningly at everyone else, and climbs into his bunk. We are aghast, and I'm ashamed to admit that the rest of us in the cubicle are too intimidated by her husband to offer her a bunk.

It's hard to tell who's more miserable, him or her. But why does she put up with his bullying behavior? Maybe she doesn't feel like she has any options. All I know is that if this were me, I'd be on the first train back to Paris. Even the floor of a friend's apartment would be a thousand times better than this.

Then I catch myself. I know nothing about them, nothing about her life, what she wants, or what choices she has. Gender roles remain so entrenched, so complicated to unravel. An image of my southern grandmother, whom I adored and for whom I am named, comes to mind and, as always, I am filled with bemusement and sadness. She made the world's best fried chicken every Sunday, which meant hours of standing over a hot stove in a hot kitchen, slowly turning the pieces so they would brown evenly. Meanwhile, she'd fix the mashed potatoes, collard greens,

Steps Out of Time

corn bread, slaw, and other dishes. Then she'd make the gravy and serve a magnificent feast that took her all morning to prepare and a couple of hours to clean up, in those pre-dishwasher days.

Her reward? The back of the chicken, from which she would carefully pull out two bite-sized pieces of meat from a slight hollow on either side of the tailbone. She'd savor each bite, content with her lot, while I kept trying to figure out why she wouldn't take a piece of white meat.

"Child," she'd say to me, licking her fingers, "you just don't know what's good. This is the best piece."

Fifty years later, I still don't know how to think about this. If appearances are to be trusted, she relished her two scrawny little bites of chicken and savored that moment for all it was worth. But why did she always take the piece nobody else wanted?

The next morning, Jacques and Maïté and I are off at daybreak, taking advantage of that brief early morning time before the earth starts to bake. Fiesta lights still twinkle, but all that's left of last night's throngs are a few clusters of young men, beer bottles in hand, and some couples lingering in doorways. The streets and sidewalks are ankle-deep in confetti and trash, which make it impossible to see the elegant brass scallop shells embedded in the sidewalk that, in Sahagún, replace yellow arrows. Luckily, I know the way out of town.

We hope to get to Reliegos tonight to make up for the last few days when we quit early. That means doing thirty-one kilometers, which is not exactly what the doctor ordered, but today is a straight shot on a gravel path, so we should be able to do it. At first, the path skirts a ploughed field and is wide enough for us to walk three abreast. Later, it narrows to single file and is lined with gangly saplings as it snakes its way across the interminable, empty plain. The sun blasts down, no holds barred. We are the only things moving in this inhospitable landscape.

Around lunchtime, we arrive at El Burgo Ranero where the only option is a grocery store. We feast on junk food. I have a supersized ice cream bar, a bag of pistachios, some potato chips, a beer, a candy bar, and another ice cream treat. My kids would be proud of me. We linger until we can no longer ignore the hot dusty plain that is our fate for the rest of the day. Then we plod along in silence under the intense sun, marching single file on the narrow path, inches apart and perfectly in step. We stop often to rest, and somehow, each time, we manage to start up again, slowly, like an eighteen-wheeler going through its gears to reach top speed. For us, today, that's four kilometers an hour. It's the pace of a stroll, but it's the best we can do in the sweltering heat. The last thirteen kilometers are interminable. Will we ever arrive?

Life didn't change, but perspective did.

Kerry Eagen, *Fumblings*

Chapter Fifteen

Meandering and Musing

June 16 – 17, Reliegos to León.

Eleven hours after leaving Sahagún, still in full sun and now moving at a crawl, we reach Reliegos. The refugio looks incredibly inviting in the midst of this forlorn landscape, and since it's new and not yet in the guidebooks, there is plenty of room. We climb the stairs to the sleeping rooms and select the beds that we think will be coolest: three top bunks, each level with an open window. Jacques and Maïté decide to nap; I go off to the shower. The bathroom is great, even luxurious by refugio standards, with two spacious, tiled shower rooms and hot water. What's more, there is a full-length mirror, a rarity in refugios.

Yikes. Is that woman staring back at me with the out-of-control straw mop really me? There's at least an inch of ugly gray displayed prominently at the roots. My skin is rough and parched from days in the wind, heat, and cold; my eyes are bloodshot, my lips chapped. Brown stains streak the shirt I've worn every day since I started walking, my now-baggy pants hang low on my hips, and my shoes have curled-up toes. Hmmm.

Well, I haven't had time to worry about mundane things like wardrobe, I think a little too defensively. I've been busy with the Camino. But the truth is I've found it increasingly freeing these past weeks to escape the pressures of a culture that judges a woman by appearance— weight, make-up, clothes, and coiffure. In short, the external trappings that the media, other women, and a male-dominated workplace have trained us to believe are the hallmarks of a successful woman. But until coming face-to-face with this mirror, I've not had to confront the cost of my freedom. It's worse than I imagined. I am a poster child for the too-bad-she-let-herself-go charge.

But that's not how I feel. Here, now, I may look a mess—I wear no make-up, I put on the identical outfit each morning (usually clean, though it's getting rather worn)—yet I've been showered with kindnesses and have had some truly wonderful experiences. Granted I am with like-minded people, but the fact remains that I have come to appreciate this way of connecting—based on the warmth of a smile, the awareness of someone else's need, or just an interest in a fellow human being. And I love the self-confidence that comes from celebrating my spirit and not my fashion IQ. I should be envied, not pitied. The Camino view may not translate well in the context of my professional life in Ann Arbor, but I am pretty sure my attitude has changed for the better. I take another look in the mirror. On reflection, I like what I see. Giving myself a big smile, I head off to enjoy dinner with Jacques and Maïté.

Last night when I went to bed, I was exhausted even beyond what I remember from those sleep-deprived years when Philip and I had two babies and two demanding careers. I was sure that the deep ache in my leg was the beginning of tendonitis. "*Notre terreur des dernières semaines*" (Our terror of these past weeks), Jacques calls it. But overnight the regenerative power of sleep worked its magic. When my alarm goes off, I feel great. I pull on my clothes, grab my pack, and creep out the door, careful not to wake my sleeping roommates. After a perfunctory wash-up, I head for the kitchen and the coffee. A few minutes later, Jacques arrives, without Maïté, whom he's reluctant to wake. It's only 6:15, but I'm ready to go, so I start out alone. We'll meet up somewhere in the next day or two.

Yellow arrows lead me out of town and onto a narrow dirt trail that stretches into the distance. The path cuts across green fields, but it's the dirt-colored strip of exposed earth on which I walk that dominates the landscape. Nothing stirs. *Except me,* I think, as I resign myself to another punishing day on the meseta. But I walk easily on the level ground and find myself relishing the sweet summertime air. Before I know it, the tedium of the infinite trail and oppressive countryside dissolves into the six shades of pink of the morning sky and all's well. A pilgrim making progress, I think, as I observe my shadow—that of a medieval pilgrim with her staff and wide-brimmed hat.

Mid-morning, the trail abruptly vanishes, and I confront one of this pilgrimage's more practical challenges—not getting lost. I look around for a good ten minutes before I spot a yellow arrow, this one painted on the side of a building. It directs me onto the shoulder of a busy highway, but the pedestrian area is almost as wide as a lane of traffic and feels perfectly safe. Later it narrows to the width of a city sidewalk, then becomes a foot-wide strip. I think conditions can't get any worse, but they do—I must sprint across a two-lane bridge on a little cement ledge so narrow that side-view mirrors streak past within inches of my shoulder. It feels like these drivers are aiming for me, trying to see how close they can come without actually hitting me. Somehow I make it safely to the other side, where I collapse at an outdoor table of the closest bar.

"El Camino está desastroso por aquí, ¿no cierto?" (The Camino is a disaster here, isn't it?), commiserates a young Spanish woman who is sitting at the table next to mine. "You need to be careful. It's a good thing you're not very wide."

I am so relieved to hear a friendly voice that I can barely resist the urge to rush over and hug her.

"Here, this will make you feel better," says her companion, as he hands me a big, luscious chocolate bonbon.

He's right. I savor every molecule and, accepting the chair he holds out, I shed my pack and slip off my right shoe, hoping to ease the annoying ache I've developed in that foot. Then I order a café con leche, a fresh-squeezed orange juice, and a pain au chocolat, which I enjoy while chatting with my new friends. After they leave, I move inside where it's cooler and have just ordered a second coffee when Fiona walks in. She's an Australian journalist; we've rested together under the same tree several times over the last few days.

"May I join you?" she asks. "I really need a break after that highway walking."

"Of course, please do," I say. "I'd welcome the company."

She carefully stashes her pack under the table, angles the empty chair so neither it nor the pack is visible from the door, then scans the sidewalk before sitting down.

"Are you expecting someone?" I ask.

She shrugs her shoulders and raises her eyebrows.

"I hope not," she says. "I came to Spain with an organized church group, but I just don't find pilgrimage to be a group experience, so I decided to give it a go alone. Today is my first day solo, but I'm having trouble shaking Charles. That's our leader. He means well, but he can't let us go."

Just then, a tall, skinny, earnest-looking man who appears to be in his late fifties walks in. He methodically searches all the nooks and crannies of the dark bar until his eyes adjust to the low light and he spots Fiona. His face lights up; hers falls.

"It's him," she whispers. "Charles."

He walks toward us, but she ignores him until he's practically sitting in her lap.

"Oh, hello," she says, without looking at him. "I'd like to visit with my friend. You go on without me. Maybe we'll catch up in León."

Fiona tries to dismiss him by keeping her back turned and talking to me, but Charles doesn't take the hint. He hangs around for a long time, standing awkwardly by our table while we chat, knowing he's supposed to go graciously but holding out for an invitation to join us. Finally, he turns and leaves, looking like a giant gray-haired puppy with his tail between his legs.

Fiona sighs. "It feels like I have a bodyguard. He'd go to the bathroom with me if I'd let him."

Shaking her head, she goes to the bar to get a coffee. Her frustration is palpable, as is his. To make matters worse, the rest of the group opted to go solo two days ago, so now Charles is alone except for Fiona. It must be hell to be a leader without any followers.

"I've wanted to walk the Camino for years," she says when she returns, "ever since I did a piece on spiritual trips ten years ago. None of the other pilgrimages I wrote about resonated, but this one, well, I just couldn't get it out of my mind. Sounds crazy, doesn't it?" She gives an embarrassed little laugh.

When I tell her about my vague but insistent feeling that I needed to do this trip—and about my husband's reluctance—she laughs again, and says that she and her husband had the same conversations.

"But one day last fall," she explains, "I knew it was time. Our son turned eight and that's old enough for me to leave him for a month. I had to go before I was too old, you see. I'm thirty-five."

She looks so earnest when she tells me her age, like it's a really big deal to be thirty-five. And I was worried about being too old at fifty-seven. I smile and nod, wanting to say something, but what? "Old" is such a relative term.

Her comment brings to mind another memory of my grandmother from a time when I was about Fiona's age. I had no sooner arrived for a visit when "Ma," then in her late eighties, insisted on taking me out to the sun porch to show me her new exercise bike.

"I ride it twenty minutes *every* day," she explained in her wonderful southern drawl.

Wearing a pretty floral-print housedress and pink slippers, she gingerly climbed up on the bike and sat there for a few minutes—tiny, fragile, and so dear to me. Then as she began to pedal, ever so slowly but proud as punch, she smoothed her hair and pursed her lips like a young girl. I don't remember what I said at that moment, but whatever it was elicited a response I didn't understand, until now. She said something like: "It's a funny thing, old age. I don't feel any different than I did at thirty or forty. Then I look in the mirror and I hardly recognize myself with my gray hair and all these wrinkles. But it's still me."

Thinking back to that day, I am shocked, then amused, to realize that I am now moving into the stage of life where it's going to be me who doesn't *feel* old, in spite of the years that say otherwise. I hope I have the good fortune to continue to feel like I'm "still me" as I age and that I stay as young at heart as my grandmother always remained.

But I'm not up to sharing this with Fiona, so I just nod sympathetically, ask her about her professional life, and we are soon deep in a conversation about gender roles. It's a conversation we both want to continue, so after we finish our coffees, we put on our packs and tackle the scorching heat together. Initially, the arrows take us on a dirt sidewalk with a strip mall on one side and the busy main highway into León on the other. Everything— shops, cars, customers, pilgrims—is covered with a layer of dust from a construction project that has torn up large sections of the roadway. Just when I've had it with the grime and noise, the Camino breaks away from the highway and heads into the hills on a rocky, unpaved road with no traffic, no dust, and no chaos.

After fifteen minutes of steady climbing, we approach a village with a graceful stone fountain. Fiona dashes ahead to the fountain, fills her hat with water, quickly puts it on her head, and lets out a big "hoo-ah!" as the cold water pours over her.

"Try it," she says, "it feels really good and will keep you cool until the water evaporates."

I follow her example. The cool water leaves me breathless for the first few seconds as it rushes down my sweaty face; then it feels fabulous. And I don't have to worry about my mascara running. I had no idea such a simple act could feel so terrific.

The rest of the afternoon, we trade life stories as we walk. Both of ours are long and convoluted, crossing continents and involving professional decisions (usually bad) made to accommodate the needs of the men we've loved—and with the lion's share of concessions and costs falling on our shoulders. It's the old saw, again: how to juggle the demands of marriage and family with the personal and professional needs of two individuals and achieve some approximation of an equal division of family and household responsibilities. I enjoy talking with Fiona so much that I almost forget about the nagging pain in my foot.

That evening, when I think back to our conversation, I fear I was ranting when I talked about my experiences in the sixties and seventies. I try not to whine and judge when the topic of gender inequality comes up, but to this day, it's hard to move beyond old insults, perceived or otherwise. Rigid gender expectations figured prominently during my life as a young professional—norms that were often premised on the idea that women were second-class citizens. Being told "no" because of my gender has left its mark, there's no getting around it. I am a product of my time.

The Feminine Mystique came out the year I graduated from high school, and reading it was one of the most influential events of my life. It articulated the confusion I was feeling as I thought about my future and what I wanted; it normalized my conviction that whatever happened, I did not want to be "just a housewife." Now, forty years later, I know that it's much more complicated than simply choosing whether to work outside the home. But back then, gender roles were pretty immutable and limiting in the small Midwestern town where I grew up.

Ten years ago, I gave Dad a copy of *The Feminine Mystique* for his birthday, expecting him to be shocked, but wanting him to better understand the gender issues that were so important to me. He read it—and was mystified that I found this book so revolutionary. I took his reaction as a sure sign of progress. Fiona's experiences also help me remember that we have made progress. She has been offered opportunities that would have been largely unavailable just a few decades earlier, and her husband assumes equal childcare responsibility as a matter of course. Women *have* made significant progress in many parts of the world. I tend to lose sight of this, for in my experience, true equality remains elusive. But there is hope. When I get defensive about gender issues, my daughter is quick to point out that these are my issues, not hers.

"Times have changed, Mom," she reminds me patiently.

I hope desperately that she is right. I also hope I am gaining a better perspective on gender inequities during this voyage, through encounters such as this one, as well as conversations with men who struggle with these same issues. And I think I am finally learning to see the humor in the realities of my pre-feminist youth. My daughter is right, times have changed. It's just that so much remains to be done.

A quick hour later, Fiona and I arrive at a busy round-about on the outskirts of León. Because of a major construction project, we have to walk on the shoulder of the torn-up main road where heavy equipment constantly churns up clouds of dirt against the backdrop of rush hour traffic. A store-front thermometer says thirty-six degrees Celsius, almost ninety-seven degrees Fahrenheit. Then standing in the shade of the store's awning, we see Charles. Waiting. Once again, he's thrilled to see Fiona. He waves enthusiastically.

"Hello! I knew you'd be by soon," he says. "I've found a sporting goods store where you can buy the socks you need."

Fiona smiles weakly and goes over to check out the socks with Charles.

"Hang on just a minute," Charles says to me. "The signing here is very confusing, but I've got a good map. We can go on into the city together." I thank him, smile, and, with a wave, leave them talking in the doorway while I head off alone. Charles was right—a plethora of yellow arrows point in every possible direction. I pick one that heads me toward the city center and start up a charming little cobblestone street. One of the attractions of this pilgrimage, I'm discovering, is the pleasure of making a decision and acting on it without having to explain or defend my choice, even if it means making mistakes. If I turn out to be wrong, well, I'm prepared to face the consequences. Getting lost is not necessarily a bad thing.

When I reach the cathedral square, the scene screams upbeat energy—sophisticated professionals rush back from lunch, university students sit at sidewalk cafes talking animatedly, taxis honk as they try to navigate the crowded streets. It's business as usual in a city. But approached on foot after days of open spaces and little villages, the urban congestion of this city of 137,000 people is disorienting, overwhelming.

I go directly to the Tourist Information Office for help finding a modest hotel where I can have a long soak in a tub and a bed with sheets. But the clerk can't reserve a room for me sight unseen. The dull ache in my foot has become a relentless, shooting pain, but I have no choice. List in hand, I head for the nearest hotel. Eight fully-booked hotels later, another kind receptionist tells me she has no rooms but sends me to a pensión not on my list that she believes has space available. I limp up to the front desk just as a pilgrim couple from Colorado is paying for the last room.

"I'm sorry," says the clerk, "I wish I could help you, but everything in town is full but the parador. Would you consider that?"

I hesitate only a second before nodding yes. The searing pain in my foot trumps principle. If the only bed in town is in a luxury hotel, I'll take it. She dials the number and hands me the phone. In my best Spanish, which is disintegrating fast, I explain that I had canceled an earlier reservation, but am now in León on my way to Santiago and wonder if they might still have a room for me.

"Of course we have a place for you, Señora Soper," replies the cheery receptionist. "We'll be happy to welcome you."

The Colorado couple is apologetic about taking the last room in the pensión.

"Don't worry," I tell them, "I think you did me a favor."

Half an hour later, so grimy and sweaty that I can smell myself, I hobble through the massive wooden doors of the sixteenth-century Convento de San Marcos, now known as the Parador San Marcos. A woman behind the front desk, stylishly dressed in a navy blue suit and high heels, greets me.

"¡Señora Soper! Buenos días, and welcome," she calls out across the expansive lobby.

How does she know who I am? I wonder. *Can it be my outfit that gives me away?*

Hearing her friendly greeting, I conclude this parador must be OK with pilgrims, although we do stand out among the other elegantly dressed guests. Well, I am, after all, just one more in the long tradition of pilgrims who have stayed in this very spot, beginning in the year 1152. Nothing remains of that twelfth-century pilgrim hospice, but the convent that took its place has been transformed into Spain's premier luxury hotel and, in that capacity, continues the centuries-old tradition of sheltering pilgrims.

And what a shelter. Guests, me included, crane their necks to admire the soaring vaulted ceiling of the lobby. Opposite the registration desk, a series of twenty foot tall late-Gothic arches flood the lobby with soft filtered light and open to a view of the carefully tended cloister garden. An enormous bouquet of colorful summer flowers stands in the center of a richly carved oak table and reminds me that money is no object in the upkeep of this place. What a contrast with the refugio in San Juan de Ortego, where they can't even afford toilet paper.

While I'm registering, two Spanish pilgrims arrive, carrying the biggest backpacks I've seen yet, but these young men are very muscular and appear oblivious to the weight. They are followed by a group of German pilgrims, jovial gray-haired men who enthusiastically greet everyone in sight. These latest arrivals look every bit as grubby as I do— and receive the same courteous welcome. Near the staircase, five middle-aged Americans cluster around their leader, a tall man with an Australian accent. They are casually but nicely dressed and carry small rucksacks and state-of-the-art hiking poles. I overhear one of them ask their leader what the Camino will be like tomorrow.

"Hard," he responds. "You should start out wearing your hiking boots. You can always change your footwear if you want to."

And with that, he distributes keys and tells his group to have their luggage down before breakfast. This must be the kind of trip where an outfitter transports clients' luggage each day, reserves hotels, guides the walk, and provides a sag wagon—just in case. Yet another way to experience the Camino.

The parador receptionist checks me in and sends me off with a smartly uniformed bellboy to discover my fifth-floor room. As before, at the Santo Domingo parador, the bellboy insists on carrying my now-even-grungier pack. One glance at the room and I feel another relapse coming on. It is exquisite. Open French doors lead onto the room's large *private* balcony with a view of the parador's extensive formal garden. Deep purple petunias cascade down flower boxes on the railing and perfume the room. I know exactly where I will spend the evening: sitting on one of the cushioned wrought-iron chairs on that posh balcony, admiring the view while I inhale the fragrant air and sip a well-deserved (if I do say so) beer. Meanwhile, the large soaking tub in the room's luxurious marble bathroom is calling to me. The warm bathwater works wonders for my sore shoulders, though it does nothing for the pain in my foot. Half an hour later, I ease my way out of the soothing water, pop a couple of ibuprofen tablets, and dress up for lunch. On the Camino, that means I accessorize my usual outfit with my purple cotton scarf and trade my disreputable walking shoes for a pair of clunky plastic sandals. I will do something about the embarrassing black ring in the tub later.

On the way out the door, I catch a glimpse of my reflection in the room's gilded full-length mirror and have second thoughts about my plan to have a 4 p.m. lunch in the parador dining room. Do I really want to go to one of the most elegant restaurants in León looking so scruffy? My mother would be horrified. Then the words of R. Sargent Shriver on the subject of mirrors come out of nowhere and get me back on track.

"Shatter the glass," he had told a group of Yale graduates a decade ago. "In our society that is so self-absorbed, begin to look less at yourself and more at each other."

The words of a man who spent a lifetime seeing and addressing the needs of others through public service put any egotistical concerns about mirrors and physical appearance into perspective. Instead of worrying about appearance, better to take his advice and look—really look—at other people. I'll work on that.

Pèleriner, c'est apprendre à mourir.

To go on a pilgrimage is to learn how to die.

Luc Adrian, *Compostelle : Carnet de route d'un pèlerin*

Chapter Sixteen

Death, Revisited

June 18, León.

"Philip?"

It's 5:10 a.m. I reach out for my husband across the vast expanse of four luxuriously fat pillows strewn over the gigantic bed. He's not there. Oh, that's right. I'm in León, in the parador. Alone. Bummer. I wiggle my foot to see what happens. Last night when I climbed into bed, the pain was pretty intense and the swollen spot was the size of a tennis ball. This morning, my foot feels more or less OK. I try to convince myself that the swelling has disappeared, too, but the truth (which I decide to ignore) is that it's still pretty puffed up.

The slightest of breezes drifts through the open patio doors, bringing with it the soothing fragrances of the garden. I don't want to get out of bed. Maybe I'll take a rest day. I can still reach Santiago in time to catch my flight home if I do two days of at least thirty kilometers each. But long days wipe me out, especially in the heat, and if I push too hard, the pain in my knee may get worse and force me to quit. Closing my eyes, I savor the sensation of pure luxury as I sink back into the deliciously clean, wrinkle-free sheets. I will take a rest day, although I can't decide if I am being a prudent pilgrim or a wimpy one.

When I wake again at seven, the sky has turned the color of cotton candy; no sounds break the stillness of the early morning. What a contrast with the refugios, where seven is the end of the morning rush hour. I dress quickly and go down to the reception area to see about extending my stay. It's tempting to lie in bed a little longer, but hotel space in León is tight, so the sooner I inquire, the better my chances. I could call, but although my Spanish is getting better every day, I still shy away from the phone and its lack of visual cues that help me follow the conversation.

The clerk greets me with a smile, but when she hears what I want, her face turns serious.

"I'm sorry, I don't see any availability for tonight," she says, taking a long look at her monitor. "A big group is arriving at noon, but let me see what I can do. Please, wait a *momentito*," and she disappears into a back room.

Fifteen minutes later she returns. "It's OK," she announces. "I've worked something out. We're pleased to have you stay tonight, and you can keep the same room."

I thank her, feeling very relieved that I won't have to look for another place—and very happy, if a little guilty, that I can stay another night in my private room that is the size of some refugios.

"It's my pleasure, señora. I hope you enjoy your breakfast. It is served in the room just at the top of the stairs, to your right," she adds, when she sees me looking around.

The spacious parador breakfast room overlooks the cloisters and hums with quiet conversations and the efficiency of a well-trained staff. It offers a spread equal to the one at the Santo Domingo parador, and this time, knowing that I won't face long hours on the trail after I eat, I savor every delicious bite. It feels decadent to have a lavish, leisurely breakfast, then return to a *private* room to sit on my *private* balcony after three weeks of mostly refugios and getting up at the crack of dawn (well, usually) to start walking. But I'm going to enjoy this brief reprieve for all it's worth. Who knows what lies ahead? I prop up my foot and think of all the places I want to visit after lunch: the cathedral with its superb medieval stained glass windows, the Gaudí museum, the Roman walls, the church of San Isidro, the church and cloisters of San Marco, the city's gardens and outdoor cafes, its Roman ruins. When I go in search of a pencil to make a list, reality intervenes in the form of a stabbing pain in my foot that reminds me the point of a rest day is, after all, to rest. Still, the prospect of spending the entire day sitting on this balcony—however lovely—alone, and with no possibility of a measurable outcome, is daunting.

I pull out my journal but soon set pencil aside. Have I ever felt less inspired? I try making a list of projects I want to do when I get home. That doesn't go any further. I've already read the tourist material in the room cover-to-cover twice and washed out my other set of clothes. There's little hope of running into any pilgrims—yesterday's contingent left hours ago, and the new batch won't arrive until mid-afternoon. So I sit, thoughts wandering aimlessly.

The buzz of a single-engine airplane catches my attention. It's flying low, just above the tree tops, heading for an airport on the other side of the Bernesga River. As the pilot banks to the left, the sun glints off the familiar V-shaped tail of an old Beechcraft Bonanza. *Baker, Lima, Charlie!* The call letters of the little Bonanza my father used to fly pop unexpectedly into my head. When I was a child, he would take me to the airport with him on Saturday mornings to ride shotgun and watch for other aircraft while he practiced instrument approaches. How important I felt. Fifty years later, the buzz of a small plane still evokes those mornings when I'd watch, fascinated, as the clouds drifted past my little window, my daydreams interrupted by occasional reminders from Dad to please pay attention to my job.

The buzz fades as the Bonanza disappears beyond some low trees. A few minutes later, the sound starts up again, this time in a deeper voice, and a twin engine aircraft rises above the greenery. I sit quietly and listen to the steady stream of small planes landing and taking off. Images of Dad drift in and out. I revisit a scene at the Bridger Bowl Ski Area in Bozeman, Montana, when he careened out of sight and disappeared into the deep powder, scaring everyone to death until he surfaced minutes later, goggles packed with snow and laughing in his deep resonant voice. I remember the corny poems he would write my mother that embarrassed us, his daughters, to death. For some reason, I picture the pink wind-up Energizer Bunny his office staff gave him for his eightieth birthday party.

I try to keep the good memories coming, but I'm increasingly aware of a scene I don't want to let in: it's early dawn and Dad is lying in a hospital bed. My middle sister and I sit by his bedside holding his warm but completely limp hands, telling him we love him over and over. His half-open hazel eyes are heartbreakingly vacant; every breath is a shallow, wheezing gasp. Mother slumps in an armless chair, gazing alternately at him and out the window, looking very small and very alone. Menacing machines are suspended from steel hooks, their bulk intimidating and dehumanizing. The cold buzz of fluorescent lights accentuates the harshness of the unadorned, urine-colored walls.

It's early August and we've been alone in this room, just the four of us, for twenty-four hours. I try not to watch the red line of the beeping machine, but my eyes cling to this visible assurance of life. The sun is beginning to peek through a low cloud cover that will soon disappear. It's going to be hot again today. My father takes a short, shallow breath. The light on the monitor goes out and the beeping stops. Time stops. I can't breathe.

We all three start to weep quietly. My sister is the first to speak.

"Flaps up, Dad. Happy landing," she says through her tears.

Death is a constant on the Camino. It asserts its inevitability by triggering wrenching memories that confront unsuspecting pilgrims. It seeps from the centuries-old gravestones, crumbling with decay. It permeates the monuments and structures built by people long dead and oozes from the ruins of pilgrim hospices where thousands of pilgrims have died over countless generations. It radiates from the churches with their crucifixes and tombs and martyred saints. It lurks in the legends of pilgrims past and marks its territory by the many crosses along the route indicating spots where pilgrims fell. Real people with flesh and blood lives, families, hopes and dreams. People like Catherine.

I can see why Jorge, the Brazilian engineer, wants to understand the mystery of death. It's so ever-present. But railing against death is futile and, like I told Jorge earlier, I think the most we can hope for is acceptance of its inevitability. This is nothing new, of course. But knowing something to be true in my head and feeling it as true in my gut are very different. My time on the Camino is helping me reconcile what I know with what I feel. My father's passing left me with a profound sadness and a painful void. However, I am starting to understand—the feeling-in-my-gut kind of understanding—that what matters is the precious, indelible mark left on me by his presence in my life. That's what I have now. I can treasure this precious gift, or I can brood over the incomprehensible nature of the loss and berate myself with regrets. Most likely I will do both for some time, but I am edging my way toward acceptance. It's just a matter of seeing the glass of existence as half full instead of half empty, which, by the way, was exactly Dad's approach to life. The monk was right: it's our struggles that make us human, including, and maybe especially, the struggle to accept death. I spend the rest of the morning thinking this over and practicing the art of being alive on this beautiful sunny day on my balcony in Spain.

Mid-afternoon, I return to the parador dining room for lunch. The maître d' welcomes me warmly and helps me choose a regional menu: a starter of white asparagus dressed with a fantastic garlicky vinaigrette followed by a delicious saffron-flavored fish and potato stew, all accompanied by a very fine Mencía from the Bierzo region. For dessert, he recommends their *arroz con leche*, which has a topping that resembles crème brulée and is the best rice pudding I've ever tasted. After lunch, I go back to my balcony to wait out the siesta and elevate my aching foot. Later that afternoon, I visit the church of San Isidro. Consecrated on December 21, 1063, it is one of four compulsory stops on the pilgrimage route in Spain, according to *The Pilgrim's Guide*. Several people have told me that if I don't do anything else in León, I must visit this little church.

I am moving very slowly, so it's almost seven by the time I get there. The lady in the ticket office motions to me excitedly when she sees me limping up.

"Hurry up, hurry up!" she exclaims in Spanish. "You can only visit the museum and crypt with a guide. The last tour of the day leaves in two minutes."

I quickly pay and join the small group of tourists standing around a petite young woman with oversized black-framed glasses and serene dark eyes. Speaking slowly and clearly, she apologizes that she speaks only Spanish and encourages anyone who can translate for the various groups to do so. People signal that they will translate into German, Swedish, and English, and throughout the tour, heads bob and nod every few minutes as our guide pauses so the translators can relay information to their companions.

This small and unassuming church possesses incredible treasures. Our guide shows us a collection of ornately decorated chests, chalices, and other containers whose expert craftsmanship belies their functional purpose. I am particularly taken by a tiny eleventh-century box, about two inches square, with a pearl inlay of perfectly formed miniature rabbits dancing around the edge—a receptacle for solid perfume. We admire dozens of medieval manuscripts, including an illuminated Bible from 960, and a fine collection of religious art.

Then, in a hushed voice, our tour guide invites us to follow her down the stairs to the royal burial vault. But it's not the centuries-old tombs she wants to show us. Rather, she directs our attention to the low, vaulted ceiling, and, as our eyes adjust to the dim light, we see a series of amazing frescoes. By some happy quirk of fate, conditions here are just right to preserve the paintings—we are looking at original, un-restored works of art from the mid-twelfth century. Nothing stands between us and the artist except nearly a millennium. The life force that pours forth from these frescoes makes me forget that I am standing in the middle of a giant tomb with a throbbing pain in my foot.

Several represent Biblical stories, but the ones that catch my eye are twelve scenes depicting the agricultural calendar. Arranged in a single row, they are laid out to follow the graceful curve of an arch. September is a wistful-looking peasant picking grapes from a laden vine and placing them into a large black pot. A smiling peasant with a sprouting branch in each hand represents April. December is a nobleman dressed in richly embroidered robes who warms his feet by the fire, a loaf of bread in one hand and a cup of mead on the table beside him. These poignant scenes are beautifully painted in rich earth tones of green, rust, blue, gold, brown, burgundy, and cream.

Life and death, side by side. This room is a tangible reminder that they can co-exist harmoniously in serenity and even beauty—that life, too, is a constant on the Camino, and while the moments of life may be ever so brief, how glorious they can be. The words of a character in Alice Steinbach's memoir *Without Reservations* sum it up nicely: "Why do they say on their tombstones that 'Time flies, remember you must die'? Would it not be more useful to say that 'Time flies, remember you must live'?"

Many languages have euphemisms for death—to help us cope, I suppose. In English, we talk about someone's "passing" or refer to the "dearly departed." The French have a way of saying someone has died that I particularly like: they use the same verb one would use to take leave socially. When saying good-bye to a friend after spending time together at a café, for example, one would say: "*Je te quitte*," literally, "I am leaving you," though the meaning is more a sense of "so long, I'm off," or, if said with a sigh, "I hate to leave, but I really must go." Similarly, when talking about someone who has died, one would say "*elle nous a quittés*" (she has left us).

I like the French euphemism because it reminds me of what death and a social parting have in common: both occur frequently, both are involuntary (we *must* keep moving on), and both are an integral part of the fabric of life.

Everyone on the tour feels an urgent desire to spend more time in this extraordinary space to absorb what we have been privileged to witness, but the museum is closing. Our previously patient tour guide becomes insistent.

"You must leave now," she says firmly. "Go to the cathedral to see the priceless thirteenth-century stained glass and come back tomorrow. I hope to see you then."

Reluctantly, we follow her upstairs and into the little museum store where she politely, but pointedly, shows us to the door. I am tempted to take her advice and visit the cathedral, but a shooting pain in my foot reminds me again that this is a rest day. On the way back to the parador, I pass a sidewalk café and stop for a light supper. It's 8:30 p.m., and the traditional pre-dinner promenade is in full swing. It's also prime time for café sitting. I find a table and watch the steady stream of people enjoying the evening air: young lovers; couples with babies; an elderly, white-haired woman walking arm-in-arm with a somewhat younger woman who looks just like her but with dark hair; packs of teenagers with book satchels on their backs; men and women in business suits carrying briefcases. Many nod and smile at me, a single woman sitting alone. A man walks by, holding hands with an attractive dark-haired woman.

"Hi there," he calls out in Spanish. "How are you? Enjoying León?" It

Steps Out of Time

takes me a minute to recognize the maître d' from the parador, dressed as he is in casual clothes instead of his black suit. But it's the same friendly smile and same deep voice.

How I wish Philip were sitting across from me. We'd be holding hands, fingers interlaced. I love feeling his huge, strong hands wrapped around mine. I'd have my shoes off and would be rubbing my foot against his leg; he'd be smiling at me. I sit at my table sipping wine for a long time, missing Philip, loving him from a distance.

By the time I leave, I feel ready to face tomorrow. Relishing the soft evening light, I amble across the large square in front of the parador, past the larger-than-life statue of a pilgrim and several Camino markers. This 1200-year-old pilgrimage makes the human parade from birth to death feel natural, even comforting, and encourages me to appreciate and live *this* moment, brief though it may be. At least tonight, at least right now.

Exploring the world is one of the best ways of exploring the mind, and walking travels both terrains.

Rebecca Solnit, *Wanderlust, A History of Walking*

20·06·02

Chapter Seventeen

Traveling Both Terrains

June 19 - 21, León to Rabanal del Camino via el Puente de Órbigo and Astorga.

A day and a half later—after another mundane, tedious day of slogging across the meseta and a dreary, lonely night in a room above a bar—I'm once again touched by the spirit of the Camino. It's early morning. I think I'm on my way to the Puente de Órbigo but haven't noticed any yellow arrows for over an hour. Am I lost? I'm about to retrace my steps when I glimpse a graceful stone bridge, twenty arches long, rising out of the morning haze: the Puente de Órbigo. This thirteenth-century bridge is the last of several that were constructed over the Órbigo River at this exact spot.

When I step onto the old bridge, not another human being is in sight. Nothing breaks the morning stillness except the sound of my footsteps and my walking stick hitting the old paving stones. Yet I feel certain that I am not alone. The sensation of another presence becomes stronger, and it's a soothing, encompassing feeling. I wonder if what I sense is an awareness of the people whose lives have been tied to this bridge over the centuries: clusters of short, round peasant ladies, caps on their heads and baskets in hand, chattering happily on their way to market; legions of Roman soldiers, footsteps thundering as they march across; and, of course, hundreds of thousands of pilgrims in various states of health who have walked over these same stones. I saunter along the bridge's causeway, loving every minute of this connection to the Camino. Rereading my journal later, after I'm home, I am bemused at my choice of words. Thoreau writes in his famous essay "Walking" that *saunter* is derived from the old French *sainte-terrer,* or Holy-Lander, the term used to describe pilgrims roving about the countryside in the Middle Ages gathering alms to fund a trip to the Holy Land. I like the idea that something in which I take such pleasure has an historic link to pilgrimage.

Several famous encounters have occurred on bridges located at this site, beginning with the battle between the Suevi and the Visigoths in 452. The story I like best, however, is that of Suero de Quiñones, a fifteenth-century knight from León who is said to be a source for Cervantes's character Don Quixote. Rejected by his lady, Suero declared himself a prisoner of love and came up with a very macho way to escape his bonds: he challenged the best knights in Europe, vowing to break three hundred of their lances. If he could achieve his goal, he believed the victories would constitute his ransom and set him free from the clutches of unrequited love. The contest lasted for days during the late summer of 1434, and when the dust settled, Suero had indeed defeated three hundred challengers from all over Europe—he was a free man.

But the story has a surprise ending, for one of the defeated knights was a sore loser. Twenty-four years later, that knight happened to ride past Suero and, seeing a chance for revenge, killed him on the spot. Still, I don't think Suero was tilting at windmills. Because of the events on this bridge, he went from being a love-sick knight to a conquering hero over the course of a few summer days, and for the next quarter of a century he was revered as a valiant warrior.

Bridges and their stories have always fascinated me, from the soaring works of art that span terrifying voids to little swinging bridges that take me to some out-of-the way place that's otherwise unreachable. On the Camino, bridges do more than tell stories and move me from one physical place to another. Here, they take me from one understanding to another and encourage me to open my mind to unfamiliar possibilities. I recall my sense of growing excitement when I stood on the old stone bridge at Saint-Jean-Pied-de-Port over three-and-a-half weeks ago, poised to take the first steps of this journey. My anticipation was tinged with uncertainty, for I had no idea what I was doing, or even whether I could do it, whatever "it" was. Yet, if the common wisdom of the Camino was to be believed, my life was going to be changed by the experience. Just three days later, I watched Juliette limp across the bridge into Trinidad de Arre and had the unsettling premonition that my journey was about to change. I wondered what that would mean for her—and for me. A mere forty-eight hours after that, I stood on the Puente la Reina and, for the first time, felt the presence of pilgrims and the life force of the Camino, an experience that opened me up to the power of this ancient way. Now this morning at Puente de Órbigo, I mark another transition. Gazing at

Steps Out of Time

this bridge, I realize that I no longer feel tentative and uncertain about my journey. Who knows what lies ahead, but I am ready for whatever awaits me on this trail to Santiago.

Church bells chime, a rooster crows, and I need to get moving. I put on my shoes and, checking my map, see that there are two routes between Órbigo and Astorga, a road route and one that goes through the countryside.

"There's no choice," an authoritarian male voice says. I turn to see Paul, the tough-looking pilgrim from the underpass, ambling up. "The country route is *much* better."

Paul is the kind of man you notice when he enters a room, although he's more striking than handsome. Inge refuses to talk to him because she says he looks evil. I disagree. He's got interesting things to say and he warms up as you get to know him. He waves his Spanish guidebook, pointing to a page with a map showing a starred route. I nod, and we head off together. I'm happy to have company for a change and I think our paces will be nicely compatible. They are—he really is sauntering. In spite of his easy pace, he covers well over thirty kilometers a day. The trick, he explains, is to walk slowly, but for a very long time each day. He starts at nine every morning and stops twelve hours later, just in time to shower and have dinner when the good restaurants open around ten.

"Our job as pilgrims is to walk and sleep and eat," he says. "Attend to our most basic needs, and that's it."

He's right. The interior journey follows on its own.

From Paul, I learn more about the aftermath of Catherine's fatal accident outside of Estella. He's tri-lingual and knew that Catherine's husband spoke no Spanish, so he went to Pamplona to help the new widower. Together, they attended to the myriad details that accompany a sudden death abroad—cutting through the thick bands of red tape that complicate sending a body overseas, filing police reports, notifying relatives, and taking care of mundane matters for the survivor such as finding a place to stay and changing the flight home. Paul put his pilgrimage on hold for several days, at his expense, until he saw his new friend onto a plane bound for home.

"The Camino is teaching me patience," Paul says, "and compassion for someone else's suffering."

What a kindness. I don't know how Catherine's widower would have managed on his own, especially given the hostile reaction of the police, the language barrier, and what must have been his terrible state of shock.

The next four hours go quickly. We cover French politics, American politics, sex and politics, gender roles in marriage, the Catholic Church's stand on birth control, its response to the priest abuse scandal, and raising daughters. We also talk about what physical attractiveness can do to, or for, a woman's career and the challenges my daughter faces as an attractive young woman in the male-dominated world of music composition.

"It's better than being ugly," Paul notes pragmatically.

I'm not so sure. Physical attractiveness is complicated for a woman. It can open doors, but also close them, and sometimes it leads to pressures and complications unimaginable to most men. We don't solve—or agree on—any of the things we discuss, but it's a fascinating few hours. Paul is that uniquely French blend of gallant sexism and unquestioning confidence in a woman's ability to assume any role she desires. It's a kind of feminism that doesn't play well in the United States, but it has a certain appeal to me. If half of what Paul tells me is true, his wife is a very lucky woman.

We split up at an appealing little bar in a small village just outside Astorga. The pain in my foot is tolerable, perhaps as a result of taking it easy today, but my shoulders are numb and I need to take a break. We shake hands warmly, wish each other well, and Paul saunters off. We'll have a beer together a few days later when we happen to meet at a little trailside bar, and that's the last I will see of him. But Paul is one of the people I am grateful to have met on the Camino and who remains fixed in my memory.

Business is slow, so the bartender comes over to my table to see how I'm doing and chat. When he reminds me that Astorga marks the end of the meseta, I let out a big "Yes!"

"It wasn't that bad, was it?" he laughs.

"I thought this day would never come," I say. "No more desolate countryside, no more roasting in the sun. Please tell me that's true."

"No worries there," he says. "The scenery changes completely, starting tomorrow. The vegetation is different, too. It's lush and green—no more brown. You'll have flowers everywhere. And great fruit grows along the way. Be sure to buy cherries from roadside stands whenever you can. They're delicious right now."

He also tells me about Astorga, which was important as the capital of the ancient Astur tribe, even before the arrival of the Romans. The town has much to recommend it, including many churches, a Romanesque cathedral, a Museum of Pilgrimage located in a palace designed by Gaudí, and a chocolate museum. Unfortunately, there is another general strike today and all the sights are closed. The churches I can live without, but no chocolate museum? It might appear that a museum dedicated to chocolate is not a very pilgrim-like destination. Not so. In the sixteenth century, the Spanish explorer Cortès brought chocolate to Spain after he discovered that this "divine drink" motivated and energized his soldiers, just as it had the Aztec warriors. It soon became available to the general

Steps Out of Time

public and no doubt motivated another kind of explorer: the pilgrim. I can say from personal experience that it works and has never tasted as good as on this long trail to Santiago.

When I finally get going again, I've tarried so long the Astorga refugio is full, but I find a room in a small hotel on the main square, right on the Camino. That afternoon, I consider consulting a doctor about my foot, which is becoming quite annoying, but I'm afraid she'll tell me to abandon my pilgrimage. At this point, I'm not going to stop unless I'm comatose, so I decide to see a pharmacist instead. I explain to her that I think it's tendonitis and since a brace did the trick with my knee, I'm wondering about one for my foot. I don't know the word for ankle brace, but I do know how to say knee brace, so I ask for a *rodillero*—a knee brace—for my foot. The pharmacist understands immediately, agrees it's worth trying, and measures my ankle and foot. My high arch and wide foot complicate finding a brace that gives good support without causing my foot to cramp up, but eventually we find one that seems fine. When I tell her how much I appreciate the wonderful Spanish pharmacists, she gives me a pat on the arm and a big smile and repeats what the doctor told me in Carrión de los Condes: "We have to take care of our pilgrims."

Following my nose to an irresistible bakery, I buy some chocolate sandwich cookies for breakfast, then scout out the route for tomorrow. When I get back to my room, I call home but Philip's not there, so I leave a voice-mail message—at least he'll know that I'm still alive. I console myself with a long soak before dinner, then operate on my new blisters. The white threads sticking out from my feet at strange angles remind me of a bad hair day.

Tonight, I dine on Spanish time, not pilgrim time, so it's late when I climb into bed—the cathedral bells are chiming half past midnight. That will mean a short night's sleep, but I'm bound to wake more rested than if I were staying in a refugio and had to contend with snorers and who knows what else. Or so I think. I am jolted awake at 3 a.m. by ear-splitting buzzes from the room next door, which are soon followed by wall-shaking vibrations and intense clunking, all from some mysterious source that the night clerk cannot identify. This leads to a room change at 4:30 a.m. and only three hours of sleep.

I walk out of the hotel at daybreak, feeling grumpy and groggy, but the cool dawn air soon brings me to life. Feet on automatic pilot and mind in neutral, I stroll on a straight and relatively flat gravel track, enjoying views of the still-distant mountains. The next village, Rabanal del Camino, is only five or so hours away; then there's nothing for fifteen kilometers. That means today will be either an easy day or a hard one, depending on whether I feel up to continuing when I get to Rabanal.

After half an hour, I spot a village, barely visible in the distance, clinging to the side of the mountain. Rabanal? The thought puts a bounce in my step. An hour later, when the village disappears from sight, my spirits flag—my goal is not as close as I'd hoped. But this time, re-energized by the fine weather and mountain vistas, I shrug my pain-free shoulders, wiggle the toes of my relatively pain-free foot, and savor the pleasures of this walk. I don't have to be anywhere for two weeks; I'm well-fed and mostly recovered from my bad night's sleep. What's not to enjoy about this moment?

Soon, the path begins to climb gently and becomes spectacularly lovely. On both sides, as far as I can see, fragrant masses of blue-violet lavender and vibrant yellow broom decorate the hillsides. Gradually, the soft whisper of heather replaces the bolder lavender. I skirt a cool oak forest that lies tantalizingly close to the trail, although not close enough to offer any shade; the mountains become more prominent—and more imminent. Then the wildflowers make their appearance: purple-throated foxglove, a tiny yellow flower reminiscent of black-eyed Susans, pink and white roses, and hawthorn covered with fragrant white flowers. The perfumed broom grows in larger and larger clumps until it is as full and colorful as the mature forsythia of a Midwestern spring. A cuckoo calls out. I even catch sight of a few butterflies, fluttering slivers of pale yellow and deep orange. Then all too soon, the pleasure of the walk is tempered by the pitch of the slope when it abruptly becomes much steeper, and the mountain stroll turns into a serious climb.

Around a bend, I see an elderly couple whom I recognize from the bar where I stopped for coffee earlier this morning. He looks close to eighty and is very tall and thin. His wife is somewhat younger and much shorter and rounder. Though I heard the man speak perfect French with the bartender, I don't think they are French. He's too tall and his face too round; his wife is not wearing a silk scarf. And he had ordered their breakfast with a self-effacing demeanor that made me certain he could not be French. When I saw them at the bar, I was amazed that they were managing this difficult pilgrimage with such ease—and reassured by their example. But the heat and grade are taking their toll. Now he stands by the side of the road, leaning on his staff, doubled over and panting. I hurry to catch up, wondering if they need help, but when I greet him and ask if he's OK, he raises his head and smiles calmly.

"I'm fine, I just need to rest," he says in French. "I'm Theo, from Amsterdam, and this is my wife, Margareth," he continues, holding out his free hand. Then with a gentle gesture, he invites me to sit with them in the grass.

Steps Out of Time

"This is a pilgrimage of thanksgiving for Margareth's return to health," Theo volunteers, beaming at his wife and patting her hand. "Eight years ago, she was diagnosed with breast cancer. Now she has been discharged by her doctor. He says she is healed, and we are very thankful."

Margareth returns his affectionate look. "Theo has a keen interest in music. He was a choir director for many years." she tells me in halting French. "He sings for me in empty churches along the way." Her eyes sparkle—she is the picture of contentment.

As we talk, Theo and I discover a common interest in wildflowers, and I'm excited to learn from him about a bog filled with wild orchids just before Portomarín. An interest in orchids is something I inherited from my father, along with his collection of gorgeous twenty-year-old cattleyas. Theo gives me explicit directions for finding the wild orchids and describes what to look for: tiny, pale pink flowers, the size of the nail on my little finger, growing on a stalk with waxy green almond-shaped leaves.

"You must have walked this pilgrimage before," I say.

"Yes," he replies, "several times with our children when they were little."

We chat a bit longer, then continue on together for some twenty minutes or so, until they need to rest again.

"I hope we'll see you in Rabanal," says Theo, as they take off their packs and look for a place in the shade. "We learned about a new hotel there from an innkeeper in Astorga. It's where we'll stay tonight."

"Before, we always stayed in refugios," adds Margareth, "but now, at our age, we need the comforts of a hotel."

"I understand," I reply. "Sometimes I go to a hotel myself. It feels like cheating, but I reach a point where I really need a night without snoring pilgrims." *Well, most hotels offer peace and quiet,* I think to myself, recalling my experience last night.

They laugh and nod. "We know," says Theo. "It's part of the experience, isn't it?"

I arrive in Rabanal del Camino at 12:30. During the Middle Ages, this village was a busy stop on the Camino, with several churches and pilgrim hospices, as well as a garrison that the Knights Templar maintained to ensure the safety of pilgrims who prepared to tackle the rugged mountain passes between Rabanal and Ponferrada. *The Pilgrim's Guide* dedicates an entire chapter to thanking and naming the men who made this notoriously difficult terrain safer by repairing the road and rebuilding a critical bridge. "May the souls of these men and those who worked with them rest in eternal peace!" proclaims the author.

Today, Rabanal is a quiet one-street village that continues to offer shelter to pilgrims. Though the refugio does not open for another two hours, already a dozen packs form an orderly queue in front of the substantial front door. It's hard to tell what this refugio is like, because nothing is visible from the street, but it's run by the Confraternity of Saint James and is reputedly one of the nicest in Spain. The owners of the lined-up packs, which are becoming more numerous by the minute, are sprawling comfortably on a grassy knoll under a big shade tree in the nearby churchyard. They look up and wave.

I like the feel of this place. Adding my pack to the growing queue, I go over to wait and relax with my fellow pilgrims. Before I left for Santiago, kicking back and relaxing was the furthest thing from my mind. Women who combined careers and motherhood, I believed then, couldn't survive without planning every minute of the day and night—it was a lifestyle that required being goal-oriented and tenaciously focused 24/7. To my pre-Camino way of thinking, I couldn't see the point of doing nothing—which I defined as an activity that yielded no measurable outcome. The notion of simply being, the wonderful, restorative richness of just being, was beyond my grasp only three-and-a-half weeks ago. The blink of an eye, yet it seems like another lifetime.

I'm not so sure now. Perhaps the desire to live a full, active, multi-faceted life is *not* incompatible with taking time to relax and simply be. I feel the cool grass between my toes, savor the caress of a gentle breeze, and make up for lost time.

Joining me under the tree are an American college student and her mother, who are enjoying their time on the Camino in spite of serious blister woes, and an American minister who is walking with his recently retired college roommate. A little later, I'm delighted to see Inge, my young German friend, appear.

"I'm fine," she announces before I have a chance to ask. "A little problem with my knees but nothing serious. How are you?"

I get up and give her a hug. "Good, I'm glad to see you," I say. "Will you stay here tonight? I hear the Confraternity refugio is really nice."

She sets down her pack, takes a swig of water, and plops down in the grass. Within seconds, she has her shoes and socks off, my question lost in her pleasure at wiggling her toes in the grass.

"I used to love doing this on hot summer days when I'd visit my grandparents," says Inge. "It feels even better now, after walking for so long."

She begins massaging her toes one by one.

"Are you taking care of your feet?" she asks. "Do you remember to do this when you stop, to keep the circulation going?"

I assure her I am following her instructions. A massage therapist and healer by profession, Inge gives advice freely about how to coax reluctant body parts into cooperating. She smiles and moves on to massage her calves. She also gives me news of Jacques and Maïté, who are a day behind us and fine, and we compare notes from our guidebooks about what lies between us and Santiago.

"I have to go farther today," she says. "I feel the energy pushing me on and must listen to my body. I've heard the refugio in the next town isn't open because of bad water, but I'll take my chances. If I have to, I'll sleep in a church or under a tree. At least I won't have to contend with snorers," she says, rolling her eyes at the thought.

"Gotta go now," she says, putting on her shoes and pack. With a hug and a wave, she lopes off.

At 2:30 on the dot (a reminder that this is an English-run establishment), the refugio door opens, and pilgrims assume their places in line next to their packs. The young couple in charge—she's Portuguese and he's German—call us up to register in groups of four. These volunteer hospitaleros are impressive linguists. I hear them welcome pilgrims in Spanish, French, German, English, Italian, and Norwegian. My group consists of three middle-aged men traveling together—two Spaniards and an Italian—and me.

"Do you mind coming up with us?" asks one of the Spaniards, with a wink.

"*No, claro*," I say, then ask as an afterthought, "*¿No roncan? ¿No?*" (You don't snore, do you?) He laughs and assures me they don't.

As we walk into the courtyard, the talkative Spaniard urges me to try to arrive in Santiago by Sunday, June 30.

"That day, the priests will swing the *botafumeiro* at the Grand Mass. You mustn't miss it," he says, "*¡Es estupendo!*"

The botafumeiro, I learn, is an immense, incense-puffing censer that has long been associated with the pilgrimage to Santiago. The current one dates only from 1851, but the first mention of a giant censer at the Santiago cathedral appears in church documents in 1322. The botafumeiro served a very practical function in the Middle Ages: priests would swing it vigorously before the Pilgrim Mass to cover up the gamey stench of the hoards of unwashed pilgrims. This tradition is a reminder of one of the hardships of being a pilgrim on the road to Santiago—the limited bathing options.

From the street, the walled refugio looked somber and inhospitable. But when I cross the threshold, a new universe appears. The door opens not into a building but onto a large courtyard that smells as inviting as it looks. To the left is a weathered barn and to the right, the handsome old home that shelters the refugio. The stone walls of both are covered with aromatic yellow roses. Beyond these structures lie a lush garden and an apple orchard. Several pilgrims are sitting around a sturdy wooden picnic table on the patio adjacent to the barn, writing in their journals or reading. Others bend over laundry tubs on the other side of the patio and scrub away.

The hospitalera registers my group of four and then takes us on a tour of the centuries-old house. Built in an L shape, it is characteristic of the homes of the Maragatos, a mountain people who have lived in this part of Spain since before the Roman occupation. The house was in ruins when the Confraternity of Saint James, in partnership with the Amigos de El Bierzo, leased it in 1991 from the Diocese of Astorga. Since then, the two organizations have meticulously restored the property to its original glory, stone by stone. Our tour ends in the large and airy sleeping room to which we are assigned.

"Pick a bed and make yourselves at home," the hospitalera says with a smile. "Breakfast is served in the kitchen at 6:30."

After a quick shower, I go back to sit in the churchyard and write in my journal. I'm lying on my back, daydreaming, when Theo and Margareth walk up. They've taken a room in the new hotel and are on their way to visit the church. I'm surprised to hear this because churches on the Camino are usually locked.

"It's open for the service," Theo explains. "Monks from the monastery across the street will sing vespers in half an hour."

I'm quite content lazing under the tree, but each Mass I've attended has helped me better understand the Camino, so I decide to join them. The tiny stone chapel feels tomb-like, with its thick walls and low ceiling. The only light comes from a handful of slits cut in the walls and a few candles, the arched windows having been filled in with bricks. Initially, the darkness is oppressive, but as my eyes adjust, the old church starts to feel cozy. A large wooden crucifix above the main altar has been polished until it gleams. Below it, someone has placed a bouquet of fully opened yellow roses; wildflowers grace the smaller altars. The church may not be in good repair but it is well-loved.

As the hour for vespers approaches, the church fills with a congregation of mostly pilgrims and a handful of village widows dressed in black. A few minutes later, two Benedictine monks wearing hooded black robes walk slowly into the church and up to the altar, their hands folded in prayer. One is in his late twenties, the other just a few years older. The younger monk genuflects at the altar, turns to face us, pushes back his hood, and quickly explains in Spanish how and when we are supposed to participate. His sweet face is framed by dark curly hair.

The two monks kneel facing each other and begin chanting the service in strong, clear voices—a tenor and a baritone. Most pilgrims in the congregation do not know the service, which is entirely in Latin. However, Theo, with his choir director's experience, is familiar with the liturgy and leads us as if we were his choir. The villagers, on the other hand, know exactly what to do. The señora next to me whispers the Latin words to herself the entire time the monks are singing without ever once consulting the prayer book.

At the end of vespers, the younger monk stands and turns again to face his congregation. This time, he addresses the pilgrims in slow, deliberate, and simple Spanish:

> You are meeting new people and seeing many new things. It is all admittedly very exciting and very beautiful. This is an exterior journey. It is the journey of a tourist. A pilgrim's journey is an interior one. It is when you go inside yourself. It is not looking outside. You are searching, perhaps for yourself. Think about the nature of your pilgrimage. I hope you will find what you are looking for. Because of my vocation, I hope you are looking for Christ, and I hope you will find him. But pilgrims, please, remember! The Camino is not just the road to Santiago. It is also a path to life, to a life enriched with perspectives offered by the Camino to those who open their hearts to its mysteries.

His message is timely. I am immersed in the challenges and pleasures of an intensely physical—and often intensely beautiful—world, yet the reflective nature of this journey is ever present. He reminds me that these journeys work together, each facilitating access to the other. Like bridges.

You don't run down the present, pursue it with baited hooks and nets. You wait for it, empty-handed, and you are filled.

Annie Dillard, *The Pilgrim at Tinker Creek*

REFUGIO ◆ GAUCELMO

RABANAL

21.06.02

La Posada D
Mvrie...

C.I.F. A-24353800

Telf. 34 987 453 201

MOLINASECA (León)

22.06.02

Chapter Eighteen

Alice in Wonderland

June 22, Rabanal del Camino to several kilometers east of Molinaseca.

I wake at first light and, feeling rested, move quickly. By six, I am ready to go, so face the decision of whether to wait around half an hour until the announced time for breakfast or start walking now. With no bars for the first two hours, the real question is whether I am prepared to walk that long without coffee. I'm trying to decide what to do when I hear Gregorian chant coming from the kitchen. Poking my head in the door, I discover a cozy room that smells of morning: the pungent aroma of freshly brewed coffee, the yeasty scent of still-warm bread, and the unmistakable mintiness of toothpaste. Half a dozen pilgrims sit around a wooden table talking quietly, their voices barely audible over the music. I'm in luck, breakfast started early today. The hospitalero greets me with coffee and good news.

"You will have splendid weather today—sunshine, but not too hot," he says. "Perfect for crossing the passes."

If ever I needed a day of good weather, this is it. Today I must cross two mountain passes and will reach the highest elevations of the Camino. Twenty minutes later, I am under way. Yellow arrows take me past the old church and through the sleeping village. Within minutes, the level city street becomes a steep country lane. Swatches of bright yellow broom replace the old stone buildings of the village; hazy blue mountains in the distance are lovely against the rosy sky. Though the countryside is increasingly rugged and isolated, it's great walking. In the pastel dawn, I feel like I'm passing through a Turner painting. Church bells chime the half hour.

When I get to what's left of Foncebadón an hour later, I'm in a different world. For centuries, this village was an important waypoint for pilgrims to Santiago because its hospices offered shelter in the midst of harsh terrain and notoriously bad weather. A late-eighteenth-century document does not mince words about the difficulty of this part of the Camino:

> The nature of the landscape is extremely rough and fearsome, and from nearly the first of September until the end of May, the pass is closed, and the neighboring villages put up cairns to mark the route, and if this is insufficient, they dedicate themselves to guide, accompany, house, and thaw out the poor pilgrims who come and go from Galicia.
>
> Quoted in Gitlitz and Davidson's *The Pilgrimage Road to Santiago*

It's only a short walk from Foncebadón to the top of the first summit, known as the *Cruz de Ferro* because it is marked by a huge pile of stones crowned with an iron cross. It lies at 1,505 meters (4,938 feet), not high by Colorado standards, but the views are nonetheless spectacular. It is said that a monument has stood on this summit since the time of the pre-Roman Celts, although the site did not become Christianized until the early twelfth century when the hermit Gaucelmo added a cross to the monument and established a pilgrim hospice in this area. Tradition has it that Santiago pilgrims bring a stone from home and place it on the rock pile to represent the sins for which they hope to earn forgiveness. The secular version of this tradition says the stone symbolizes worries you wish to leave behind.

Placing a stone at the cruz de ferro is supposed to be a very moving experience. Not for me. Cameras click obsessively from every direction, and large groups of people huddle around guides waving little flags. The parking lot, crammed with tour buses and cars, reeks of exhaust fumes; kids climb on the rock pile as if it were a playground. No doubt there is a shop selling postcards and souvenirs nearby, but I don't stick around to find out. I scramble to the top and add my stone—collected only the day before when I learned of this tradition from a French pilgrim—and beat it. In my rush to escape the bedlam, I completely forget that I'm supposed to saddle my stone with my worries.

Upon leaving the cruz de ferro most pilgrims take the road, probably because the vegetation is so thick that it obscures a little path leading to the trail. Not one for road walking, I push aside the bushes and check out the alternative. Seconds later, I am on a foot-wide trail surrounded by broom so tall and thick that it precludes a view of the road or anything else save the profuse yellow flowers and patches of cobalt sky that peek through the golden clouds all around me. The air is intoxicatingly fragrant, the proportions surreal. I feel like a child in a magical place that is both enchanting and overwhelming. Maybe this is what Alice felt like when she ventured down the rabbit hole into the unknown. But I'm Kate, not Alice, and this is real and all the more glorious because of it.

At times, the little path is barely passable. I push aside the dense vegetation, creating just enough space to slip past, and for the next half hour I float along the gently undulating trail through a forest of heather and broom. Flowers grow right up to the edge of the narrow track, their intense fragrances and colors further magnified by the bright sunlight. The only sound is the humming of bees, a low, soothing murmur that tethers me to reality. Then the path makes its way up to rejoin the paved road, climbing gradually but relentlessly, and soon I am at the highest point of the Camino francés, an unnamed summit at 1,517 meters (almost 5,000 feet).

"Do not be fooled," warns my guidebook, "it is not all downhill to Santiago—far from it!"

I climb up onto a bank beside the road, sit down in the grass, and pause to take in the view. Across the road, the slope pitches steeply downward to a green, V-shaped valley. Houses dot the distant hillside. Before me, I see wave after gentle wave of mountaintops. A tiny, far-away village suggests a life of rural tranquility and total isolation. Traces of an old stone roadway, too narrow for a car, recall an earlier era when no motor traffic polluted the air with noise and fumes.

A friendly "*bonjour*" breaks the silence. I turn to see Theo and Margareth arriving at the summit.

"What weather!" exclaims Theo. "We weren't sure we could make it this time, even on the road, if the weather was as bad as the last time. It was stormy the entire way, with winds that blew us sideways. I'm seventy-seven, you know."

"Wow!" I say. "I hope I can walk five hundred miles when I'm seventy-seven."

Theo smiles. "We're thankful. Still, I'm anxious every day when I get started. I've walked the Camino before and know it has surprises."

His pleasure in being here is so obvious and so genuine that it's hard to believe he worries very much about anything. Just then, their cell phone rings. They huddle together around the phone, eager as kids on Christmas morning. When they recognize the voices of their grandchildren, their faces light up. I understand nothing of the lively conversation, which is in Dutch, but laughter is universal and I can hear the love in their voices.

"They call often to make sure we're OK," Margareth explains, as they hang up. Theo stores their phone in his shirt pocket, still grinning.

Before they start walking again, I ask to take their picture.

"Of course," says Theo. He puts his arm around his wife and they strike a pose, walking sticks held confidently at their sides, mountains in the background. Suddenly he doubles over.

"Please, wait a bit, until the spell passes," he gasps. "It's my heart condition."

Neither of them seems alarmed, though I am truly frightened. But a few minutes later, he straightens up, smiles, and puts his arm back around Margareth as if nothing had happened. Admiring their courage and perseverance, I take my photo.

When they start off again, Theo points to a little sign up ahead with his walking stick.

"Continue on the path, it starts over there," he says. "It's only twenty minutes longer but much, much nicer. Take advantage of this splendid weather. We must take the road because the steep and uneven trail is too much for our knees, but the mountain route won't be a problem for you at your age."

At my age? I love it!

Five years later, when I receive their annual Christmas card, a flood of memories of that day and this wonderful couple comes pouring over me—they have had the photo I took of them made into postage stamps.

Margareth and Theo at the highest point of the Camino.

Steps Out of Time

And inside the envelope, in addition to their Christmas note, is a larger copy of the picture that serves as an announcement of their fiftieth wedding anniversary the previous September 17. "*Gretha en Theo*," it says across the top in Dutch, and below, "*50 jaar samen op weg*" (Gretha and Theo, fifty years together, on the way). They've been happy ones, judging from their smiles.

I settle back into the hillside and fix this time and place in my memory. Silence reigns again, except for a few birds and an occasional passing pilgrim. It is hard to imagine this spot as anything other than serene and sheltered from all harm, yet even today, an insistent wind at the summit reminds me that the weather can change quickly in the mountains. I must not linger.

For the first ten minutes, the trail is rocky and steep, then it becomes an easy footpath that crosses a stream and makes its way through a meadow thick with fragrant pink primroses. Later, when I begin the descent into El Acebo, I appreciate just how dangerous this alternate route can be. The little high mountain trail is still lovely, but the pitch becomes so steep that I resort to sliding down some sections on my bottom. My walking stick is useless. In fact, it's in the way as I struggle to find a way down the precipitous rock wall. In rain, snow, or high winds, this section of the trail would be treacherous, and in bad light, one could easily stray off the poorly defined track and become hopelessly lost. I take a long drink of water, then begin to pick my way down. Slowly.

When I get to the bar in El Acebo, Theo and Margareth are already there, enjoying a meal of fresh-squeezed orange juice, the usual tortilla española, and a café con leche. It looks so good that I go to the bar and order the same thing.

"Come, join us," says Theo, offering me an empty chair at their table.

And before I know it, this little lunch break has turned into a two-hour conversation. We talk mostly about our children. Theo and I reminisce about how quiet our houses became when they grew up and went off to college. We both have musician daughters and recall with fondness and nostalgia the pleasure of listening to them play the piano at all hours. I tell them laughingly—although at the time it made me sad—how I missed tripping over our son's size-thirteen shoes, which he used to leave scattered around the house, and missed his good company at breakfast. (We are the only ones in the family who engage in conversation before noon.)

"How quickly they grow up," I say.

"Grandchildren, too," replies Theo.

He tells me the story of a frightening experience during one of their first pilgrimages, when their children were small. Their youngest son had a very high temperature and they were terribly worried about him but couldn't find an open pharmacy or a doctor. Desperate, they went to the village church, where a kindly priest helped them find a doctor and put up their entire family for a week while the child recovered. Now, each time they do the Camino, they still stop to thank this priest for his caring help so many years ago.

"That small child is grown now, with children of his own," adds Margareth.

Theo also tells me about an encounter with a Frenchman on another trip. He had found the man, tears in his eyes, sitting at the base of the *cruz de ferro* clutching a rock on which he had written "Madeleine," the name of his late wife who had died three years earlier.

"He said he was walking the Camino in her memory," Theo explains, "and in the hope Saint James could help him heal. He kept saying over and over how lucky we were to be able to do this together and how empty his life was without Madeleine."

And with that, Theo recites the poem he wrote in Madeleine's memory and gave to the bereaved pilgrim. By the time he's finished, we both tear up, tears of sympathy for Madeleine's husband. But mine are also tears of wonder, tinged with sadness at the powerful yet fragile nature of happiness.

Theo tells me, with a shy smile, that he wrote a poem on the Camino for Margareth, but he doesn't offer to recite it. Margareth looks affectionately at her husband; he returns the look as he pats her hand. I think back to my first impression of them. Their stooped posture and humble demeanor made them seem so vulnerable, and this had filled me with dread at the thought of aging. Yet as I get to know them, I realize I was wrong to interpret their quiet manner as a sign of resignation and fragility. They are the embodiment of life and hope. They remind me, once again, that people are so much richer than the facile stereotypes I sometimes ascribe to them.

Another round of coffee later, Theo and Margareth look at their watches and realize they need to start walking if they're going to make Molinaseca at a decent hour. We shake hands, figuring we'll meet up again at some point, and they're off. I linger a bit to chat with Mark (the retired New Jersey plumber), who has just staggered into the bar, a wild look in his eyes. He also took the path and was freaked out by the descent into El Acebo. Drenched in sweat and exhausted, even the brim of his hat droops with fatigue. I commiserate with him about the difficulty of that descent, then he raises something else that's bothering him.

"This damn snoring thing finally got to me," he announces with a disgusted look.

"I know, it's a big problem for me, too," I say. "Sometimes these guys keep me awake all night. It's really annoying how one person can disrupt so many people's sleep."

He looks wounded, then shrugs. "Yeah, well, it's my snoring that's the problem. But don't worry, I'm staying in hotels now, where I can snore away in peace."

Oops. I'd never thought about it from his perspective. The snoring feels like such an assault, but I guess it causes problems for the snorer, too. I clearly have some work to do on tolerance.

"I really put my foot in my mouth this time, didn't I?" I say. "Can I buy you a beer?"

"Naw," he says, "you don't need to do that. I'm used to abuse over my snoring."

We commiserate some more, this time about the heat, and Mark goes off to get another beer. I wait for fifteen minutes to tell him good-bye, but when he doesn't return, I write a short note of encouragement on a napkin, put it under his hat, and head out. Our paths don't cross again, but I do run into Theo and Margareth in the next village, at a pretty fountain surrounded by roses, where they have stopped to fill their water bottles. Theo looks pensive.

"I regret that this will be my last Camino," he says, "At my age, I don't think I'll be able to do it again. Each one has been different, different people, different weather, different routes. But always so rich."

How can he walk twenty-five kilometers a day in this heat at his age? And he still wants to do it again.

But Theo is totally focused on the richness of the journey and not on the hardships.

"We'll take the road from here to Molinaseca, but there's also a lovely mountain trail," Theo says, showing me his map, and as before, he advises me to take the off-road route.

"I don't know," I reply. "It looks pretty isolated, and I'm walking alone. Is it safe? What if I get lost or fall on a steep section?"

"You'll be fine," Theo says.

Margareth nods in agreement.

That's all the encouragement I need. Though the path is rocky and often steep, it continues to be a beautiful walk, now in high, lush valleys with stately chestnut trees, expansive meadows, fragrant pines, and always the protective presence of the mountains.

The only problem is that I am being followed by a man. At first, I thought it was my imagination, but now I am sure I smell the strong scent of aftershave—Old Spice, in fact—and it's making me nervous. Pilgrims on foot don't wear aftershave. Who is it? And what am I going to do? I haven't seen another person since I left the last village almost an hour ago.

I discreetly turn around to look. No one is behind me. Unnerved, I leave the path, walk up the hillside, sit on a rock, and wait. The scent persists—in fact, it becomes stronger when I stop, but no one appears. In the absolute silence of this mountainside, I hear no footsteps, no voices, no breathing. Finally, it dawns on me that what I smell is something growing along the path that mixes with the lavender to mimic a decades-old memory of my high school boyfriend's aftershave. Feeling silly and relieved, I scramble down to the path and continue walking.

A bit farther, in another isolated area, I have another worrisome moment when I notice an old man sitting on a stool by a beat-up camper. His face is completely expressionless as he stares unflinchingly at the path and me. I avoid his eyes and walk on, heart pounding, anxious once again. Do women ever stop feeling vulnerable? Can they ever afford to let down their guard? That night I learn from other pilgrims that this old man sits at that spot day after day and waits for the chance to offer assistance to pilgrims in distress. (Speaking of stereotypes . . .)

Half an hour later, the path traverses a steep slope high above the road, whose hairpin curves are visible in the valley far below me. Theo and Margareth are down there, little dots in the distance, but recognizable by their shapes and posture—a tall stooped figure and a shorter, rounder one. I wave my walking stick. Theo sees me and raises his in response. Though I can barely make out their faces from this distance, I know they are both smiling.

I won't encounter them again on this pilgrimage, but it turns out not to be the last one for either of us. Three years later, I see Theo and Margareth at the Santiago train station when we are on the way back to our respective homes after another journey to Compostela. And three years after that, Theo sends me a photo of Margareth and himself at the O Cebreiro pass, wearing blue rain ponchos, walking sticks in hand and smiles on their faces. This time, too, they made it to Santiago. A year after that, I learn that Theo and Margareth hope to make yet another pilgrimage to Santiago—their eighth. But their next pilgrimage will be different, for this one they will make in memory of Laura, their precious four-year-old granddaughter, whom they lost some months earlier to cancer. Theo explains that they will sing the song he wrote for her in churches along the way and walk in remembrance and in thanks for her short life. I hope they will find comfort.

As I continue watching them from my perch high on the mountainside, I feel like I'm observing time itself ticking away. I've met so many people on the Camino. From each I've received (and hopefully given) something—shared insights, kind gestures, or simply a happy moment together. We move into, and out of, each other's lives, ever so briefly.

Steps Out of Time

Ships passing, all that. Yet I don't feel sadness or even nostalgia (well, not too much) at the thought of leaving behind these unforgettable people and the experiences we share, although they are as fleeting as the beauty of Ronsard's rose. I am profoundly grateful for each encounter.

The tiny figures of Margareth and Theo disappear around a curve. Not another person is in sight. I stand there alone, peering down the silent slope, remembering another rocky path across a steep mountainside— the one in the Dolomites that I somersaulted off several years ago. And I realize that I've broken my key safety rule. I promised everyone—myself most of all—that I would make sure never to be the last one on the trail, especially in an isolated area or on a steep section. This is both. What's more, I still have a long way to go, and it's now late afternoon. If I fall and hurt myself, nobody is likely to find me until morning. Well, there's nothing to do now but continue on, stay alert, and carefully make my way down the mountain.

And bask in the day. After all, Alice tumbled down a rabbit hole, and by keeping her wits about her—wherever she was and however strange her circumstances—she came out just fine. It's unlikely I'll take another spill, but if I do, I'll go with it. What else can I do?

It is not really a place at all, only a
state of understanding.

Colin Fletcher, *The Man Who Walked Through Time*

Chapter Nineteen

Being, Just Being

June 22 – 25, Molinaseca to Alto de Poio via Villafranca del Bierzo
and O Cebreiro.

I hear Molinaseca before I see it—the sound of kids splashing happily in
the Río Meruelo that borders the town to the east. It's after five and the
sun's low in the sky, but the heat is as intense as if it were midday. This late
the refugio is almost certainly full, and that likelihood is all the excuse I
need to go to a hotel. On the far side of town, I find an immaculate single
room in a small, family-owned place right on the Camino. The innkeeper
is so welcoming that by the time she takes me up to my room, the tension
I felt in my shoulders when I arrived is all but gone.

The next morning, however, I howl in pain when I try to move my
legs. Yesterday's steep ascents and descents—thousands of feet up and
down in an eleven-hour day—have taken their toll. After averaging over
twenty kilometers for the last twenty-six days, this soreness is the last thing
I would expect. Hopefully my muscles will loosen up before I tackle the
last remaining passes.

For the next two days, the route continues to climb. There is a nasty
stretch of highway walking just outside of Cacabelos where the trail is on
an eight-inch shoulder and I must share the road with a steady stream of
cars and the occasional bus that hurtles towards me at breakneck speed.
But most of the time, the Camino goes through thriving vineyards. The
plants have fat green leaves, long wavy tendrils that curl tightly like ribbon
on a package, and huge bunches of baby grapes that look like hundreds

of tiny green peas packed tightly together into perfectly formed clusters. Huge storks fly over this section of the Camino, surprisingly graceful when they spread their enormous wings and soar like hawks.

One rainy morning, I walk with Gephardt, an Austrian pilgrim who is in transition on all fronts. He recently quit a great job with an international IT company after a management change put him in a supervisory role over his girlfriend. That didn't work at all and she left him in a matter of weeks. A short time later, both of his parents died from cancer.

"I was floundering badly and terrified of how out of control my life had become," he says, "then a friend mentioned the Camino. I quit my job and started walking."

"Just like that?" I ask, remembering how long it had taken me to make up my mind.

"Just like that," he says. "Maybe I thought about it for a minute or two, but this felt right. You should have seen me a month ago, when I left home—you'd understand why I had to do something and fast."

Gephardt is good company. We begin a long conversation about our Camino experiences—the dizzying highs and lows, the characters we've met, the feelings of peace that we've known along the way.

"The trick will be keeping this feeling once you're home and your husband and kids and everyone else start pushing your buttons again. They're bound to do it, even if unconsciously."

"I'm wondering the same thing," I admit. "And even without the influence of others, life can throw a curve that derails you in seconds. Maybe our experiences on the Camino will be permanently imprinted by the time we get home."

"Yes, hardwired!" he says.

Just then, we walk past another particularly lush bed of roses, and Gephardt breaks out in a grin.

"This should be called *camino de rosas*," he says. "You know, maybe smelling the roses will be my way to tune back in when I need a refresher course."

We part ways at the outskirts of Villafranca del Bierzo where I stop to visit the Romanesque Church of Santiago. In the Middle Ages, this was an important waypoint for pilgrims who were ill or injured. Tradition held that pilgrims who made it this far but were unable to continue would receive the same absolution they would have received had they arrived in Santiago. I sit on a pew and spend some time thinking about the pilgrims over the centuries whose journeys ended here. The church is a majestic structure that radiates that now-familiar sensation of being a part of something bigger than any individual life, my own included. When I put my pack back on and walk into town, I feel refreshed and calm, but not prepared for what I will face the next morning.

The route out of Villafranca del Bierzo is the worst highway walking of the entire Camino. The official path is once again a small swatch on the shoulder of the busy two-lane National VI, but now the traffic is mostly huge tour buses and eighteen-wheelers. The shoulder of this busy highway is only inches wide, and there is an unprotected twenty-foot vertical drop from the outside edge of the tarmac to a little flower-filled meadow below. Walking down there would be so pleasant, but no stairs offer access and it's far too steep to negotiate unaided. The pilgrim's path is on the left shoulder, which means I walk facing traffic. (On the other side, a rock wall often abuts the shoulder.) When the trucks and buses go whizzing by, I have to stop and brace myself to keep from being blown over by the wind they create. The drivers are as nervous as I am. They pass so close I can see the fear in their eyes, but when traffic comes from both directions, as is usually the case, there is nothing they can do to give me any leeway.

Earlier in my pilgrimage, whenever the Camino ran along the shoulder of a well-traveled route, I had been furious at the drivers who seemed to threaten my life. This time I think of Pedro, the bartender and truck driver who gave Jacques, Maïté, and me a ride into Burgos, and I no longer feel attacked. We share these terrible conditions, after all, the drivers and I, and like it or not, we are part of the same scene, each on our own journey. Living in this present moment is definitely more challenging than the untroubled times, but it is my present, so I will do my best, with tractor trailers and their drivers for company.

After about two hours of terror, I stop for coffee at a major crossroads bar. Ten kilometers down and eighteen to go. Even inside, I can hear and feel the trucks whizzing by. It's like being at one of the rest stops on I-94 between Chicago and Ann Arbor—built across the interstate, they shake every time a truck rolls by. But this time, instead of getting in my car and facing the traffic on more or less equal terms, I'm about to go back out into this free-for-all on foot. After my break, the Camino follows a pleasant country road, but it soon turns into another stretch of busy highway and the struggles begin again.

"*El Camino está terrible por aquí, ¿no cierto?*" (the Camino is awful here, isn't it?), a Spanish pilgrim says as he overtakes me. He slows his pace a bit, and gives me an encouraging look. "There's not too much more of this, take heart," he says, and introduces himself as José-María from Cádiz, in southern Spain. He's walking the Camino because he made a promise three years ago that if something worked out, he would go to Santiago to thank Saint James. He doesn't offer details, but things went as he had hoped, and he got special permission from his boss to take time off, with the stipulation that he would complete his pilgrimage in twenty-nine days. He's had some tendonitis, so he walks slowly, but covers long distances each day.

"You have to keep promises," he says.

José-María is a good companion and the time passes quickly. When the Camino leaves the highway an hour later, I stop to rest my throbbing foot and he continues on. A few pain pills and some chocolate later, I continue walking, now on a narrow, pedestrian-only trail that takes off at a right angle from the highway. It heads steeply uphill, offering spectacular views in all directions, and best of all, erases all trace of cars, trucks, and highway.

As I climb, the vegetation becomes thick and lush, obscuring any markers. But there is only one trail, so I just keep following it, eyes fixed straight ahead and concentrating on the smell of the tall grass. No other pilgrims are in sight, and I hear nothing but the occasional whisper of a breeze in the grass. Stripped of the powerful stimulus of sound, I saunter through a still and serene universe, aware only of the warmth of the sun and the little path snaking upward in high alpine meadows.

Two and a half hours later, a moss-covered stone wall materializes along one side of the path, and then the little mountain trail becomes a paved country lane. I hear the grinding gears of a bus, the slate roof of a pre-Romanesque church comes into view, and I've arrived at the village of O Cebreiro, in the province of Galicia. The first thing I do on crossing the road into the village is take off my pack and carry it in my arms like a baby to relieve the pain in my shoulders. (I contemplate throwing it down the valley, but I know that would be short-sighted.) Nothing helps the pain in my foot.

A Benedictine monastery is said to have sheltered pilgrims here in the ninth century, and outposts of civilization have existed on this remote mountain top since the Celtic settlements as early as the eleventh century BC. The village is named after Cerberus, the mythological three-headed dog that guarded the door to Hades, a place known for its particularly terrible climate. Like O Cebreiro. Typically, the wind howls year-round and, even in summer, heavy rains chill and disorient pilgrims. In winter, blizzards are frequent and life-threatening. In fact, in the early fourteenth century, one of the miracles of the Camino occurred when a peasant struggled through a raging winter storm to reach the church of O Cebreiro to receive communion. When he arrived, the priest scorned him for making such an effort just to receive a little bread and wine, but the priest had barely finished talking when the bread and wine turned into flesh and blood. It is said that the church's statue of the Virgin, now known as *la Virgen del Milagro*, tilted her head to get a better view of the miraculous event. The flesh and blood from that communion purportedly remain in the church to this day, in a silver reliquary donated by Queen Isabella.

Today's weather is splendid, and I relish my good fortune as I head for the municipal refugio located well beyond the hustle and bustle of the tourist area at the far edge of the village. Along the way, I pass a number of *pallozas*, ancient oval-shaped stone structures with thatched roofs that used to house people and animals. Typical of this region, they are similar to dwellings found in Ireland, Brittany, and other parts of the world where the Celts settled.

The refugio is perched on a promontory at eye level with the surrounding mountains and offers majestic views of the rounded peaks in the soft, late-afternoon light. Birds soar across the sky and clouds hint at the colors of the sunset to come. I could linger for hours. But the steady stream of pilgrims reminds me that I must register and claim a spot. I get the last bed on the first floor, in one of the eight-person sleeping rooms, which is lucky because it's bound to be quieter than the large dormitory upstairs. It's a top bunk, but by now I've gotten pretty good at scrambling up and down, even without a ladder or chair.

Hot and sweaty from the climb, I dump my pack on my bunk, dig out my set of clean clothes, and head for the ladies' bathroom, where I queue up for the shower behind some Italian teen-agers on a school trip. One of them, a pretty dark-haired girl of about fifteen, is eager to talk when she discovers that we both speak French. We commiserate about the climb up to O Cebreiro (tough) and compare the condition of our feet (bad) while we stand in line. She and her four friends were here first and are all carrying an assortment of bottles, tubes, razors, and other paraphernalia, so I figure I've got a long wait ahead of me. To my surprise, they offer me the first shower that becomes available. My instinct is to demur. A line is a line, after all. But one look at their earnest faces and I know that's the wrong response. It's obvious that their gesture gives them pleasure, and I remind myself that it's OK to accept special favors.

"*Grazie, mille grazie,*" I say, in badly pronounced Italian.

I mean it, too. I'm hot and tired and grateful for their thoughtfulness. They grin at my attempt to use their language and the young girl who speaks French holds out her arm, pointing the way with a little bow. The water is cold. I try to take it in stride this time and think instead about the kindness of the young Italians. But even though I was about to melt from the heat when I turned on the water, I'm shivering uncontrollably by the time I dry off. I put on all my layers and go to the lounge to get warm. I'm scribbling away illegibly in my journal, fingers stiff from the cold, when I hear someone call my name in French. It's Jacques and Maïté. I knew we'd see each other again. They rush over and, of course, it's kisses all around.

They go off to claim beds in the upstairs dormitory, and after they've settled in, we visit the town. Later, we have dinner together in a village restaurant and bar situated on the edge of a precipice. The dining room has a bank of windows running the entire length of the back wall that takes full advantage of the view down into the valley and beyond, to the distant mountains. The wind's howling outside and it's quite cold now that the sun has set, but a crackling fire in the oversized fireplace warms the entire room and creates a welcoming glow and a pleasing scent.

We order the house specialty, a hearty stew of beef, chorizo, white beans, and other vegetables, well-seasoned with rosemary and garlic—it's fantastic. In fact, the food is so good that when a second dinner—succulent roast pork with thyme gravy and sautéed potatoes—appears because of a miscommunication, we don't send it back. After a piece of the delicious almond cake that I first discovered in the parador in Santo Domingo and a cup of chamomile tea, I'm finally beginning to get full and warm, but my right foot still hurts.

"Tendonitis," Maïté pronounces when I mention the problem. "I have just the remedy," she says, pulling from her pocket a floppy, silvery green leaf. It's a piece of cabbage.

"Where in the world did you find that?" I ask, astonished.

She waves it around, ignoring my question. "I wish you'd try this," she insists. "Wrap it around your foot and, in a day or two, it will cure the pain. You'll see."

She's dead serious, and I don't want to hurt her feelings, but the idea strikes me as ridiculous.

"How can a cabbage leaf cure foot pain?" I ask, suppressing a giggle.

"It works because it hydrates," she says with calm conviction.

A French pilgrim at a nearby table chimes in: "Cabbage leaves are a proven remedy for tendonitis. I'm a mountain guide. I have seen it work."

"Maybe tomorrow," I tell Maïté.

I never do try this alleged cure. However, several years later I learn from a nurse friend that cabbage leaves are an old wives' remedy for sore nipples during breast feeding, so there may be something to Maïté's claim.

After a couple of hours, we start back to the refugio but get only as far as the door when we run into José-María, the Spaniard I walked with earlier today. I introduce him to Jacques and Maïté.

"Join me for a drink?" he asks.

Jacques and Maïté are ready to turn in and decline. I had planned to go to bed early tonight, too, so I start to refuse. Then I remember my goal of trying to go with the flow, and catching myself in mid-sentence, I accept. We return to the restaurant I've just left, order a couple of beers, and, in no time, we are engaged in a long conversation about the sometimes funny and always interesting experiences of raising teen-agers. We could go on for many more beers, but the refugio is about to close, so we reluctantly head out into the dark and windy night. Walking back after sunset, this place is even more beautiful, as purple clouds roll in below the surrounding mountaintops and swirl in dizzying patterns. The moon lights the way, peeking in and out of the roiling banks of clouds. José-María insists on walking me out to the precariously placed clothesline, then discreetly turns his back while I pick up my ragged, dingy underwear and holey, graying socks. Keys in hand, the hospitalero appears and calls out to us to hurry—it's two minutes to lights out. We quickly shake hands and I race to the ladies room, making it to bed just as everything goes dark. I'm glad I decided to stay and chat with José-María. It was fun and I feel comforted about my shortcomings as a parent. *Maybe perfection isn't the appropriate standard,* I think as I drift off.

At 5:45 the next morning, I wake feeling warm and well rested. My roommates are all sound asleep. I slide down as quietly as I can from my top bunk, grabbing my pack and shoes and pulling my sleeping bag with me. With my tiny flashlight in my free hand, I do a quick sweep of my bunk for anything left behind. Finding nothing, I creep toward the bright band of light under the door, slip into the hallway—and break out in a grin. Everything I need is cradled in the elbow of one arm. Amazing! I vaguely recall my grad student days when I could put all my possessions in my car. Even that seems like an encumbered state now, when all my possessions fit in a small day pack. This extreme version of paring down is not possible in real life. I know that. But living this way, even temporarily, convinces me that there is great value in a simplified life, one that permits the time and space, physical and mental, to be present. I savor this uncluttered state—and vow to find a way to apply the lessons of simplicity I have learned on the Camino when I get home. I will start by cleaning out my closet.

When I get to the reception area, I'm greeted by a handful of pilgrims who are standing around, struggling to jam sleeping bags into impossibly tiny stuff sacks. They sway as they pull on well-worn boots with expressions ranging from mild discomfort to agony and fumble to don hats and parkas before heading out into the cold. I go over to a row of empty chairs and begin the familiar task of reloading my pack. By now, I've got it down to a science. My sandals go in first, flat on the bottom of the pack so they won't create uncomfortable lumps against my back. Then I cram my sleeping bag into its stuff sack and lay it on top of the sandals. Next goes the twelve-by-fifteen-inch white plastic sack that contains my wardrobe. It's less bulky than usual, since I'm wearing everything except my extra socks and underwear. I place my journal into a small, gray plastic bag from Rice University, where my daughter is a student. This bag sports an inquisitive-looking midnight-blue owl on the front, sitting on a leafy branch. Each time I see it, I imagine that this wise bird is speaking to me: "Write in your journal! Practice chilling! Keep walking! Stop whining! Are you listening to the Camino? Are you listening to me?" The little bag fits perfectly into the vertical space along the back of my pack, next to my spine, providing a bit of structure so that when my pack is fully loaded, it doesn't sag quite so much.

I place the heaviest single item—my screaming-yellow Dopp kit—on top, in the middle, for easy access. It contains my first-aid kit, including a variety of blister treatments and painkillers. My rolled-up sports towel fits along one side and my rolled-up pilgrim's cape on the other. Finally, I snuggle a full one-liter water bottle into each side of the pack, check to make sure it's zipped up, and tighten the straps. All that preparation, the weeks of weighing and measuring, paid off. Everything fits perfectly, and I'm ready to roll.

While I am putting on my jacket, the young Italian girl who was so friendly last night comes over, eager to speak French again. She's smiling, though she is clearly not used to getting up so early. The other girls look a little dazed, too, but all are made up, prom-style. They wear black eye liner, lots of blue or green eye shadow, and thick black mascara. Their lipstick is bright red and the lines are a little wobbly, but in a way that makes them look innocent, not silly. The boys stand perfectly still, leaning against the wall, half asleep and slumped together for support. They appear to have slept in their clothes and their hair is uncombed.

"We did the first part in a bus," the young girl says, pointing outside to their vehicle. "Now we're walking. You have to do the last one-hundred kilometers on foot, you know, or you won't get your Compostela."

I want to ask her why she thinks, at her age, she needs a Compostela. What sins can she possibly need to expiate? But I resist the urge; it's too early for teasing. Instead, I ask her which she likes best, the bus or walking.

"The bus," she says without hesitation, "though it makes me sick to my stomach. Walking hurts my feet. It's terrible, really, really terrible!"

Her eyes get big at the thought of what lies ahead. Slowly, her group gathers in the reception area, and I see what the problem is. Their packs are huge. They look like giant over-stuffed sausages, with bits of innards dangling from all the openings and tied on every possible strap. *Poor kids*, I think, *this is only their second day walking and they have no idea what they're in for.* But I take another look at their open and hopeful faces and revise my opinion. Good for them, I decide, they are doing this by the book—carry your own stuff and suffer. They'll be fine.

Their harried leader, a desperate look in his eyes, says something in Italian that I don't understand. The young girl smiles and tells me *au revoir*, touches my arm, and heads over to join her group. They move silently out into the early morning stillness, and I feel a sudden tenderness that threatens to turn into tears. They are so vulnerable and yet so open to life and its experiences. I hope the fates are good to them.

Craving a good coffee before I start walking, I head for the restaurant where I had dinner last night. Even at this hour, the bar is packed with pilgrims, most of whom are studying maps while they sip from large steaming mugs. José-María waves and pulls out an empty bar stool. He's got the standard breakfast of café con leche, bread, butter, and jam. What I'd really like is a piece of that delicious cake I had last night. It reminds me of my grandmother's pound cake that I so loved as a child.

"Do you remember that Camino cake they had here last night?" I ask José-María. "Too bad it's gone, it would be a great breakfast."

"*¡Claro que sí!*" he laughs. "You mean the tarta de Santiago. It's all that butter and ground almonds that make it so good. You need to enjoy it, you won't find it anywhere else in Spain, only on the Camino."

He says something to the bartender, and the next thing I know, I've got a huge slice of this delicious cake to go with my café con leche. How can a day that starts out like this be anything but good?

This morning, the conversations are all about today's walk. Some Italian men want to make it to Sarria, some thirty-nine kilometers away. José-María will try to reach Samos, which is over thirty kilometers. His leg is better, and he thinks he can do it if he takes it easy. My foot still aches, but the intense pain is gone. I will continue to Triacastela, a mere twenty-two kilometers, but enough for me, given my foot and the mountainous terrain.

"You must go farther today," the talkative Spaniard from the refugio in Rabanal says. "Remember the botafumeiro? You need to make it to Santiago by Sunday so you can see the priests swing it." I shake my head and point to my foot. He looks disappointed but gives me a pat on the back and waves as he and his friend walk out into the cold. They start a mass exodus, and as each pilgrim strides out the door, it's with a hearty "*Adiós ¡buen camino!*" spoken to no one in particular (or rather, to everyone). Soon, it's just me, Gephardt (the Austrian pilgrim), and the bartenders. I savor the remaining crumbs of my tarta de Santiago and contemplate having another café con leche but decide to wait until the next bar. I plan to take the main road today, which is the only route according to my guidebook, but as I'm leaving, Gephardt tells me about a walker's route that avoids road walking without adding much distance. He's not ready to leave but insists on showing me the start of the unmarked path that disappears into a deep forest, just opposite the refugio.

"It's lovely, you'll see," he says reassuringly.

Before heading into the woods, I look back to fix in my mind this lovely mountaintop. Level with my feet now, as if I'm standing on them, soft, billowy clouds of blue and gray tinged with pink swirl into shades of pale yellow and coral. The clouds completely hide the valley below, and I feel as if I am in the last settlement on earth. In the distance, hazy round peaks stand out above the clouds like stepping stones for a nimble giant. *Where do they lead?* I wonder. Over the higher mountains to the east, a radiant orange and coral sunrise bathes this ancient stone village in the promises of the new day. Once again, the silence is absolute and total—no cars, no planes, not even any human voices or barking dogs. Nothing breaks the early-morning stillness; the scene feels otherworldly and timeless.

It's an easy walk to the Alto de Poio—the last pass between me and Santiago—but a fierce wind is blowing at the top, making it miserably cold in spite of the intense sun. The sight of an open bar and Maïté standing outside the entrance digging around in her pack gets me up the last few yards.

"Come join us," she calls out when she sees me. "Jacques and the two Germans are inside having coffee." Noticing my limping, she frowns. "Foot still bothering you?"

She doesn't mention the cabbage leaf, but I know what she's thinking. I don't say anything; we kiss on both cheeks and enter the warm and welcoming bar. I get a coffee, pop some ibuprofen, and sink into the chair that Rainer pulls out for me. This little group has been there long enough to have solved everyone's problems but mine, so I'm the center of attention as I take off my right shoe and begin to massage my foot.

"Try this cream," says Rainer. "I want to give it to you. It's from a Dutch pilgrim. It saved my life. You can use it as often as you need to."

"You have to take arnica," Maïté insists. "It will loosen the tendons and ease the pain."

"The pomade worked for you before," Jacques points out.

"My spray will do the trick," says Werner, the other German and Rainer's travel companion. "It's really good for tendonitis. It deadens the pain."

I thank them all and begin by smearing on a thick layer of Jacques' gooey, foul-smelling gel. Then I notice that we are all sitting together with at least one bare foot in somebody's face, applying stinky ointments, scraping off old dressings, popping pills, rubbing our toes—and it all seems perfectly natural.

"Do you think we'll be able to re-integrate into polite society when we get home?" I ask.

Maïté makes a pout, as if to say, "who cares?" And moves over one spot so I can rest my foot on a chair while I rub in the pomade. The others look up and grin.

Back home, when I read through my journal, I am chagrined to realize how much time I spent whining, mostly about my feet and shoulders. Yet the pain is as real as the moments of peace and beauty—and probably as necessary. The pain, I am discovering, grabs my attention in a way that forces me to set aside petty cares and concerns and puts me in touch with a more visceral reality, making me aware of my body in a way that clears my mind. When I am conscious of the pain, I am truly present.

What is it the Spanish pilgrims say when I complain? Oh yes, "*¡Tienes que sufrir!*" (You're supposed to suffer!) Yes, I think the pain *is* necessary. The Camino, I decide, is like a love affair—real intimacy is achieved after suffering and the passage of time. And as with a broken love affair, even your best friends eventually tire of hearing about the pain. I go back through my journal and, believe it or not, delete 80 percent of the complaining about my aches and pains.

A Buddhist friend once urged me to think about the difference between pain and suffering. This was probably good advice, although I didn't take it at the time. Later, I heard a saying attributed to professional bicycle racers that helped me understand what my friend was trying to tell me: pain is inevitable, suffering is optional. When I began my journey to Santiago, I experienced pain and I suffered. Now, toward the end of my journey, I still experience pain, but most of the time I walk through it. I am learning to *be* in the space which is mine. Being, just being. A very Buddhist concept.

No corras, que a donde tienes que
llegar es a ti mismo.

There is no point in running—
you yourself are the destination.

Brochure of the Asociación Riojana de Amigos
del Camino de Santiago

Chapter Twenty

Moseying Along

June 25 – 27, Alto de Poio to Barbadelo via Triacastela.

Not yet ready to confront the howling wind and my various ailments, I linger inside the bar after the others leave. When I head out an hour later, I'm relieved to discover that the throbbing pain in my foot is now mere background noise and the other aches have vanished. Was it Maïté's arnica? Jacques' pomade? The anti-inflammatory? All the water I've been drinking? The leisurely break? All I know is that I am grateful.

As soon as I'm off the mountaintop, the blustery wind dissolves into a gentle summer breeze. The sun is out, but it's cool enough that my vest feels good. A few high cumulus clouds float across the sky, and I stroll over grassy slopes and across mountain meadows. Eight hours after leaving O Cebreiro, I arrive at Triacastela, feeling fine except for a bearable ache in my foot.

Triacastela is another town that has been a stop on the pilgrim trail for over a thousand years. In its heyday, it boasted several pilgrim hospices and even a pilgrim jail, the latter for unruly pilgrims and pilgrim impostors who exploited the pilgrim identity (and authentic pilgrims) for personal gain. The pilgrim jail and hospices are long gone, as are the town's three castles ("Triacastela"), which were destroyed by Norman raiders around 968. Over the centuries, Triacastela has undergone other transformations. In its most recent incarnation, bland buildings offer the essential amenities (although the pay phones don't work). Initially, the contrast between the visual monotony of this town and the stunning setting of O Cebreiro is shattering, especially after today's lovely walk. Yet Triascastela is not without its charms. Townspeople smile and the men tip their hats at passing pilgrims. Little kids play happily on the sidewalks, while pilgrims and locals alike enjoy outdoor tables at restaurants and bars. Flower boxes hang from second-story windows, adding a splash of color. When I give it a chance and look beyond appearances—once again, that trap of appearances—I discover that Triacastela feels comfortable and welcoming, like a Midwestern town on a fine summer afternoon.

The municipal refugio is a one-story ramshackle wooden building that bakes in the sun. Its handful of tiny windows all appear to be closed. In the large front yard, some teenagers mill around under the only tree in sight, their music blaring from a boom box. I walk on to the private refugio, which is located in a well-maintained two-story stucco house with a colorful flower garden where pilgrims gather and chat, read, or write in their journals. The cheery hospitalera offers laundry service for three euros a load (washed, dried, and folded). When she takes me to the upstairs dormitory to select my bed, she insists on carrying my pack, which makes me think that I must not look as good as I feel.

After showering and taking a rest under one of the garden's big shade trees, I go off to replenish my supplies and discover the first real supermarket I've seen in days. I'm confronted with a dizzying array of food—hundreds of kinds of cookies and candy bars, countless varieties of nuts and dried fruits, a great selection of cheeses, and many other items that would keep well in a backΔpack. I'm happily filling my basket when a twinge in my shoulder reminds me that any extra weight, no matter how delicious, means equally exquisite pain. Reluctantly, I put back most of the treats and buy just enough food for breakfast and lunch tomorrow, plus a chocolate bar to get me through until dinner.

Next, I make a quick trip to the pharmacy to replenish my supply of ibuprofen and plasters, then head for a lively bar with the prettiest flowers in town. I've been doing a little survey about bars and have determined that the ones with the prettiest flowers also have the best coffee and the coldest beer. This one bears out my conclusion. My German friends Rainer and Werner are already there, and courteous as ever, Rainer pulls out a chair for me. Sitting in the sun and sipping frosty beer, we compare notes about today's walk, and then the topic turns to our spouses back home. We've all realized by now that our Camino experience will be with us for a very long time, and we'd like to share it with our spouses, but how?

"By car," says Rainer. "Why not?"

"I'm not sure about that," says Werner. "How can you feel this place unless you walk?"

"I can't imagine doing this any other way than on foot," I agree.

"It takes the total immersion of a walker's pace for me to slow down enough to listen to the Camino. Yet not everyone can walk five hundred miles."

I tell them about my mother's ninety-year-old friend who made her pilgrimage to Santiago on a bus and had an extraordinarily moving experience and about the tour group of well-dressed Germans who are walking selected segments.

"Right, and let's not forget that there are other reasons for visiting the Camino besides pilgrimage," says Rainer. "How about wildflower viewing? Or gastronomy?" he adds, pointing proudly to his beer belly. "And what's wrong with coming as a tourist? My wife would love the Camino if she could stay in hotels and visit the sights by car. If that's the only way to share this experience with her, I'd try it."

"That may be my best chance of getting my husband here, too," I say. "Maybe we'll see you and your wife at one of the paradores along the way in a year or two."

"I'd like that!" he replies.

So would I.

The exit from town the next morning meanders along a country lane, heading for a wooded area that is only faintly visible through the dense, early-morning ground fog. Up ahead, the ghostly outline of a pilgrim appears, standing motionless in the middle of the lane. As I get closer, I recognize Inge and see why she is frozen in place. To her left, three large, mean-looking dogs snarl menacingly at her. Just as I see the dogs, they notice me and the low growling turns to vicious barking. Defenseless except for my walking stick, I unscrew the rubber cap from the bottom to expose an ice pick and hold it out in front of me, ready to defend us. I approach slowly, being careful not to stray off the track. I can't abandon Inge, who is clutching a handful of rocks, but I don't like this situation. The dogs begin to jump up and down on stiff legs, howling and drooling and hissing.

When I get within whispering distance, we agree that we are scared to death but don't know what to do. We decide to slowly continue on, angling off to the far side of the road to get as much distance as possible between us and them. As we get closer to the snarling dogs, they leap and lunge—then gag as chains jerk them back. In our terror, we hadn't noticed that they are tied up to the side of a storage barn and cannot reach us. The chains hold, but the ferocious barking does not stop until we have entered the forest. We're both shaken by this encounter, although I feel a little silly at how I reacted to three chained dogs.

"Shall we walk together?" Inge asks, her voice still quivering.

"Yes! I'd love company," I say quickly. "Though I go slowly, especially in the morning when I'm warming up."

"Me, too," she says, "because of my knee. I've learned it's better that way."

We walk in silence along the forest trail, each decompressing in our own way. My mind is in neutral as I recover my equilibrium. Inge appears lost in thought. An hour later, I reach up to adjust the strap of my backpack and discover that my hair is soaked. In fact, we are both covered with a fine layer of moisture, and we can barely see three feet before the landscape is swallowed up in the mist. It's lucky there weren't any turnoffs, because I don't think either of us would have noticed.

Later that morning, when the cloud layer lifts, we appreciate the tree-lined path with its fluorescent green canopy. However, the trail is quite steep in places. In other sections it runs along the bottom of a deep gully lined with large, smooth stones that are partially submerged under a good foot of water. Boulders pop up at more or less regular intervals and offer a choice: either we can leap from wet rock to wet rock—a bit like hopping from banana peel to banana peel—or slosh through the muddy water. I opt for the drier alternative, laboriously picking my way down the gully. I am thankful to have a walking stick for balance. It also helps to follow Inge, who has a knack for spotting the most level rocks and shouts encouragement at regular intervals. Somehow, I stay on my feet, and soon we're back on a woodland trail.

We arrive at Sarria around 11:30, seventeen kilometers down and fourteen to go before we stop for the day. The earsplitting noise of heavy construction equipment greets us as we enter the town. Excavators thunder past, belching clouds of reddish-yellow dust that blanket everything in sight; dump trucks disgorge loads of gravel; workers yell to be heard above the fray. "No Parking" signs are plastered everywhere, but this has not deterred the Spanish drivers who park helter-skelter in every possible space. This tangled array of cars hides the yellow arrows that are painted on buildings and what's left of the sidewalk, and with no arrows to follow, we're quickly lost.

We wander through the chaos, looking for either yellow arrows or the *Ruo do peregrino* ("Pilgrim Street" in Gallego), the road that takes pilgrims up to the church and, from there, out the west side of town. We find neither. Finally, I ask an elderly, frail-looking Spanish lady for directions. She points to a set of steep stairs so tall we can barely see the top and makes a shooing motion, indicating that we must climb them. We look at each other in disbelief and then at the stairs again. Meanwhile, the señora sees our faces and chortles.

"*¡Ánimo!*" (Take heart!) she says as she scurries away. "Go on, get started!" She probably walks up and down these stairs several times a day.

We're about to tackle them when Inge spots an open cyber café just across the street, the first in days. She wants to check her e-mail, and I'm hungry, so we go our separate ways for now. I pick up the arrows again at the top of the stairs and continue through town, looking for a place to eat. The main street offers several restaurants and bars, but none of them will serve food for another couple of hours. Finally, I double back to a butcher shop, hoping the shopkeeper can recommend a place. A portly, well-dressed matron is there buying some pork cutlets and talking to the woman behind the counter. When I walk in the door, they stop talking mid-sentence and look at me. Apparently, they are not used to seeing pilgrims in this shop.

"*¿Qué quiere?*" (What do you want?), asks the butcher, peering at me over rows of carefully arranged cuts of meat. Her voice is not unkind, just curious.

I ask her if there is a restaurant nearby that is open for lunch. She points across the way.

"Not till 1:30," I say.

"Then try Taberna Lopez," she replies.

"Same thing," I say, "not until 1:30."

The shopkeeper and customer confer, but I can't catch the drift of their conversation. After a few minutes, they look at me and nod in agreement, their faces unreadable.

"*Venga conmigo*" (Come with me), the customer commands.

I follow her out the door, and we march up the street.

"Where are you from?" she asks.

"USA."

"*¿Sola?*"

"*Sí.*"

Her face registers serious disapproval on learning that I am traveling alone.

"My husband can't walk because he has to work," I offer by way of explanation.

She's somewhat mollified. Most pilgrims accept walking alone as a good, even preferable, way to make a pilgrimage. But this view is not necessarily shared by older Spanish ladies, at least when the solo traveler is female. I've discovered that these ladies become much friendlier if I let them know I'm married. Then there's the occasional Spanish matron who asks me with great interest exactly how I was able to go off without my husband for a month.

My guide takes me to a restaurant on a tiny side street, strides through the open door, and leads me past the bar area to a galley kitchen the size of a small closet. Tantalizing smells—garlic and onions and savory herbs—come from a pot bubbling away on a two-burner cook top. Something equally aromatic sizzles away in the oven, sliced potatoes soak in cold water, and salad preparation is in progress.

"Juanita," my savior says to the woman standing over the stove, "this pilgrim is famished and needs to eat. Will you give her lunch? Now." Her tone makes it clear that the only possible answer is yes.

Juanita wavers, but another look from the señora, and she agrees: "Well, if she's hungry, I'll feed her."

I thank the señora, who smiles for the first time. "*¡Buen Camino, pelegrina!*" she calls out, with a wave as she motors out the door, a satisfied look on her face.

"Come with me," says Juanita.

We go beyond the tiny kitchen to an elegant formal dining room, empty but with tables set and ready for business. Many have reserved signs, and no wonder—Juanita is a fabulous cook, and as she warms up, a welcoming hostess. She brings me tastes of the starter choices—lentil soup with chorizo or a vegetable dish called *menestra*—and waits patiently while I sample and make up my mind. (I can't resist the lentil soup.) For my main course, I have garlic tarragon roast chicken, served with homemade fries. Juanita also lets me sample the desserts (flan or *natillas* or chocolate cake), and when I hesitate, she brings me an assortment. I am the first pilgrim they have had from North America, and she wants to be sure I have a good impression of Spain. "No worries there," I assure her.

Inge usually takes at least an hour when she finds a computer with e-mail, so after lunch I go across the street to a public garden to wait for her. When she doesn't appear by 1:30, I continue on to the tiny village of Barbadelo. Inge is already there and calls out to me from the second-story window of the municipal refugio.

"Up here!" she says, waving her arms. "There is only one bed left, do you want it? Hang on." Seconds later, she bursts through the front door.

"I think you'd better stay," she says breathlessly. "The next refugio is eight kilometers away and has only twenty-two beds. It'll probably be full by the time you get there, and, if it is, the next possibility is not for another nine kilometers."

Massive black clouds on the horizon look like they could go either way, but if they bring a storm, it will be a bad one. Besides, the pain in my foot is starting to overpower the ibuprofen, and I'm dragging after my big lunch. I thank Inge and take the bed. The upstairs room where we are assigned bunks is long and narrow with a tiny bathroom at the far end. There is no hot water.

"Wait a *momentito*," says the hospitalera. "It will recharge."

I know better. Bring on the ice water, I think, anticipating the nasty shock when it starts pouring down my sweaty back.

Later that afternoon, I find a comfortable spot under a tree and refigure, yet again, the kilometers to Santiago. One hundred and ten yet to go. Is this are-we-there-yet obsession an eagerness to arrive or an attempt to control time? The new Kate or the old Kate? I decide it's the new Kate, eager to arrive. The single sheet of paper with my distance calculations and schedule—the little handwritten, two-column itinerary that I worked on for months in Paris last winter, when I thought I could plan this trip as I would any other—is frayed and smudged. I treasure this grubby piece of paper, even if it did turn out to be useless. I see it now not as a schedule but as tangible proof that I am making progress, that I can do this.

Just then, the clouds make up their mind. The sky turns dark, and it's clear that a monumental storm is moving in fast. I grab my journal and run for the refugio, reaching it just as thunder begins exploding all around me. Lightning pops like so many firecrackers, and sheets of gray water pour off the roof. Relieved that I stopped early, I go upstairs and curl up in my sleeping bag to wait for the storm to pass. But each time I'm about to doze off, somebody scampers past, towel in hand. And each time, within minutes, screeches and screams come out of the bathroom when the unsuspecting pilgrim gets in the shower and is doused with cold water. I start counting, pilgrims instead of sheep, and, after eleven, realize that something is wrong with this picture. Our bathroom is for the eight pilgrims in this room, all of whom are in their bunks right now, so where are these people coming from? Then I notice that the showergoers are all in their early teens, speak Italian, and look familiar—it's the group from the refugio in O Cebreiro that included the French-speaking girl.

Later, I learn that the hospitalera wouldn't let these kids stay in the refugio. It's not clear if this is because they are traveling with a back-up vehicle and, therefore, are not technically eligible, or because she is out of beds and not willing to let them put their sleeping bags on the dining room floor. I suspect the latter, motivated by the thought that having a group of energetic young Italians in her refugio would probably not make for a quiet night. However, she does let them camp out in the picnic shelter that stands in a corner of the spacious front yard and use the refugio facilities. Whatever they paid for these "accommodations," it's no bargain, even by refugio standards. The three-sided shelter is open to the prevailing wind, so when the rain hits at a forty-five degree angle, as it does today, nothing protects its occupants from the downpour. Yet that evening, when the young Italians return to the refugio to use the bathroom before bed, though they are dripping wet and shivering, these kids are actually cheerful. What a lesson in attitude. It's hard to imagine a group of adults accepting these Spartan conditions with such good humor.

The village doesn't offer any bars or restaurants, but the hospitalera tells us about a nearby family who serves dinner to pilgrims. Inge and I walk over around eight, a little early to eat, but we're hoping we can get something to drink while we wait. The rain has finally stopped and we easily find the house, but it's so dark inside that we think they are not open. We are turning to leave when a man with curly dark hair and a thick, sexy moustache rushes up and welcomes us.

"*¡Pasen! ¡Pasen!*" (Come in, come in!), he says. "We've lost our electricity because of the storm, but it will return. Come, have some wine while we wait."

He leads us into a large room and seats us at a dining room table. A single candle provides just enough light to recognize three American women—a mother-daughter duo and the daughter's college roommate—who had set off from the full refugio earlier today in search of a place to stay. They found one in the hospitality of this kind family, who rent out rooms in their home to pilgrims during the high season. The women are laughing at the accommodations—they will sleep on beds set up in the living room, surrounded by photos of generations of ancestors, and share the home's single bathroom with the family. But they are also moved by this family's kindness at taking them in, especially on a stormy night, and it's apparent that everyone is getting along. One of the girls tells how she helped the family's daughter with her English homework. The mother gratefully recounts the advice of the Spanish mother about blister first aid, and the Spanish son is still hanging around tutoring the other girl, a cute blond, in Spanish slang.

An hour and two bottles of good Spanish wine later, the lights come on, and the señor serves us a great home-cooked dinner: an enormous plate of colorful crudités followed by a white asparagus omelet and homemade fries. Our host is very congenial and loves joking around with us, especially the cute blond, whose earnest attempts at Spanish are compromised by a strong southern drawl. He roars with laughter when she asks for ketchup for her fries.

"That's *so* American, and I'm ready for you!" he says, producing a brand-new bottle with a flourish.

And when we all rave about the fabulous coconut flan he serves for dessert, he brings us seconds.

"I have to take care of you," he says. "This is a home for pilgrims, you see. Here, let me give you more wine."

But it's almost 10, and Inge and I are worried about getting back before the doors are locked.

"*¡Hombre!*," exclaims our host. "Relax. They don't lock the refugio doors here until eleven. You have plenty of time."

We have another glass.

The pilgrimage is, above all, an experience,
and must be experienced to be understood.

Conrad Rudolph, *Pilgrimage to the End of the World*

Chapter Twenty-One

Growing Understandings

June 27 - 28, Barbadelo to Eixere.

When my alarm goes off at dawn, the sky is dark and threatening. The others in our little room are sound asleep, and there's no sign of life from the Italian teens in the shelter. I slide down from my top bunk, trying not to disrupt the stillness that surrounds me. On the way back from the bathroom, I wake Inge. When she hears the time—5:30—she leaps from her bunk, still groggy with sleep. We throw on our clothes, grab a quick breakfast in the refugio kitchen, and after a stop at the village fountain to fill our water bottles, we're on our way.

We walk together for the first few kilometers, but Inge is feeling energetic today. She warms up quickly and, ready to move, strides out and disappears into the mist. I continue strolling through rocky terrain that recalls England's Lake District—dewy pin oaks, low clouds that enclose me in a mysterious yet secure universe, and miniature waterfalls created by last night's rain. Every now and then, I pass a tiny village—really nothing more than a few houses huddled together. Mid-morning, I catch up with the man who was in the bunk below me last night. At least I think it's the same man—all I ever saw of him were tufts of gray hair sticking out of the top of his sleeping bag and the suggestion of a small, wiry shape. I had noticed a French book about pilgrimage on his bunk, so figuring he's probably French, I greet him with a "*bonjour.*" His face lights up.

"*Mais pourquoi tu ne m'as pas dit que tu parles la langue de Rabelais?*" (Why didn't you tell me you speak the language of Rabelais?), he asks, throwing his open arms over his head.

I observe a mischievous look in his eyes and know immediately that I like this man. The correct expression is: *to speak the language of Molière*, the great seventeenth-century comic playwright (not that of the raunchy, hedonistic Rabelais). His question tells me he is a witty bon vivant. When he realizes from my expression that I understand his play on words, he shakes my hand enthusiastically.

"Giles," he introduces himself, holding out his hand. He has already walked from Le Puy, a distance of almost one thousand miles. In no time, Giles is telling me about his trip to Dallas last year to be an au pair, of all things, for his nephew's two school-age children. His nephew's job required frequent travel away from home, and after the difficult birth of a special-needs child, both parents were feeling overwhelmed. Giles, who had recently retired, agreed to help out until they could find a permanent au pair.

"*Quelle mode de vie!*" (What a lifestyle!), he says about Dallas. "Everyone lives in cars or indoors with the air conditioning at full blast. There is no place to walk, no public gardens for evening strolls, not even a city center where people gather and talk to each other. People will forget what it's like to breathe this air," he says, inhaling deeply. We are in the middle of a eucalyptus grove and the air is spicy sweet.

"I tried a bike, but the Texans didn't know what to do with me. Why was I on a bike? They thought I was some eccentric, pedaling away like a madman, too poor or too crazy to buy a car.

"People there are so worried about making money," he continues. "It's not a thirty-five-hour work week (as in France), but a thirty-five-hour *day*. How can you live like that?"

I shake my head, thinking about the truth of his Dallas experience. Our love of cars, our focus on things, and our need to make money often do take precedence over simple pleasures, like strolls in the evening or café-sitting just for the pleasure of hanging out. How did I get so caught up in the idea that it's good to always be busy? But before I can verbalize these thoughts, I realize that Giles is still talking.

"*La France est belle, tu sais*" (You know, France really is beautiful), he says.

Giles is from a small city in the French Alps, which *is* a particularly lovely part of France, making his comments ring all the more true. He shrugs his shoulders. "I asked myself, why do I need to travel when I have mountains and valleys and grazing sheep right outside my window? What could be more beautiful?"

"Not more beautiful," I reply, "but different. Beautiful in its own way."

Still, his comments resonate. Much as I love traveling to new places, I always return to France. The French countryside is not more beautiful than other places I've been, but the natural beauty provides the context for treasured aspects of French history and culture—everything from cathedrals and palaces to modest farms created over the centuries and now lovingly maintained in exquisite settings. It's the charming little country inn that serves gourmet food on a riverside terrace; it's the twelfth-century Benedictine monastery tucked away in the hills of Burgundy, where a tour guide demonstrates the extraordinary acoustics by singing Gregorian chant just for the pleasure of the sound. And it's the French, finally, who infuriate me with their inefficiencies and arrogance, but charm me with their unwavering appreciation of family, friends, and beauty.

Later, the conversation turns to our children, and in his case, grandchildren. Giles is close to all five of his daughters. He tells me about his middle daughter, who works as a shepherdess in Switzerland and shares his love of the mountains. I can tell that he is proud of her free spirit and love of adventure.

"For my pilgrimage," he continues, "she gave me a prayer to Santiago for each of my children. I carry them with me always, and, whenever I get discouraged or tired, I take them out to read." He tells me with obvious delight about his three-year-old grandson, whom he saw last month when he took a few days off from the Camino to attend a family christening. It's such a pleasure walking with this man.

At Magrade, Giles stops for a coffee. I have a long way yet to go and am feeling good, so we kiss on both cheeks and I continue on. Ten minutes later it starts to rain and I walk in a light drizzle the rest of the morning, now on gently rolling country lanes that traverse cultivated fields and cool pine forests. The fresh smell of rain mingles with the occasional jolt of barnyard odors; songbirds are out in full force. As I approach Portomarín, the vegetation becomes lush, the air heavy and humid—perfect conditions for the orchids Theo said grow in this area. I slow down and look carefully on both sides of the trail but don't spot a single bloom.

Portomarín was originally a Roman settlement on the bank of the River Miño. Centuries later, it spread to both banks, then became a stop on the pilgrimage route to Santiago when a bridge was built connecting the two parts of town and giving pilgrims a safe way to cross the river without going miles out of the way. (Bridges, yet again.) In the 1950s, the old town was buried under thirty feet of water, the casualty of a hydroelectric dam project. However, the twelfth-century church was moved stone by stone to a hilltop on the northeast side of the river to become the center of the newly constructed town. Today pilgrims reach that new town by crossing an ugly modern bridge over the river and following the yellow arrows up a very steep hill to the relocated site. But this time, instead of going past the church and out the other side of town, the arrows direct pilgrims to make a U-turn at the church and go back down the same slope by which they arrived. Of course this makes no sense to me. Unless I needed provisions or planned to stay in the refugio, why would I hike up and down a small mountain only to end up where I started? I have just crossed the bridge and am about to take the turn off that will let me skip the loop into town when Sergeant Suzette charges up from behind.

"You can't do that!" she orders when she realizes that I am planning to bypass Portomarín. "Look at the yellow arrows. You have to follow them or you'll get lost," she scolds. "*Then* what will you do?"

I pull out my map to show her the shortcut I've discovered, but Suzette flounces off with that exasperated guttural sound the French make. In this instance it probably means: "I can't believe how stupid this lady is." I resist the urge to respond and, with a quick wave, take the turn-off. Sure enough, minutes later I see yellow arrows—old friends by now—and I'm back on the Camino.

It starts to pour, and that's when I spot three stalks of tiny pink flowers. Discovering wild orchids in this lost corner of Spain is bittersweet, for they remind me, once again, of how much my father would have loved this journey. And I would have relished telling him about my discovery. More and more, I appreciate these seemingly random connections with loved ones, even when they make me sad. Each is a gift that anchors me to precious memories of family and friends, some thousands of miles away, others in their graves, yet all very much present in my heart, all dear to me. I take a quick photo to send Theo with my thanks for alerting me to this unexpected pleasure. I wish I knew how to contact the monk. I would like to tell him how right he was about the meseta.

Inge, who did not know about the short cut, is walking down the hill to rejoin the path just as I'm putting away my camera. She stops to admire her first wild orchids, then we continue on together. Soon, the sun comes out, and the terrain changes, too, as we leave behind forests and small hamlets to begin a section of open plains and expansive vistas. The farms here are much grander and more commercial than the one-family operations of this morning. Big farm dogs guard these properties, but the fierce ones are chained and the ones that aren't tied up don't give us a passing glance. Inge and I walk in companionable silence for a couple of hours on a path that runs alongside a quiet paved road. Suddenly, she perks up and starts waving her arm. She appears to be pointing to a twenty-foot-tall stack of enormous logs right next to the path, very excited about something.

"Over there," Inge says, now breaking into a jog. "That sign! It's telling us to stop for a picnic lunch."

I have no idea what she's talking about, but I look again and, this time, see that she's pointing to a red stop sign at the intersection of the little road and an even smaller country lane. Meanwhile, she has already scrambled up to the top of the precarious-looking pile of logs that towers above the lane. Inge takes off her pack, finds the most level spot, and motions for me to join her. I shake my head, mouth open in amazement. *She's crazy!* I think. A hiccup could send these logs crashing down, crushing both of us beyond recognition, and she's nestling in as if she were on her living room sofa.

Then I notice the massive chains wrapped around the logs—they're not going anywhere. I give her a thumbs-up and shimmy my way to the top. She greets me with a high five, and in no time, we're feasting on fresh crusty bread and a big hunk of a pungent local cheese that Inge picked up in Portomarín. She also has a succulent, deep-red tomato that we split and eat like an apple. One thing about Inge, she always has food in her pack—good food at that—and she's always ready to share. All I have to contribute is a chocolate bar, but it's excellent quality and big. Her eyes light up when she recognizes the brand, and we eat the whole thing. Such simple food, but it's gourmet to us, and the setting can't be beat. To this day, when I hear the word "picnic," I think of the two of us sitting on top of the world, feeling the soft breeze on our faces and inhaling the summer smells. We are removed from time, stomachs full, the taste of chocolate lingering in our mouths.

After lunch, we stretch out our legs and enjoy the sun from our queen-of-the-hill position. A pilgrim walks by; a bit later, two more struggle past on bicycles. We wave from our throne, laughing at how small they seem and how hard they are working. I feel completely relaxed, the struggles of pilgrimage set aside.

"Does this seem like a vacation to you?" Inge asks, out of the blue. It's a rhetorical question, but her serious tone takes me by surprise. She's apparently not feeling as mellow as I am.

"It doesn't at all to me," she continues, not waiting for my reply. "It's not relaxing because I can't sleep. All the snoring, you know."

Inge at our lunch stop.

She rolls her eyes. I smile to myself, thinking back to my first encounter with Inge in the refugio in Trinidad de Arre, when she lit into a snorer.

"It's the mental effort, too," she continues, leaning back into the logs. "There's so much inner-focusing. A real holiday is a break from inside. You don't think so much about yourself. You just try to have fun." She exhales loudly. "This is really hard. Sometimes I feel like I can't take it all in. It's not easy to go inside. But you know," she says, with another deep sigh, "the strangest thing is that I know I have to see this through to the end. The monk . . ."

Her voice trails off and she becomes quiet, a distant look in her eyes.

"I think he's right," I say. "We must not try to avoid the difficulties. The meseta dries tears."

She nods, closes her eyes, and promptly falls asleep. I know from other conversations that Inge is wrestling with a painful family situation, and sometimes it wears her down. While she dozes, I think about her words. The Camino *is* hard, for me, too. But unlike Inge's experience, for me this feels increasingly like the first real time off I've had in a very long while. I've had vacations, of course, and they've been wonderful. Yet they were not without stress—the inevitable hassles of travel, the time-consuming job of making arrangements for everything from accommodations to transportation, and the challenging task of accommodating different needs and desires. I've taken short trips alone, too, for work or to visit a friend, but never before have I enjoyed—yes, that's the right word, I think a bit sheepishly—forty days on my own, not responsible for anyone or anything but myself and my needs.

Until now, what came the closest to any real time off were backpacking trips years ago when I was on the faculty at Boise State, and, later, in Boulder, when I was doing graduate work at the University of Colorado. Those trips required the same physical effort and were characterized by the same limited wardrobe, pared-down lifestyle, and days structured by nothing more than meals, distance to hike, and hours of daylight. Yet on those backpacking trips, I was still very much connected to my everyday life and to my specific realities of time and place. I carried my worries and responsibilities with me, percolating in the background, for I knew they would be waiting for me when I got home.

What's so astonishing about the Camino, what makes it so profoundly different from any other experience, is the increasing sense of connectedness, not to my own familiar world but, rather, to a much larger universe. The usual daily cares dissipate, and conscious of my bond to the hundreds of thousands of pilgrims who came before me, walk with me, or will come after me, I feel human on a larger scale, one where specifics of time and place are irrelevant. I am, quite simply and completely, here.

When Inge wakes up, I tell her my feelings about the Camino.

She doesn't say a word but looks at me intently. "Maybe I'll understand more when I'm home," she replies.

I nod. This is a work in progress for both of us.

We plan to stop for the night at Gonzar, where my guidebook says there is a "functional" refugio. But when we arrive, we don't like the way it feels so decide to go on to the next one, three kilometers away. This time, the guidebook is wrong—we find no accommodation of any kind and, what's more, the refugio that is supposed to be just a bit farther on is not open. As a result, we end up walking another eleven kilometers, to the Refugio de Ligonde, in Eirexe, which makes a thirty-six-kilometer day (on feet and legs that wanted to quit long ago). By the last few kilometers, it's raining hard again, and we're really dragging.

"I hope they've got beds," Inge says when we spot the refugio.

Built in the traditional Galician style, this refugio is in a white, two-story frame house with the door, shutters, and trim painted Kelly green. It looks so inviting that we speed up our pace to a wobbly jog, which is the best we can do. The hospitalera sits just inside the front door at a desk that blocks the stairway leading to the sleeping rooms. In her early forties, she is a sturdy blond woman with a gentle face. She greets us before we're even in the door. When we ask about beds for tonight, she holds up a finger while she consults her logbook.

"¡Sí! Muy bien, dos camas." she exclaims a minute later.

We show her our credentials, pay, and she checks us in. But when she takes us upstairs, there is only one empty bed, not the two she had expected from consulting her log. She checks both sleeping rooms a second time. All but one bed are occupied, either with a pack or a napping pilgrim. Puzzled, she looks again, and this time, spots a tall, pudgy man with a gray crewcut lying on a top bunk. He scowls when he sees her coming his way; the hospitalera steels herself. A flag on the man's pack identifies him as Belgian. He's sprawled out, taking up the entire mattress, which makes him look even bigger. The hospitalera cranes her neck to make eye contact.

"You must leave," she tells him in Spanish. "No cyclists are allowed until eight this evening, and it's only five." She looks at him but speaks to us: "I told him this before, but he pretended not to understand." She pauses. "I know you speak Spanish," she says to the now red-faced man. "You have to leave," she repeats, "it's the rule."

He rolls over and ignores her.

His blatant disrespect of the hospitalera annoys Inge, as does his flaunting of the rules.

"You must leave," Inge says, in English. "Please take your things and go."

"I'm not leaving," he replies with a yawn. "I'm tired, and I'm a pilgrim, too. I have a right to be here."

"A rule is a rule," she tells him. "No cyclists until eight." (This widely accepted rule gives preference to walkers because a pilgrim on a bicycle can travel to the next refugio more easily than a pilgrim on foot.)

Inge and the belligerent Belgian are glaring at each other in tense silence when a French woman comes over and in heavily accented English, starts telling Inge off.

"He's tired and has worked hard to get here. He has every right to stay," she says. "Where's your compassion for your fellow pilgrim?"

This is all the encouragement the Belgian biker needs. His face turns redder, he raises up on one elbow and strikes an aggressive, threatening pose.

"I am *not* leaving!" he bellows.

The poor hospitalera doesn't know what to do. This guy is not only mean, he's big, and he acts like a man who's used to getting his way by bullying others. Pilgrims gather around, but nobody says a word. After what seems an eternity (actually not more than a minute), two Italian girls leave their bunks and go over to the hospitalera.

"We will sleep in the same bed," they offer in Spanish, "so there will be room for everyone."

The tension in the room goes down several notches with this proposed solution, but the Belgian continues to scowl and breathe heavily, and Inge can't let go of The Rule.

"You have to leave. A rule is a rule," she repeats, with a steely look in his direction.

The hospitalera twists the corner of her apron and clears her throat nervously. Then a young Spanish cyclist who was lying down on another bunk comes forward and admits he was just resting a couple of hours before going on. He had sneaked upstairs without signing in and figured he would leave before he was discovered. He apologizes to the hospitalera and bows sheepishly as he makes a quick exit. The belligerent Belgian unclenches his fists just a hair, perhaps because he's no longer the only one guilty of bad behavior. Inge struggles to let it go—at least this guy's not taking somebody's bed—and there's an audible sigh of relief from the rest of us. The hospitalera shows Inge and me to our bunks, one in each room, and the Belgian cyclist storms off to the shower. I later learn from conversations with other pilgrims that fights over refugio beds do happen. That's not surprising, given the physical and mental demands of the Camino, but I'm glad that this is the only one I witness.

That evening, Inge and I have our worst meal of the Camino—tough, dry, tasteless pizza and flat beer served in filthy glasses at a roadside stand. But there is nothing else within walking distance, and the proprietors take full advantage of their captive clientele. After dinner, many of the pilgrims staying at this refugio gather in the living room. It's spacious and homey, with a cheery fire humming in the stone fireplace. Four couches and several overstuffed chairs are arranged around the hearth, along with coffee tables, lamps, and vases of fresh flowers. The hospitalera, who is responsible for these welcoming touches, sits on one of the couches, now a gracious and relaxed hostess. Taking her smile as an invitation, I go over to join her.

"It's really loud if Spanish men are here," she volunteers, "and Spanish men say women talk a lot. What is it like for women in America?"

And we're off on a long conversation about one of my favorite topics as we compare notes.

"Things are changing slowly here," she says, "but they are changing. Women do much more of the work, but now we have opportunities I never dreamed of as a girl."

She tells me, for example, how pleased she is to have a job running this refugio, although it is demanding work. In addition to tending to the needs of her constantly changing flock, she must also clean the entire refugio each day, keep the books, and handle maintenance and repairs. (She doesn't mention dispute resolution, which I suspect might be her least favorite refugio duty.) Oh yes, and she is responsible for her four kids, the family home, and the farm animals, while her husband goes off to his 10-to-6 job.

"Oh, that's normal," she says, when I observe the disparity in the division of labor and hint at the possibility of sharing some of the home and family responsibilities with her husband.

She beams when she talks about her daughter, who will soon graduate from their equivalent of high school and wants to go on to university. However, it's not clear what the future holds for a smart, ambitious young woman in Galicia. She's starting to tell me more about this when a group of Spanish men comes in. Just as she predicted, it gets really loud as they tell jokes and drink wine.

"Spanish men can go on a pilgrimage to Santiago," she says, with a wistful look on her face. "But not their wives. The husbands wouldn't allow it. They say a woman's place is at home."

While I know that's the prevailing attitude, I have to say that Spanish men have been courteous and helpful to me. It's as if they put American women in a different category from their Spanish wives—some sort of third gender that they don't quite understand but find both puzzling and intriguing.

Around 9:30, the hospitalera goes to her home across the street to cook dinner for eight (herself, her husband, their four kids, and his parents), as she does every night. When she leaves, she shakes my hand vigorously and wishes me a *¡buen camino, hermana!* (Have a good journey, sister!) Though it's still half an hour until lights off, I go up to bed. I hate to leave the glow of the fire, but I'm tired, warm, and ready for sleep.

My bed is in the smaller of the dormitories where seven of the eight beds are assigned to the Spaniards who were making so much noise in the living room. I'm expecting them to wake me when they come upstairs, but I don't hear a thing.

The next morning, an alarm goes off at 5:30. It's immediately silenced. Soon, my Spanish roommates are tiptoeing around the room, whispering quietly, and to my surprise, all seven of them are dressed, packed, and out the door in less than ten minutes, without ever turning on the lights. When they gently close the door behind them, a stillness comes over the room. I hear the faint crow of a rooster, a sliver of pink appears in the sky, and I lie there for a few minutes as an amazing reality sinks in. I can turn on the lights whenever I want. I will have the bathroom to myself. No one will stare when I pull on my pants. Nice.

On the way downstairs, I peek into the other room to see if Inge is up. It's completely dark, and there are bodies in most of the beds. Gentle snoring comes from a bunk in the far corner. I creep downstairs, pack in one hand and shoes in the other, feeling like a teenager who's sneaking in after curfew. Alone in the kitchen, I put on the kettle and get ready to enjoy a delicious breakfast of mint tea and crumbled chocolate sandwich cookies. Several minutes later, Inge wanders in, tousled and half-awake. She heads for the stove, hoping to make some tea, too. However, the only working burner has now been claimed by two French women, one of whom defended the Belgian biker yesterday, and they refuse to let Inge use the burner. They have filled their cups with hot water, so their reaction is puzzling, but they are acting pretty possessive about this burner. Inge doesn't insist. I split my tea with her, she gives me a yogurt, and we share my cookies, eating in an uncomfortable silence, trying to pretend that everything is fine. But gradually, our fingers relax around our teacups; Inge stops bouncing her foot. I catch her eye and we smile at each other in tacit recognition that, actually, everything *is* fine.

Inge wants to lounge around a bit before she starts out, so we plan a rendezvous tonight in Melide at the *pulpería*. Maxi (the portly Spanish storyteller) recommended it for its distinction of having the best octopus in the world. I'm looking forward to this—I have confidence in Maxi's recommendation and love octopus, which tastes like meaty lobster.

My foot is a little stiff when I head out into the windy, gray morning, but I've taken a good dose of ibuprofen and that controls the pain for now. The path takes me into pine forests. Later, I stroll through the first of several eucalyptus groves whose strong fragrance recalls childhood memories of the potion my grandmother would rub on my chest when I was sick.

In the distance, I notice a high ridge with a row of sleek white wind turbines running along the top. Rotating in a soothing rhythm, these modern-day windmills are bathed in a narrow beam of sunlight that pierces the dark, threatening sky. On a vast stage highlighted by a powerful spotlight, they wait for a twenty-first-century Don Quixote to ride into view. I think back to the hilltop turbines outside of Pamplona, turning peacefully as if they had all the time in the world. I was in such a rush in those early days, like a frantic little wind-up toy that couldn't slow down.

"Your mind needs time, as your body needs distance, to reach the destination," a Camino priest told me. I understand that now, as I understand that the measures are different here. Time on the Camino is tied to the ancient rhythms of the sun and not the relentless ticking of my watch. Sometimes hours zip by at a speed that makes my head spin; other times each minute seems to last an eternity. Moments can be glorious or grueling, but I am present for them. And they pass. The sun appears every morning.

This new measure of time influences how I think about distance. Now, rather than worrying about how fast I can go the distance, I see that a journey takes time and, more to the point, that the time is not wasted if I look around and appreciate what the distance traveled has to offer. When I started walking, I felt great frustration at how long it took to get anywhere on foot. It was as if I was living in slow motion and would never reach Santiago. Now I see that I'm making good progress. At the end of most days, I have traveled a modest distance under my own power. I haven't gotten lost, I've found food and shelter, and each day I've drawn closer to my destination. What's more, when I embrace this new cadence, I find that I *like* the pace of a pilgrim. I *like* being receptive to whatever the journey might offer. It's counterintuitive for this busy professional, but the Camino way of time and distance is empowering. Now more than ever, I feel centered and grounded.

I understand pilgrimage differently now, too. Pilgrimage, I thought when I left home, was a trip to a sacred place made by a religious person seeking to reaffirm his or her faith. That definition did not apply to me. Over the past weeks, the experiences of my journey, as well as conversations with my fellow pilgrims, hospitaleros, villagers, and especially Camino priests, have led me to see that while the history of pilgrimage may lie in religious beliefs and traditions, the practice transcends a strictly religious interpretation. I think back to the Pilgrim Masses. The details varied but the basic message was simply this: we are all seekers, and regardless of what we search for, pilgrimage offers the promise of wisdom and understanding. The specifics may have changed over the centuries, but not the need—or the outcome. Secular I may be, but I'm a pilgrim nonetheless.

Freya Stark and Peace Pilgrim

Freya Stark (1893–1993) was an Englishwoman and one of the twentieth century's great adventurers and travel writers. Fearless and bold, she explored the Middle East primarily in the period between the two world wars, astutely observing human nature and the landscape. The passage quoted below is from *A Winter in Arabia* (1940).

Peace Pilgrim (1908–1981) was an American woman who gave away all her possessions at age forty-four and spent the last twenty-eight years of her life walking back and forth across the United States. On a quest for world peace and the inner peace she said had to come first, she walked over 25,000 miles before she was killed in a car accident as she was being driven to a speaking engagement.

Two twentieth-century writers talk about pilgrimage in this broader sense. ". . . the charm of the horizon is the charm of pilgrimage, the eternal invitation to the spirit of man," writes Freya Stark (1893–1993). Her words remind me that pilgrimage is about the fundamental desire to explore ourselves as we discover the world in all its beauty and mystery. It is a quest for meaning that is as old as humankind. Later, Peace Pilgrim (1908–1981) defined a pilgrim as "a wanderer with a purpose." I like the juxtaposition in her definition of two contradictory words: "wanderer," which implies the lack of a goal, and "purpose," which requires a goal. When I left home, I was a wanderer without a purpose. Now, with each step and each passing moment, I am closer to understanding why I am here.

A Santiago nunca se llega.

You never arrive in Santiago.

Spanish saying about the Camino

Chapter Twenty-Two

Betwixt and Between

June 28 – 30, Eixere to Santiago via Melide and Arca.

Only two and a half days to go until I reach Santiago. I've found my rhythm, but the Camino feels different now. For the last thirty-one days, when I would pass someone working in the field or out for a stroll, I'd invariably be greeted with a smile, an enthusiastic *¡buenos días!,* and often a friendly word of advice. The people whose land I crossed seemed proud to be part of the long history and rich traditions of this pilgrimage route. But now, when I spot a villager or farmer up ahead and raise my hand in greeting, he or she looks the other way. At first, I thought I was imagining things. I'm realizing now that this is the new norm.

There is a change on the trail, too. Since yesterday afternoon, about the time I hit the one-hundred-kilometer mark, it has been much, much more crowded. This is not a coincidence. Remember, a pilgrim need only walk the last one hundred kilometers to Santiago (or cycle the last two hundred) to be eligible for a Compostela, the official document certifying successful completion of the pilgrimage. It never occurred to me that so many people would choose to get a Compostela by making the minimum effort required, but it's clear that is what's going on. (My friend the monk would *not* approve.) I think the locals are responding to the sheer volume of humanity walking and cycling across their land daily. In the midst of the bustling crowd, I try to remember another lesson from the Camino: go with my flow. If I keep this thought firmly in mind, the noisy throngs are tolerable.

Overcrowding on the Camino

In 1986, 2,411 pilgrims received a Compostela, the official document certifying completion of the pilgrimage to Santiago. By 2013, that number had increased almost tenfold to 215,880, and thousands more traveled to Santiago without registering with the Pilgrim Office. For annual statistics beginning in 2004, go to the Pilgrim Office website at oficinadelperegrino.com/en/statistics; select the year of interest in the drop-down box "*Descargar informes anuales en PDF,*" then click on "*Descargar*" (download). As the pilgrimage to Santiago becomes increasingly popular, the pilgrim infrastructure on the most frequently-used trails is stretched beyond capacity during peak periods, making it difficult to find a bed.

There are two ways to avoid the worst crowds. First, pick your dates carefully. Crowds are especially large during Holy Years. (A Holy Year is when Saint James's Feast Day, July 25, falls on a Sunday.) The last one was 2010, and the next ones are 2021 and 2027. Also, the number of pilgrims varies dramatically from month to month in ways that aren't easily summarized. Do your research on this point. Helpful resources include the Pilgrim Office in Santiago, which also publishes monthly information. Go to the website above. In the second drop-down box under the heading "*Consulta rápida de estadísticas mensuales,*" select the year, then the month. The months will be in Spanish but the list starts with January ("*enero*") so you can just count down to get the month you want. Then click on "*refrescar.*" It will bring up charts showing where the arriving pilgrims are from by continent ("*continentes*") and by country ("*paises*"), the route they took ("*caminos*"), their departure point ("*procedencias*"), profession ("*grupos*"), sex ("*sexos*"), and age range ("*edades*"). Unfortunately they do not give a total number for each category so you will have to do the math.

A word of caution: unless you are an experienced hiker and a hardy soul, winter is not a good time to walk the Camino. Many accommodations close from November through March, and winter pilgrims face dangerous weather conditions, especially on the meseta and in the mountain passes.

The second way to avoid crowds is to take one of the less-traveled roads to Santiago. Seventy percent of pilgrims who received a Compostela in 2013 arrived on the Camino francés, making it by far the most popular route. The routes from Portugal are becoming increasingly well-known: in 2013, about 14 percent of Compostelas were granted to pilgrims who arrived via Portugal. However, dozens of other trails lead to Santiago coming from all over Europe. They present viable options of varying length and difficulty, and as they become more popular, improvements to the trails and infrastructure follow. See the websites for the Confraternity of Saint James (csj.org.uk) and the American Pilgrims on the Camino (americanpilgrims.org) for descriptions of the many roads to Santiago.

I can spot the short-termers immediately. They look rested and well-groomed, with dazzlingly white shirts and neatly trimmed hair. They sport golden tans, which is in stark contrast to the peeling, splotched skin of those of us who've been on the trail for weeks or even months. They are younger, too, and that translates into a higher-energy crowd. Many wear headphones, and I note an onslaught of cell phones. A party atmosphere surrounds these chattering newcomers who walk with a bounce in their step.

The grubby, blistered old guard appears worse for the wear because most of us are. Our clothing is stained and faded, our footwear tattered. We are tired and advance with a single-minded determination. To others, we may appear beaten and resigned. On the contrary, we're in a contemplative state and perhaps a bit sad at the realization our journey is coming to an end. And, inevitably, as we approach Santiago, thoughts turn to people back home. We begin worrying about mundane things like arranging return transportation. Forgotten cares resurface. I wonder if we are in danger of forgetting a basic principle of the Way of Saint James: *se hace el Camino en camindo,* literally translated as, "you make the Way as you walk it," or more loosely but accurately, "this is about the journey, not the destination."

No, I think not, at least not the long-distance pilgrims I talk with. They express the same wonder I feel about this journey. We recognize, each in our own way, that we have experienced the magic of the Camino and are changed because of it. What we *don't* know, can't know, is what the Camino will mean in our lives when we return home to spouses and jobs and responsibilities. What we *do* know is that our destination is so close we can feel it in our weary bones. We need to get to Santiago, not so we can say we're done with this trip, but, rather, so we can begin to process what has happened to us.

I am on automatic pilot. The pain in my foot is fierce, but I no longer consider the possibility of quitting, or even wonder anymore why I am doing this. I am a woman on a mission: to get to Santiago under my own power. All I have to do is put one foot in front of the other for two more days—harder than it sounds.

I meander down the trail, alone among the hordes, until early afternoon, when I stop for lunch at an outdoor café in the middle of a garden overflowing with flowers in every imaginable shade of pink, a riot of energizing color. I choose a table with an umbrella right next to a large bed of hot pink geraniums and baby pink roses where I enjoy some delicious, freshly made gazpacho served with big chunks of crusty bread. Then, feeling a siesta coming on, I pull the brim of my hat over my eyes and settle in for a little nap. The lady who runs the restaurant notices me just as I'm about to drift off and wishes me pleasant dreams. Half an hour later, when I wake, I have a *cola cao* to get me going.

It's an hour's stroll into Melide on a flat, tree-lined path. The pain in my foot has become merciless by the time I arrive. I take a room at a modest hotel on a little side street. Its furnishings are tattered, but the spacious room comes with a little balcony and the private bathroom has hot water. Bliss. I take a long, hot bath followed by an equally long and steamy shower, hoping that my extravagance does not cause somebody else to face an icy blast.

That evening, I meet Inge as planned at the *pulpería*. The restaurant is packed and turns out to be as popular with locals as it is with pilgrims. In no time, we've filled one of the long wooden picnic-style tables with Camino friends—two young German men, Gephardt (the Austrian pilgrim), Giles, the Finnish couple, the Spanish men from the refugio at Eixere, the unpleasant Frenchwoman who had defended the Belgian biker, and her companion. I'm a little uneasy when the Frenchwoman, whose name is Giselle, walks over to Inge. To my surprise and relief, they talk for a while, then shake hands, and Giselle goes back to her seat. (Inge later tells me that Giselle said the Belgian's bike was so heavily loaded that he was forced to push the old clunker, except for the downhill stretches, and that he hadn't had a bed in two nights. Giselle felt sorry for him but agreed he behaved very badly; Inge decided maybe he counted as a walker—and problem solved.)

There's no menu at the *pulpería,* and food service is at the discretion of a cheerful Spanish matron.

"Let's get started!" she says, pointing to two large wooden casks. "Red or white wine?"

Why choose? We ask for one of each, and she returns minutes later with two large ceramic pitchers and small earthenware bowls from which to drink. The red wine has a very strong grape taste. The white, however, is delicious, ever so lightly carbonated and refreshing. She soon reappears, this time with a generous platter of steaming little pies.

"*Empanadas,*" she says, as she sets them down in front of us. "I hope you like them."

Do we ever! These meat-and-potato pies with their tender, flaky crust and moist, savory filling disappear in minutes. When they are gone, the señora comes back.

"Our specialty is octopus," she says, then asks with uncertainty in her voice: "Do you want to try it?"

She breaks out in a big grin when we respond in an international chorus of assent—yes, *si, oui, jawohl!* Octopus is a traditional and much-appreciated specialty of Galicia, but I can picture uninitiated diners turning up their noses at this delicacy. The señora goes over to several huge copper pots that are bubbling away in a corner and emit a seductive aroma of wine and garlic. I watch, fascinated, as she pokes around in one of the pots with a lethal-looking fork and pulls out an octopus that she's speared in the head. She examines it, somehow determines that this gangly creature is done and, holding the dripping carcass above a large wooden platter, she cuts it into bite-sized pieces with decisive snips of a foot-long pair of scissors. She ladles some of the cooking liquid onto the platter and heads our way.

"Here you go," she says, setting the platter down in front of us. "Enjoy!"

The octopus is served with toothpicks and baskets of country-style bread that we use to soak up every bit of the tasty olive oil and red wine broth that pools on the platter. We order a second platter, which we quickly devour. Next the señora brings us a generous bowl of boiled potatoes, drenched in butter and seasoned with paprika, which exhausts their menu. A second bowl of potatoes and two more pitchers of wine later, we have forgotten our aches and pains and feel so content sitting there that none of us wants to leave. Then Giles perks up.

"Anyone for ice cream?" he asks, pointing to a bar across the street with a sign in the window picturing a variety of frozen treats.

In spite of our tired legs, we rush over to the tiny bar where we stand packed shoulder to shoulder, crowding around a small freezer full of ice cream bars and other more exotic concoctions. We change our minds several times before settling on a choice. I have a Fudgsicle, the first one in thirty years, and it's even more delicious than I remembered, perhaps because I eat it sitting on a park bench with friends on a balmy Saturday evening on my way to Santiago.

The next morning, when my alarm goes off at 5:30, it's pitch black and a gusty, noisy wind rattles the windows. I know I have to do well over thirty kilometers today, but I can't face these conditions. A quick push of a button and the offending buzz goes away. When I wake again at 6:30, the wind has calmed down, the sun is up, and life looks brighter. I have two glasses of Camino tea, along with a slice of the Santiago almond cake that I purchased at the hotel bar last night, then throw on my clothes. I stick plasters around several toes that have blisters in various stages and apply Compeed (a very effective blister treatment available in Europe) to the ball of my right foot, where I have a blister on a blister. Finally, I slap some of Jacques' ointment on my foot and ankle, pull on my knee brace, put on shoes and socks, and, tying the socks that didn't dry overnight on the back of my pack, I'm out the door.

The pain in my foot starts up after just a few steps, but I manage to (mostly) ignore it. Inge, who also got a late start, catches up with me after about twenty minutes. But she soon takes off like a horse heading for home. Later that morning, I meet up with Giles, and after the obligatory kisses, we take up where we left off a couple of days ago.

"Super evening last night, wasn't it?" he comments. I nod and smile.

"But you know," he continues, "for me, the essential fact that makes this a pilgrimage is going alone. If you go with friends, it's a vacation. How can it be otherwise? The companionship is wonderful, you talk constantly, every meal is a party. You know each other's ways and stories and you share the same beliefs and values, so you remain anchored to your usual life. And you don't have the space and time to reflect."

"I agree," I say. "One of the best parts of this journey has been the people I've met—*des gens comme toi!* (people like you!). But it's the time alone with nothing to do but walk that has transformed my journey into a pilgrimage."

Giles smiles and gives a little salute, and we spend the next few kilometers happily comparing notes about our Camino experiences. Then Giles is ready to stride out, while I need to go at a slower pace to control the pain in my foot.

"I'll see you in Santiago!" he calls out as he pulls ahead.

"*Évidemment!*" I reply, and just saying the word gives me a boost.

I take frequent breaks the rest of the day, stopping when the pain in my foot gets too intense to continue, but I soon learn not to stop for very long. If I do, my foot stiffens up and it's hard to get moving. My shoulders ache today, too. I'm afraid I'm about to face a serious mutiny from my body, but I can't listen to it, not yet. I walk through immense eucalyptus groves and stands of wispy pines on a wide, soft earthen track. Then the trail becomes nothing more than a white ribbon of dirt with occasional miniscule patches of shade from newly planted saplings. I walk in a daze until early afternoon, when I can't ignore my queasy stomach. Fatigue? Some sort of bug? The octopus last night? Well, if it's the latter, it was worth it. I stop at the next bar, a seedy looking place with a handful of dirty tables set up in the parking lot, and order a bottle of sparkling mineral water. Inge appears just as I am trying to get it down.

"Eat," she commands, giving me half her banana when she hears I haven't eaten all day.

Inge speculates that I am feeling ill because I don't want to arrive, adding that she is not ready for her pilgrimage to end either. Well, every mother knows that tummy aches have mysterious causes, but the pain in my foot is too real for her explanation—it's due to abuse, pure and simple. Our brief respite gives me the courage to move again and we start off together, but soon Inge pulls ahead. I plod on, wondering how it can be so hot.

By the time I finally drag into Arca, I can hardly lift one foot after the other. To make matters worse, I can't find the refugio. Two Spanish ladies who are walking along the path see me turning in circles. They each take an arm and speaking very fast Spanish—as much to each other as to me—they lead me to the refugio, which is tucked away in a wooded hollow about ten minutes off the main path. The refugio receptionist assures me she still has beds and tells me Inge is in the sleeping room to the left at the top of the stairs. I find her and the Finnish couple lounging on their bunks in an eight-bed cubicle that is right next to the bathroom—always a noisy location. But it's good to be with friends, and the top bunk opposite Inge is empty. I crawl up and lie there, wondering how I will walk again tomorrow. Meanwhile, Inge runs off to the local supermarket. She returns with pasta, a jar of tomato sauce, bread, a green salad, and a bottle of cheap wine that she invites me and a Brazilian woman to share. Dinner is a blur. I can't even remember what language we were speaking. I'm too tired to eat but offer to do the dishes, since Inge shopped and prepared the food.

"Go to bed, Kate," she insists, "I'll finish up."

It's a kind offer, but her tone is cool. I suspect that at her age—twenty-six—she can't comprehend total physical collapse. It's just not within her experience. Mine either, until now. Maybe I overdid it in my desire to reach Santiago by Sunday. I walked thirty-seven kilometers today and two days earlier, thirty-six, both well above my daily average of about twenty-three and a half kilometers. I hope the botafumeira is worth it.

We do the dishes together, then, in spite of my bone-tired state, I head for the bathroom to wash away the layers of sweat and grime before bed.

"The showers are the worst yet," Inge warns. "They're cold and drafty and the window's too high to close. Oh, and watch out for the water-saving system."

The water-saving device, I soon discover, turns a drafty shower into the shower from hell. You get two minutes of water per push of a big yellow button, during which time the water cycles from glacial to boiling, and in the thirty-second pause between cycles, you stand naked and shivering in the cold breeze as you wait for the next blast of ice water. But there's another issue she doesn't mention. Our sleeping room has two large bathrooms (multiple showers, toilets, and sinks in each). In both, the curtainless showers are in full view of anyone in the bathroom or sleeping room who cares to look—unless I shower with my clothes on, there is no possibility of privacy. I hesitate, but not for very long. *OK,* I think, *this is my cosmic final exam, the ultimate test of being really OK with who I am.* I can try to hide insecurities about professional competence, appearance, or other status markers with various sorts of covers. But I can't hide physical imperfections when I'm naked.

Well, if my body is about to fail me, why should I care what anyone thinks about it? I grab my sports towel and soap and head for the nearest shower, first setting my glasses carefully on my bed—at least *I* won't be able to see anything. I recognize the shape of flesh-colored butts at the sinks and in the showers, but that's all.

Shivering, but at least clean, I crawl up onto my top bunk. As I lie there, wondering if I will ever be able to move again, I finally understand why so many refugio bunks are always occupied by sleeping pilgrims, whatever the hour. It's exhaustion, pure and simple, every molecule threatening to shut down. Like me, right now. I'm too tired even to sleep, though it's only 8:30. A snorer across the hall buzzes away, but the thought of climbing down to get my earplugs is out of the question. I doze fitfully, waiting for this night to pass.

There is usually a grace period each morning, sometimes as long as an hour, between the first rustlings of a plastic bag and the jolting glare of an overhead light. Not today. By 5 a.m., someone has turned on all the lights in our sleeping room and in both bathrooms. No one makes even a pretense of trying to be quiet, for everyone is eager to get to Santiago. Most hope to make it in time for the noon Mass. As do I, but I can't will my body to move. I tell myself I'm going to get up, but nothing happens. Is my Camino over, so close to Santiago?

I put on my glasses and look around, trying to assess the situation, but what catches my eye are two small signs, one taped by the entrance to each bathroom: *mujeres* and *hombres*—women and men. The signs are so tiny and inconspicuous that I hadn't noticed them yesterday without my glasses. It seems I showered last night with the guys.

Oh well. I can't think about that now—I've got to get going. I decide to start small, by wiggling my toes up and down. Next, I try rotating my ankles, first in one direction, then the other, while I get my bearings. I flex my fingers and roll my head from side to side. It's a pathetic little warm-up, but it seems to be working. Inge watches me from her top bunk on the other side of the narrow passageway. Do I imagine it or is she looking at me with disdain? Was it my warm-up?

"Kate. You were snoring last night."

I can't see Inge's face, but I hear the scorn in her voice and know she's using all the restraint she can muster not to say more. Snoring is, after all, the worst sin one can commit on the Camino, in her view (mine, too). What can I answer? That I am glad to be breathing, however noisily? That I didn't choose to snore? Once again humbled by the Camino, I feel a twinge of compassion for all the snoring pilgrims whom I have found so annoying over the past month. I don't respond, but slip down quickly, even nimbly, from my top bunk, feeling OK now and ready to go. Maybe the warm-up wasn't so pathetic after all.

As I begin to arrange my belongings in my pack, I'm conscious of the usual morning sounds—the bustling of the departure, the multi-lingual murmur, the clanking of dishes—and suddenly my stomach sinks down to my toes. This is the last time I will gather my belongings and walk out into the dawn, the last time I'll follow yellow arrows to a trail that takes me ever closer to Santiago. Assuming I can walk twenty-two more kilometers, my journey will be over in a few hours. What an extraordinary experience this has been—the beauty that takes my breath away when I least expect it, the sheer simplicity of existence on the Camino, the time for my mind to wander wherever it chooses, the rich solitude and the wonderful camaraderie. I am bereft at the thought of this journey coming to an end. I want to keep walking.

Yet I know that's not possible. Not even desirable, really. This experience has been so precious in part because it cannot last. It's Ronsard's rose once again. And the reality is I've pushed myself as far as I can go. I may think the pain pales in comparison to the joys of the Camino, but physical ailments are very real. At this point, I'll be lucky if I can power through to Santiago, about another six hours at four kilometers per hour. By back-home standards, that's a laughably slow pace, but it's faster than I walked yesterday and faster than my Camino average. It's also the speed required if I want to arrive at Santiago in time to see the botafumeiro. If the terrain is reasonably flat and—if I don't get lost—I can do it.

I join Inge in the kitchen where she is sipping tea. We share a breakfast of tea and chocolate sandwich cookies in comfortable silence, my snoring last night apparently forgiven, or at least forgotten. Inge wants to linger over her tea, but I need to get started. Hoisting my pack, I peer into the inhospitable void outside the kitchen window.

"You don't have to backtrack," she tells me, reading my mind. "When I went to the grocery store yesterday, I discovered a little path that connects with the Camino, just beyond the refugio." She points into the pre-dawn darkness. "Keep going up the highway a few minutes, then take the path that goes off to your right. It's marked with a yellow arrow and saves a couple of kilometers."

I'm nervous about taking a shortcut in the dark, but I need to minimize the distance if I'm going to make it to Santiago. I head for the empty highway. Luckily, the yellow arrow signaling the turn-off is large and, better yet, under a streetlight, so it's visible, even in the dark. The path takes me deeper, then deeper yet, into a quiet and eerie place. In the absence of light, everything is shades of gray. The looming bulk of the trees is visible, but just barely. I walk alone. In fact, after Inge passes me around 6:45, I don't see another soul until I arrive at the first village two hours later. The bar is open, but I don't stop—I must push on if I am to make the noon Mass. Later, just when I'm starting to drag, the path passes alternately through eucalyptus groves and pine forests and their fresh, clean scents give me just the burst of energy I need. Every now and then, I pass a modest cluster of houses, but nothing stirs, not even the dogs, in this serene and lovely environment.

The Santiago airport jolts me into the world I must soon re-enter. One minute, I am walking along, conscious only of being alive. The next, I am confronted by a daunting chain-link fence. Tall and foreboding, it protects an area where the hilltop has been flattened to accommodate a seventy-five-foot-wide runway. The edge of the tarmac is just a few yards from the path and is lined with rows of enormous, industrial-strength lights whose harsh, artificial brightness obliterates the warm, natural light of the Camino. Looming over me and guarding the runway are the intimidating steel towers of the navigational equipment. The scale is shattering. In an instant, I have been reduced to insignificance. It feels like I am skirting the flight deck of an aircraft carrier, looking up at it from sea level. But this world is completely deserted. No planes are in sight, and none land or take off during the entire time it takes me to walk around the perimeter of the airport. No service trucks drive by. Nothing moves. It is a scene from an end of the world movie where the hero—me—wanders through an abandoned urban landscape, trying to comprehend what catastrophe has created this strange new world.

Yesterday I had a glimpse of what was coming, when I heard a noise overhead and looked up to see a 727, a temporary blight on the blue sky. This reminder of the modern world was startling, but it was gone before I could register what I'd seen. A fleeting aberration, easily forgotten and discounted. Today, there will be no escaping. I walk for ten minutes along this scar on the earth, caught between two very different worlds, feeling increasingly uneasy.

In times past, pilgrims arriving at Santiago also experienced a powerful sensation. But for them, it was overwhelming happiness when they reached the *Monte de Gozo* and caught their first glimpse of the cathedral tower, standing out above all else and safeguarding the city. The name, Monte de Gozo—mount of joy—pays tribute to the emotion they felt at that moment. The seventeenth-century Italian pilgrim Domenico Laffi describes his experience when he arrived one fine summer day in 1670:

On seeing the city we fell to our knees and, with tears of great joy falling from our eyes, we began to sing the 'Te Deum.' But we had sung no more than two or three verses when we found ourselves unable to utter the words because of the copious tears which streamed from our eyes, so intense were our feelings.

Little remains now to inspire arriving pilgrims. Looking out from the Monte de Gozo, I see only industrial complexes and a sea of high rises that obscure the cathedral tower. Tour buses dot the landscape; a motorized cart carries workers dressed in blue jump suits along a paved path. There are no tears of joy, only people going about their business. A dreadful little kiosk offers stale sandwiches, burned coffee, and junk food. Farther down the hill, countless rows of ugly cinder-block barracks provide free housing for eight hundred pilgrims in a complex that recalls a prison yard. This pilgrim ghetto also offers restaurants, a campsite, bars, an amphitheatre, and even free buses to the cathedral. The commercialization, the ugliness, the mass-produced architecture of this scene are completely at odds with every aspect of the pilgrimage up to this point. I hope it's not a foreshadowing of what lies ahead.

From the Monte de Gozo, my guide indicates a choice of routes to the cathedral: the official Camino, which continues on a paved path through the pilgrim complex and then onto minor roads before heading into the city center (seven kilometers, supposedly waymarked) or a highway option that heads straight for the city center (four kilometers, unmarked). I do not want to walk through that pilgrim ghetto and I still hope to arrive by noon, so I take off cross country, heading for the highway. Worst case scenario, when I get to the highway I'll walk the rest of the way on the shoulder of the road. Fortunately, that's not necessary. Minutes later, I pick up yellow arrows that direct me onto city sidewalks.

When I reach the old part of town, the sidewalks disappear, and I am walking down a narrow cobblestone street that is deserted at eleven on a Sunday morning. I stop at a bench to massage my throbbing right foot and tend a giant blister on my left, then continue on, the beauty of the Camino dashed, conscious now only of the pain.

"The real journey begins when you have
processed what you learned from the Camino."

Shirley MacLaine, *The Camino: A Journey of the Spirit*

Chapter Twenty-Three

Beginnings

June 30 – July 3, Santiago de Compostela.

I am trudging down a narrow medieval street, mechanically putting one wrecked foot in front of the other, eyes fixed on the torturous cobblestones. The sun is out, but I'm chilled as I walk in the shade produced by the old stone buildings. It's a dark, silent space. I detect no signs of life, not even a tom cat lurking in the shadows. *Where is everybody?* I wonder. *And where is this cathedral?* I feel like I'm the last person on earth.

Minutes later, I glance to my left and am confronted by a massive stone wall. Turning my head to take a better look, I am stunned to see soaring, lacy towers. I look again and there it is—the Cathedral of Santiago de Compostela, the place I have been walking toward for the past thirty-three days. I hear, of all things, a bagpipe, and then the low rumble of a crowd. A few more steps and I am staring, open-mouthed, at the *Plaza de Obradoiro,* the cathedral square.

I hesitate, torn between beating a hasty retreat to the eerily silent cobblestone street or entering the chaotic scene that unfolds before me. Before I can react, a group of jubilant Spanish pilgrims comes up from behind and sweeps me into the plaza. Roughly the size of a football field, it exudes an energy reminiscent of the University of Michigan football stadium on a sunny game day. But it looks for all the world like a medieval street fair. Two bearded pilgrims on horseback trot by, wearing long robes and feathered hats, each holding high a large wooden cross. A nun in a black habit and white wimple floats past an energetic juggler. Parents chase happy little kids. Beaming senior citizens,

Santiago welcoming pilgrims from the top of the cathedral.

scallop shells around their necks, follow a guide wearing the traditional cloak and wide-brimmed hat of a pilgrim. Tantalizing smells from street vendors' stands mix with the odors of aftershave, sweat, horses, sunscreen—and marijuana. Black-robed priests scurry to and from the cathedral. I spot a piper just a few yards from where I'm standing, no doubt the source of the music I heard as I approached the square. On the other side of the plaza, a string quartet plays Mozart, the music almost lost in the din. And the cathedral, with its spectacular Baroque façade and ultra ornate towers, is radiant in the morning light. A statue of Saint James, wearing the wide-brimmed hat of a medieval pilgrim and holding a raised staff, beckons from the highest arch of the bell tower.

I see it all, but am numb and unmoved. I feel just as I did on that first day in Saint-Jean-Pied-de-Port—curious, but dispassionate, as if observing from the shoreline of this adventure, without so much as dipping a toe to check out the water. After all I've experienced—the joy, the pain, the sheer intensity of living—am I back where I was emotionally when I started walking a month ago?

A couple from Colorado with whom I walked on the meseta one morning waves at me from the top of the very tall stone staircase leading to the cathedral's main door. They are smiling and motioning for me to come up. I want to climb the stairs to greet them, I do, but the effort required is simply inconceivable. The blistering heat of the plaza in full sun is brutal. All my bravado about getting beyond pain evaporates. Waving back, I point at my foot, shrug my shoulders in a gesture that I hope signals imminent collapse, and head for the nearest hotel. I need to stop walking, need to arrive, need to begin digesting this trip.

I hobble the few steps to the *Hostal dos Reis Católicos*, the Santiago parador, whose sixteenth-century facade forms the north side of the plaza. I had canceled my reservation back in Santo Domingo, after deciding that staying in luxury hotels was inconsistent with the life of a pilgrim. At this point, I am way beyond standing on principle. I go directly to the check-in desk, and inquire if they still have a room for me. They do, and I take it.

This parador claims to be the oldest hotel in the world, and it is now one of the world's great luxury properties. With the exception of a few small and gloomy rooms—one of which I am about to inhabit—the facilities are superb. Regrettably, the service is not. A surly desk clerk registers me without so much as a *buenos días.*

"The elevator is over there," he snaps, tossing a key across the counter and pointing vaguely toward the back of the enormous foyer as he shoos me away.

A man in a dark suit carrying a briefcase walks up. The clerk straightens his shoulders and rushes over to greet this new arrival effusively. A bellboy appears, discreetly takes the man's briefcase, and offers him a glass of water. I shrug my shoulders. Eventually, I find the elevator (not in the direction the clerk indicated, just for the record), and ten minutes later, at the end of a dark hallway, locate my room. With its single tiny window and shabby furnishings, it's not worthy of a parador. The jarring rattle of mops and buckets booms out from the utility area next door. I take off my pack and shoes, get a big glass of water, and sink into the lumpy bed.

After a few minutes, the room seems stuffy, so I get up to open the window, and for the first time since arriving in Santiago, I notice the air, redolent of summer flowers. It smells wonderful. The sky is the purest blue I can imagine, not a cloud in sight. A church bell rings out its ancient sound. Feeling better, I head back to the bed, thinking I might just settle in for a twenty-four-hour nap. Then it hits me. I did it! I am in Santiago de Compostela, and I got here under my own power. With that realization comes an irresistible jolt of energy. Looking at my watch, I see that I still have time to make the noon Mass and the botafumeiro. I gulp some ibuprofen and, without waiting for the pain to subside, wash up and hurry back to the cathedral, using my walking stick as a cane.

It's complete chaos now, a pedestrian rush hour. The majestic staircase leading to the main entrance is packed body to body. Inside the cathedral, hundreds of people mill around, their voices bouncing off a ceiling that soars to fourteen times the height of a man, according to *The Pilgrim's Guide.* Extravagant gilded statuary decorates the main altar and the many side chapels. Candles flicker, gold glitters; I catch a whiff of incense. Such is the power of this magnificent structure that "[a] man who goes up into the galleries, if he is sorrowful when he goes up, will be happy and comforted after contemplating its perfect beauty" (*The Pilgrim's Guide*). Though I am crammed into the ground level nave of the cathedral, I do indeed begin to feel some of that contentment—at the beauty of the place, certainly, but also because I have walked some five hundred miles to get here.

I take one of the last seats, in a pew about halfway back from the main altar. People crowd around the massive stone pillars, jockeying now for something to lean against. A dizzying cascade of languages washes over me—Spanish, German, Portuguese, Italian, Japanese, and another Asian language. The locals, men in dark suits and women in sober dresses, pay no heed to the majesty of their surroundings (nor to the noisy foreigners) as they devoutly recite the rosary. The tourists, often in shorts, cameras hanging from their necks, consult their guidebooks and ooh and ah as they push their way forward to get a better shot. And the pilgrims, usually grubby and often limping, drift about, some exuberant, others dazed.

Looking around, I spot Giles several rows in front of me and catch glimpses of Jacques and Maïté, Gephardt, Inge, Suzette, the Finnish couple, and Jill and Lil. Seeing my friends further raises my spirits; I'm glad they made it, too. I also recognize a scruffy-looking Brazilian pilgrim, whose name I never learned, leaning against a nearby pillar. Through the grime, I catch a glimpse of how handsome he probably is when he's cleaned up. He waves to an attractive and immaculately dressed young woman—clearly not a pilgrim—who rushes toward him. As she congratulates him, he falls into her arms, sobbing. I think about my homecoming with Philip and wonder if I will have a similar collapse into his arms. It's possible.

Half a dozen priests take their places at the altar. The noise level diminishes to a low roar and Mass begins. Welcoming us in a voice that reverberates over an antiquated loudspeaker, the celebrant reads a list of the nationalities and departure points of pilgrims who have received a Compostela today. He talks about the importance of this gathering of people from all over the world and starts to explain what it means to be a pilgrim, but my ability to comprehend Spanish fades away and my mind wanders. As I sit there, I notice a large, gilded statue of Saint James high above the altar. Fascinated, I see what look like disembodied hands emerge from the darkness and paw at the neck of the statue. *Great, now I'm hallucinating*, I think. Later, I learn that these hands belonged to pilgrims who were giving Saint James the traditional hug.

The rest of the Mass goes by in a blur. When it finally ends, I make my way back into the fresh air and sunlight, and only then do I realize that the priests didn't swing the botafumeiro. A nearby pilgrim informs me that the priests won't use it regularly until the tourist season officially starts *next* Sunday. I burst out laughing at the irony of this moment: my desire to see the giant censer in action was the reason I knocked myself out to get here by noon today. This is the ultimate reminder not to get so caught up in the goal that I forget to be present. *OK,* I think, *I get it. This time, I really get it.*

Chagrined—and let's be honest, disappointed at missing the botafumeiro—I start down the cathedral steps. Sara, one of the Mexican girls, runs up behind me, grinning broadly and waving her Compostela. She invites me to meet her and Mariana at 7:30 tonight for a glass of wine.

"I would love to," I say, "but I can't promise. Whatever's wrong with my foot feels terminal." (When I got home, I saw a doctor about my by then constant foot pain and learned that I had a stress fracture. I spent the rest of the summer in a knee-high orthopedic boot, which was just as well since my feet were a mess and not fit for sandals. I had lost four and a half toenails, and both feet were covered by calluses, patches of raw skin, and the remnants of blisters.)

Sara nods sympathetically. I still regret not making that rendez-vous. I would have liked to have exchanged addresses and heard about their journey. Apparently, Sara's tendonitis healed enough for her to walk at least the last one hundred kilometers.

After a rest, I go to the Pilgrim Office to apply for my Compostela. I imagine that a compassionate priest will question me closely when he learns that my pilgrimage was not a religious journey and that I am not a member of any church. But I am confident I can reassure him that my motives are true and that he will smile benevolently as he hands me my certificate.

That's not how it works. At the chaotic Pilgrim Office, I join a long line and, in about twenty minutes, it's my turn. From behind a counter that runs the length of the wall, a harried young woman shoves a pen and a piece of paper at me. It's a form with thirty lines, one line per pilgrim, on which we are to write our name, method of travel, point of departure, age, gender, nationality, profession, and reason for the pilgrimage.

"Fill this out," she says, after a perfunctory glance at the stamps in my pilgrim passport. "I'll get your Compostela."

I hesitate for a long time before filling in the box labeled "reason for the pilgrimage"—so long that the man behind me becomes impatient. The problem is I know the right answer: "religious devotion," "to reaffirm my faith," or something along those lines. But that's not me, and I won't lie. But I *want* this proof that I have completed my pilgrimage to Santiago. Finally, I decide to write "spiritual reasons and to give thanks" in the troublesome blank. Then I notice that the pilgrim who filled out the line just above mine listed "*deportivo*" as his reason. *Sport?* I think. *Since when has sport been a justification for making a pilgrimage?*

It turns out it doesn't matter. The young woman returns with two pre-printed Compostelas, in Latin, which she has personalized by filling in the appropriate blanks with the Latin equivalent of our names and the date we arrived in Santiago. I pay my three euros and she hands mine over, without even looking at what I wrote.

I am stunned. *This* is the moment I've been waiting for? To be handed a piece of paper? What was I thinking? I've just lived an extraordinary thirty-four days that will be with me for the rest of my life. There is no one time that defines my journey, nor do I need material proof of my accomplishment. Each day has had its own pleasures and perils, but it has been the fact of slowing down and learning to appreciate all of these moments that has made my journey so rich.

I hear my father's words, always said with great enthusiasm in his deep, sonorous voice: "You'll never live this day again, kiddo. Use it well!"

How right he was.

My Compostela.

Steps Out of Time

I wander back to sit in the sun on the cathedral steps. On this perfect summer afternoon, the crowd ebbs and flows in the massive square—a literal tide of humanity. It is a scene that has played out countless times on this plaza over centuries. So much life and energy spread out before me, and *I* am part of the amazing tableau. My arrival in Santiago may not have come with thunderbolts or triumphal music, but I know without a doubt that I belong here today, basking in the glow with my fellow pilgrims, savoring my sense of accomplishment, and grateful for this remarkable adventure. I am of the Camino now, and I am thrilled.

But along with relief and happiness at making it to Santiago, I again experience a profound sense of loss that this great adventure is ending, that my time on the Camino is over. Or is it? *"El Camino es la vida,"* said the young Benedictine monk at Rabanal del Camino. He was right, the Camino is life, and as long as I breathe, it will stay with me. I am of the Camino, but the Camino is also a deeply engrained part of me. Has the promise of the letter that accompanied my credential—". . . by your decision to leave, you are no longer the same"—been fulfilled?

I don't know, but sitting here today, completely enveloped by the Camino, I understand this much: over the last thirty-four days, I have been practicing with every step, every blister, and every pleasure, the art of being alive.

The next two days—my last before returning home—pass in twilight. The intensity of the pilgrim experience recedes into the background, waiting for me to gain the time and distance necessary to process it. I am no longer, strictly speaking, on a pilgrimage, but neither am I a tourist or traveler. Yet I cling to my pilgrim identity. The pretty sundress and strappy sandals that I had mailed to myself from home were waiting for me at the parador. I stare at these alien-looking items in disbelief, then pick up the dress. It feels so fragile and soft, and I can't imagine balancing on the skinny little heels of the sandals. Why in the world did I think I would want these fancy clothes? They go in the bottom of my pack, and I continue to wear my pilgrim outfit, hand-washing my underwear, socks, and shirt in the sink each night, as I have done for over a month. These ragged vestments are the relics of my pilgrimage, and I am not yet ready to part with them.

I spend my time limping around the city, running into Camino friends at every turn. We share meals and sit for hours at sidewalk cafes, reliving our pilgrim experiences. We laugh until we cry as we recall some incidents, get mad all over again at others, and marvel at how even the tiniest details leap to mind. Inge and I run into each other one afternoon as she is walking down the Rua del Villar heading for Finisterre (Land's End), a traditional ending point for many pilgrims to Santiago. A journey of four more days, she figures. When she arrives, she will burn her clothes on the beach in another ritual by which pilgrims mark the completion of their journey. A plastic sac from a Santiago department store hangs off her pack and contains new clothes purchased for the occasion.

"Can you imagine how wonderful it will feel to wear really clean underwear?" she says, her eyes alight with anticipation.

When the talk turns to our feelings on arriving, we discover that we both felt let down initially. To my surprise, right in the middle of a sentence, I start to cry—tears of exhaustion and relief that I made it to Santiago, but also tears of sadness at the realization that the people with whom I've shared this experience are about to disappear from my life, perhaps forever. Inge and I reminisce for a long time about our Camino experiences, split one last banana, exchange e-mail addresses, and, with hugs and more tears, we're off in our respective directions. I watch Inge until she's out of sight, feeling much affection for this caring young woman. Although I never told her so—I didn't see it myself until months later—she helped me understand that it's important not only to give but also to accept. It's an intriguing contradiction that this person, who cares so much about rules and control, showed me that sometimes one has to let go and be vulnerable.

I see Jacques and Maïté on several occasions. During our last meeting, they tell me they are going to Finisterre the following day, by bus since they won't have time to walk there before returning home the day after tomorrow. I plan to join them, but at the last minute decide against it. I don't know where they are staying, so can't get in touch with them about my change in plans. I tell myself that I'm not going to Finisterre because my foot hurts too much to walk to the bus station in Santiago and then to the beach and back once I get there. But really, it's because I can't bear to say good-bye.

Instead of Finisterre, I return to the cathedral and perform the traditional pilgrim rituals of arrival. I go very early, when the cathedral is quiet and empty. Without the distractions of the usual throngs, the place is spellbinding. First, I go to the Tree of Jesse, the intricately carved twelfth-century pillar depicting the genealogy of Christ. At the top stands Santiago, dressed in traditional pilgrim garb, holding a staff, and smiling at me. I say a mental thank you and look for the groove that is supposedly worn into the marble by the caresses of grateful pilgrims over the centuries. There is indeed a deep indentation in the stone. I touch it affectionately, then run my fingers along the trough, leaving my own mark on the ages.

Next I turn to the squat stone figure that kneels at the base of the

Steps Out of Time

pillar, hands folded and eyes closed in prayer. This ordinary-looking fellow is Master Mateo, the twelfth-century stone carver responsible for many of the magnificent artworks that grace the cathedral, including the Tree of Jesse and the Portico of Glory. His self-portrait in stone intrigues me—I love the personal connection between this astonishing work of art and a real human being who lived centuries ago. Tradition has it that if you knock your head against Master Mateo's, he will impart to you some of his wisdom and skill. I stand before him, look into his eyes, and tap my forehead against his. You never know.

My third stop is the crypt under the high altar, which is said to contain the remains of Saint James. I don't believe that the ornate, late-nineteenth-century solid silver casket contains the apostle's bones, though I know many do. Yet one step into the small, dimly lit chamber and waves of serenity wash over me. I kneel before the tomb and remember the people who asked me to pray for them in Santiago. I also remember Catherine and her family. The Santiago priests said a Mass for her soul the day after I arrived (Maïté followed through on her vow, as I knew she would), but I did not find out about it in time to attend. I pay my final respects to Catherine now and thank her for being part of my Camino experience. Finally, I remember family and friends who haven't a clue that this little shrine exists, but for whom I wish peace and wisdom.

I had planned to skip the last ritual—the hug for Saint James. It sounded too touristy and usually requires standing in a very long line. This early, not a single person is waiting, so after a brief hesitation, I climb the steeply winding staircase that leads to the larger-than-life gilded and bejeweled Baroque statue, perched high above the altar. At the top, a priest glowers at me, then motions that I may approach. I put my arms around the statue. It's hard and cold. The priest stares at me, his cynical eyes oozing disdain. I slink down the stairs on the other side, not knowing if I'm reacting to the tradition itself or the hostility of the priest. Hoping to tap into the serenity of this mystical place once more before I leave, I return to Saint James' crypt, but the cathedral has become very busy and a noisy line has formed. The moment has passed.

Instead I return to the Pilgrim Office to see if I can get some information about the pilgrims who arrived with me on June 30, 2002. Surveying the people behind the counter, I select the friendliest-looking worker, a young woman with long, dark hair. When she is free, I ask to see the register of pilgrims who arrived the same day as me. She seems surprised at my request but agrees and disappears into the back room. A minute later, she returns and hands me the pages. I pore over the register, fascinated, and discreetly take notes. I am happy to see that the group of young Italian students, the monk who knew the power of the meseta, and Fiona (the Australian) arrived the same day I did. (I later learn that Theo and Margareth also made it to Santiago, though a few days later.)

Though I am trying very hard to disappear into the woodwork as I study the register, a young man on the other side of the counter stares at me, unhappy that I have access to this information, but unsure what to do about it. He leaves me alone until a rude Dutchman walks up, grabs the register out of my hands, and starts making flippant and disrespectful comments (in English) about the pilgrims on the list. I manage to get the register back, but by then, I've got the attention of all of the workers behind the counter. There is a moment of uncomfortable silence, then the young man starts screaming at me.

"¡No puede tomar notas!" he shrieks, as he reaches across the counter and snatches the register away from me. Apparently he's decided that it's forbidden to take notes. I'm afraid he's going to try to take my notes, too, so I head for the door, not looking back until I am in the safety of the busy street. The angry clerk is nowhere to be seen. In retrospect, I don't see why he was so mad—the cathedral authorities eventually put most of this information on-line so it's available to the public (www.oficinadelperegrino.com/en/statistics).

My information is not complete but I do learn that two-hundred-and-forty pilgrims received a Compostela with me on that June day. All but twenty-five of us came on foot, and almost 27 percent were women. We ranged in age from twelve to seventy-two and represented twenty-two nationalities and many stations in life. A truly motley crew. Yet as I wander around town that afternoon, I am struck by how easy it is to spot a recently arrived pilgrim. It's not just the bandaged feet and gimpy walk, the sunburn, or the shaggy hair. It's the knowing eyes that hold an awareness of—and appreciation for—all we've shared. I spend the rest of the day trying to soak in every last bit of the pilgrim experience, making up for the fog I found myself in when I arrived.

That night, when I return to the hotel and claim my key, the surly clerk tosses a fax my way. I am sure something terrible has happened at home—my punishment for having abandoned all my responsibilities. I tear up when I read the message:

> Well done, valiant warrior, brave pilgrim. Congratulations on your
> accomplishment. Safe journey home.
> Much love, Philip

Although I haven't been dwelling on it, I'm feeling a little a
my reunion with Philip at Detroit Metro, especially when
to our strained farewell. His fax reminds me how supportive he's been
during our phone calls over the past forty days. Clutching his fax to my
chest, I sense that we have both been changed by the experience.

The next morning, the day of my departure, I wake up at four. My alarm
is set to go off in only half an hour, but I try to go back to sleep, knowing
that it will be twenty-four hours before I sleep in a bed again. After a
few minutes of lying there feeling anxious, I give up, put on my pilgrim
clothes, stuff my few possessions in my pack, and go down to catch a cab
to the airport.

A light rain is falling. From the misty window of the cab, I see the
familiar yellow arrows, but no pilgrims are in sight. We are soon on the
highway and the cabbie accelerates. The fields glisten, then blur. It's
disorienting to be moving so fast down the highway in this metal box,
racing away from the Camino.

I take a deep breath. I'm really not sure how I feel. I am happy at the
thought of throwing my arms around Philip and hugging my children
and my mother. I look forward to catching up with friends and other
family. And I am bone tired. But even before I board my flight, I miss
intensely the sights, smells, sounds, and people of the Camino. How will
I integrate these two very different experiences? How will I react to the
Ann Arbor life I left behind? And how it will react to me?

Minutes later, we arrive at the Santiago airport, where I will catch
the 7 a.m. flight to Paris, and from there, the Air France non-stop to
Detroit. Besides myself, there's no physical trace of the Camino now. My
fellow passengers are mostly business travelers who move purposefully,
cell phone at their ear. The flight is announced; we file on board. Flight
attendants give the usual information in Spanish and French. The engines
whine, we taxi into position, and the pilot revs up for take-off.

In seconds, Santiago drops away. I look for the cathedral, but the plaza
is on the other side of the plane. Speed and distance increase. The villages
that welcomed me are tiny dark splotches now, the fields I traversed flat
patches of color, their verdant aromas replaced with the pungent odors of
jet fuel and brewing coffee. The people are long gone. Roads fade into an
occasional thin black line. Mountains that have blistered countless feet,
broken bones, and taken lives—but which have also offered moments of
pure beauty and timeless peace—rise serenely in the distance. The plane
reaches the clouds, and every visible remnant of this land I've known so
intimately disappears.

I glide silently into the luminous unknown.

The Camino's gifts will endure
just as love endures.

Joyce Rupp, *Walk in a Relaxed Manner:*
Life Lessons from the Camino

Epilogue

Philip greeted me at the airport with a smile and a warm embrace, and I was as close as I'll get to heaven when he took me in his arms that lovely summer evening. We enjoyed a leisurely dinner on our deck, and I spoke with my children and my mother, who were well and happy. Then I savored a long, hot shower and a gloriously thick, sweet-smelling towel. Best of all, I went to sleep with the man I love—and not some snoring stranger—lying next to me.

In the days that followed, I reconnected with friends, caught up with forty days of mail, and puttered around the garden. By the time I started back to work three weeks later, it was business as usual, at the usual pace. The Camino was a presence in my life, but in the background, like the bass that pulses away while you are listening to the melody. It was waiting patiently, confidently, for me to process my journey.

Over the next decade, I kept in touch with the Camino. From time to time I corresponded with Camino friends, and whenever I went to France, I saw Juliette. I kept my membership in the Confraternity of Saint James and enjoyed reading their quarterly bulletins. Several months after I returned, I relived every detail of that wonderful trip when I typed my journal. To this day, when I smell a rose bush, see a white Panama hat, or get caught in a downpour, I'm awash in the Camino.

The journey continued to figure in my travel plans, too. I returned to the Camino francés in 2005 and walked sections of the Le Puy Camino in France in 2006 and 2012. Curious about this experience that has meant so much to me, Philip joined me on one of these journeys. Over our ten days on a section of the Le Puy route, he experienced firsthand what it meant to go on a pilgrimage. This new perspective had a tangible consequence: the next time I left on a pilgrimage, he sent me off with a red rose, an assurance of his love and support. In addition to my subsequent Caminos (with more in the works), I have volunteered three times at the *Accueil des Pèlerins* in Saint-Jean-Pied-de-Port, even once with Philip. More recently, I have been serving as a volunteer *hospitalera* at the eleventh-century monastery in Conques that has welcomed pilgrims to Santiago since the Middle Ages. Helping pilgrims from all over the world has given me a deeper understanding of the ancient tradition of pilgrimage.

I made some changes in my life as well. I went through my closet and simplified my wardrobe—every piece of clothing I own now fits comfortably with room to spare—and I take only a carry-on whenever I have to fly, even for extended trips. Makeup for me is optional (full disclosure: I still can't face gray hair). I threw out piles of accumulated clutter, improved my time management, and even learned some patience.

Yes, this had been an unforgettable trip, one of the best I'd ever taken. But now that I was home it didn't feel like the transformative journey I had been promised.

A friend once told me that messages from the universe can't get through until you're ready to hear them. Ten years after my first Camino journey, I discovered the truth of her statement when my mother died, in February 2012. In the aftermath of her death, I finally understood how far I've come since I first set foot on the Camino.

We were dramatically different people, my mother and I, different in temperament, interests, lifestyle, goals, even in size and shape. Our divergent agendas—sometimes conflicting, incompatible, opposing— were apparent from the day I was born. Eager to arrive, I showed up a month early; Mother had to be torn away from her bridge game and rushed to the hospital to deliver me. (I never asked her, but I am sure she was winning.) Growing up, I always suspected that her lack of encouragement for many of the things I wanted to do was actually disappointment in me, her daughter. And although we never discussed it, I probably wasn't very subtle about communicating my determination to never be "just a housewife," like my college-educated mother.

Over the years, she supported me (mostly), even if she didn't always understand or approve of what I was doing. And I was (mostly) a good daughter. When my own children were born, I realized for the first time how hard she had worked to raise three daughters. My father traveled constantly for business, so she bore all the responsibility for maintaining the home and managing the kids. This was in an era before many of the labor-saving conveniences, like disposable diapers, dishwashers, and wrinkle-free garments. She maintained a stable, loving household; fixed

Steps Out of Time

patience → presence

delicious dinners every night (always with homemade desserts); sewed our ballet and Halloween costumes; typed our term papers; and never missed a single recital or performance. How did she do it? As I struggled to live by my values while raising my children, I began to appreciate what a terrific mother she had been and that it had not been easy for her. In the meantime, she became the world's best grandmother: she adored—and was adored by—all of her grandchildren.

But the distance between us remained, born of caution, an over-developed sense of independence (one of the traits we shared), and mutual puzzlement. Then, over her last years, circumstances resulted in our spending more time together: her physical decline, my retirement, and the fact that I was the only one of her three daughters who lived within driving distance.

It was a wonderful time. The seeds of my Camino perspectives on patience and presence—concepts that before my journey had seemed so alien—had taken hold without my realizing it. My willingness to kick back and engage in unstructured moments with Mother yielded increasingly open conversations, shared laughter, and a new understanding of the life she had led.

She was my mother and I'll always love her. But in her last few years I came to genuinely appreciate the woman she was. And as I became less judgmental, she became more accepting of me and my life choices. Mother and I were merging instead of clashing, and this immeasurably enriched our final times together. I credit the Camino for this priceless gift, and I am enormously grateful.

Her death left me bereft, a replay of what I had experienced fifteen years earlier at the time of my father's death. But in spite of my feelings of sadness and loss, I started this new journey of grief from a much different place. For one thing, Mother had a peaceful exit from her ninety extra-ordinary years, dying in her sleep after eating chocolate ice cream for dinner and making a grand slam at mother-in-law bridge. But it was also because my experiences on the pilgrimage to Santiago had taught me to better accept death for what it is: a part of life, a journey of its own, a Camino.

These Camino perspectives continue to shape my life, making difficult relationships easier and reminding me to step back in stressful times and take deep breaths. And I've learned to stay attuned to little pleasures and other people. It isn't that my priorities have changed. What has changed is my ability to bring these priorities into better alignment with how I want to live my life.

I understood something else after Mother died. Years earlier I had started to work on a book about my pilgrimage, but I could never finish it. I would come close, then get involved in a project that became my priority, or I would plan a trip or sign up for another class. Months later, I'd return to my manuscript and the cycle would start again. The problem, I finally realized, was that I didn't know how my story ended. I wrote laundry list after laundry list in an attempt to analyze and quantify how the Camino had changed my life, but my efforts always fell flat. I couldn't articulate what the Camino had brought to me without sounding trite.

I was flummoxed for quite a long time, until Mother's death got me unstuck. Her passing helped me understand that my story doesn't end. I began my Camino journey mourning my father's death and ended it celebrating my mother's life. One of life's cycles was complete. But others were beginning and would be enriched by what had gone before. My son married in 2012, and he and his wife are expecting their first child. That child's life will continue unfolding long after I am gone. There are no endings, and that realization is both comforting and energizing. It has enabled me to finish my book.

And what about Time? I experienced time differently on the Camino, but again, I didn't understand what that meant in my life until Mother's death. Toward the end of her life, as she became increasingly frail and immobile, her physical world became ever more limited. Outings no longer brought pleasure, so I sat with her for hours. Sometimes we played double solitaire or watched old movies, but often we sat together over the kitchen table. No agenda, no goal, just peacefully living those moments in each other's company. Such a simple thing. Yet I know that had I not taken my journey to Santiago de Compostela, had I not experienced those times of nothing more—or less—than being alive, I could not have given her this gift of time that I think meant as much to her as it did to me.

Thirty years later I think back to the episode with my gold watch. At the time, I felt irritation and frustration. Why couldn't I do a better job of controlling time? How could I let it—figuratively, literally—keep slipping through my fingers? Back then, time was an enemy to be conquered. And in my fruitless attempt to control it, to use every minute productively, I could not grasp the message the universe was sending, that time was controlling *me*. I failed to recognize time as a precious commodity, a treasure to savor, not something to be squandered.

I wear a reminder of that lesson every day. In preparation for my first Camino journey, I bought a clunky plastic Timex sports watch (it doubled as an alarm clock, saving several ounces). My inexpensive Timex, I soon discovered, was far more practical than the delicate dress watch that had replaced my gold one, the casualty of the toilet. I wear a Timex (the third replacement) to this day. Thanks to the Camino, I don't need a fancy watch to remind me that time is precious.

Time and I, we're more comfortable with one another these days.

Ann Arbor, September 2013

Steps Out of Time

In loving memory of my parents, Margaret and Vic Ball.

Margaret and Vic hut hopping in the Austrian Alps in the summer of 1977.

Acknowledgments

Writing this book has been an adventure of the magnitude of my Camino journey. I am enormously grateful to the wonderful family, friends, and colleagues who encouraged and supported me along the way. I could not have written this book without their help and presence in my life.

This book would never have seen the light of day but for Patricia O. Steiner, writer, translator, and fellow lover of Spain and Latin America. Pat was the first person with whom I shared my journal, tentatively, cautiously. It was she who encouraged me to consider publishing it. It was Pat who broke the startling news to me that my manuscript was not just about the people and the experiences of the Camino, but also about me—and finally convinced me to write about not just the facts and the stories of others but also my own thoughts and feelings. Pat has offered me her unflagging enthusiasm every step of the way. I deeply appreciate her support and friendship.

I am also so very grateful to my children, Chris and Katie, for believing in me and for never doubting that I could walk the Camino or that I would finish this book. Their faith in me made a huge difference, especially early on when I was on the fence about whether to walk to Santiago. And thanks to Katie for helping me pare down the text. I love you guys!

Betsy Jackson and Margaret Leary, excellent authors, dear friends, and members of my writing group, have been incredibly generous with their time and endlessly helpful and patient. I can't begin to express my appreciation to them for all of their help over the past five years. I was extraordinarily lucky to fall into a group of such talented and committed writers. You are both awesome. I also wish to thank Betsy from the bottom of my heart for showing me that writing is not only incredibly hard work, but also fun. I am eternally grateful to you both.

I am deeply grateful to my long-time friend Bee Clark and my relatively new friend Anne Knott for reading and commenting on several drafts, offering no-holds-barred advice (the best kind), and helping me think more clearly about the nature of my experience. My sister Esther Hewlett also read several drafts and has been enormously helpful. In particular, she provided wise advice about delicate matters and always praised my drafts, even when they didn't deserve it. With their contagious and unfailing enthusiasm, these fabulous women were first-rate cheerleaders. I am so fortunate to have each of you on my side.

I am indebted to Josette Lefèvre of the *Association des Amis du Chemin de Saint-Jacques/Pyrénées Atlantiques* for welcoming me into the group of *accueillants*, the volunteers who run the Pilgrim Welcome Center in Saint-Jean-Pied-de-Port. The times I have spent there working with my fellow volunteers and tending to the needs of pilgrims from all over the world have enriched and deepened immeasurably my understanding of this ancient pilgrimage route and what it means to be a pilgrim. I treasure those days and hope to continue them.

I wish to thank my niece, Flora Birdzell, and her cousin, Sara Lamson Nathan, for sharing a portion of their Camino with me in 2005 and showing me the Camino through the eyes of twenty-somethings. It was great fun, and I am privileged to have walked with them. Marion Marples, Secretary of the Confraternity of Saint James, in London, has been an invaluable resource by graciously answering my many questions and reviewing materials for me. She is extremely knowledgeable about the pilgrimage to Santiago, and I thank her for so generously sharing her knowledge with me. (Any errors are, of course, my own.) Fran Blouin, Professor of History at the University of Michigan, with his probing questions and thoughtful comments, encouraged me to think more deeply about my experience and helped me find my voice. I appreciate his interest and help. I am also indebted to my personal physicians, Drs. Elisa Ostafin and Leslie Crofford, who did not try to dissuade me from undertaking a five-hundred-mile walk. Instead, they helped me think about how to prepare for it.

The following friends and colleagues (in alphabetical order) have helped me in various ways, and I cannot thank them enough: Elaine Alexander, David Bloom, Nancy Cantor (whose help arranging my leave of absence made it possible to walk the Camino in the first place), Susan Darrow, the late Rhetaugh Graves Dumas, Doug Elser, Sandy Sorini Elser, Meg Gower (a member of my writing group for several years), Dick Kraft, Jean Kraft, Luisa Lopez-Grigera, Adèle McCarus, Ernest McCarus,

Nina Redman, David Soper, Deanne Sovereen, the late Peter O. Steiner, Linda Beth Tiedje, Bruce Wallace, Megan Walsh, and Sandra Xenakis (who gave me a needed kick in the butt early on).

I thank Mike Savitski, my superb book designer, for his help with all aspects of production and for his great ideas. A special thanks to my exceptional editor, Penny Schreiber, whose expertise has made this book infinitely better. She has taught me more than she will ever know about writing and the process of shaping a book. I am forever grateful for her excellent help and support and for her patience. I also wish to thank Katie Vloet for doing such an excellent job of proofreading the manuscript.

Finally, I am tremendously grateful to the priests, hospitaleras and hospitaleros, pharmacists, and other Spanish people who helped me along the way, and to the pilgrims with whom I shared my journey. They enriched my time on the Camino in countless ways. How can I ever thank them enough? The experiences we shared continue to influence my life, and I treasure each and every one of these encounters. I especially wish to thank Jacques and Maïté Mouchel, for being such wonderful Camino companions; Theo and Margareth Brink, for their excellent company; "Inge," for sharing with me some of the best and worst of times (and for her good care); and "Juliette," for her years of friendship, for her good company during those first days, and for her support and help with my book.

And, of course, I must thank Philip, the love of my life, for giving me the time and space to write this book and for all the delicious dinners he fixed while I was typing away. I also thank him for his willingness to take the plunge and explore this world that means so much to me by helping me staff the *Accueil des Pèlerins* in Saint-Jean-Pied-Port in 2011 and joining me on the pilgrim trail to Santiago in 2012 .

Philip's rose.

Sources

Adrian, Luc. *Compostelle: Carnet de Route d'un Pèlerin.* Paris: Presses de la Renaissance, 2002.

Boulès, Jean-Claude. *Le Grand Chemin de Compostelle.* Paris: Editions Payot et Rivages, 2001.

Bureau, Michel, S.J. *Pèlerin! Marcher vers Compostelle.* Paris: Vie Chrétienne, 2001.

Dillard, Annie. *Pilgrim at Tinker Creek.* New York: HarperPerennial, a division of HarperCollins, 1998.

Eagen, Kerry. *Fumblings: A Pilgrimage Tale of Love, Grief, and Spiritual Renewal on the Camino de Santiago.* New York: Doubleday, 2004.

Fletcher, Colin. *The Man Who Walked Through Time.* New York: Vintage Books, a division of Random House, 1967.

Freidan, Betty. *The Feminine Mystique.* New York: Random House Publishing Group, 1963.

Gitlitz, David M. and Linda Kay Davidson. *The Pilgrimage Road to Santiago: The Complete Cultural Handbook.* New York: St. Martin's Griffin, 2000.

Kerkeling, Hape. *I'm Off Then: Losing and Finding Myself on the Camino de Santiago,* translated by Shelley Frisch. New York: Free Press, 2006.

Hogarth, James, trans. *The Pilgrim's Guide: A 12th Century Guide for the Pilgrim to Santiago de Compostella.* London: The Confraternity of Saint James, 1992.

Hoinacki, Lee. *El Camino: Walking to Santiago de Compostela.* University Park, PA: The Pennsylvania State University Press, 1997.

Laffi, Domenico. *A Journey to the West: The Diary of a Seventeenth-Century Pilgrim from Bologna to Santiago de Compostela,* translated with commentary by James Hall. Leiden, the Netherlands: Primavera Pers, 1997.

MacLaine, Shirley. *The Camino: A Journey of the Spirit.* New York: Pocket Books, a division of Simon and Schuster, 2001.

Merwin, W. S., trans. *The Song of Roland.* New York: The Modern Library paperback edition, 2001.

Peace Pilgrim. *Peace Pilgrim: Her Life and Works in Her Own Words,* compiled by some of her friends. Santa Fe: Ocean Tree Books, 1998.

Raleigh, Sir Walter. *The Poems of Sir Walter Raleigh: A Historical Edition.* Edited by Michael Rudick. Tempe, AZ: Arizona Center for Medieval and Renaissance Studies, 1999.

Roddis, Miles, Nancy Frey, Jose Placer, Matthew Fletcher, and John Noble. *Walking in Spain.* Victoria, Australia: Lonely Planet Publications, 1999.

Ronsard, Pierre de. *Les Amours: Introduction, Bibliographie, Relève de Variantes, Notes et Lexique par Henri Weber et Catherine Weber.* Paris: Classiques Garnier, 1998. Translation of Ronsard's sonnet "A sa Maîtresse," by Scott Horton, first published in *Harper's* on-line in 2008 (harpers.org/blog/2008).

Guides to Pilgrimage Routes to Santiago

Sources cont.

Rudolph, Conrad. *Pilgrimage to the End of the World: The Road to Santiago de Compostela*. Chicago: University of Chicago Press, 2004.

Rupp, Joyce. *Walk in a Relaxed Manner*. Maryknoll, NY: Orbis Books, 2005.

Selby, Bettina. *Pilgrim's Road: A Journey to Santiago de Compostela*. Leicester, England: Ulverscroft, 1994.

Solnit, Rebecca. *Wanderlust: A History of Walking*. New York: Penguin Books, 2000.

Stark, Freya. *A Winter in Arabia: A Journey through Yemen*. Woodstock, NY: The Overlook Press, 2002.

Starkie, Walter. *The Road to Santiago: Pilgrims of Saint James*. London: John Murray (Publishers), Ltd., 2003. (orig. published 1957).

Steinback, Alice. *Without Reservations: The Travels of an Independent Woman*. New York: Random House, 2002.

Thoreau, Henry D. *Walking*. Bedford, MA: Applewood Books, 1992 (orig. published 1862).

Brochure of the Asociación Riojana de Amigos del Camino de Santiago. Logroño: Consejería de Turismo (undated).

The Confraternity of Saint James (London) publishes guides to a number of the most popular routes to Sangtiago. These trim, lightweight guides are updated regularly and are available from the Confraternity on-line bookstore: www.csj.org.uk/ bookstore.htm.

John Brierley's Guides to the Camino francés, the Camino Portugués, and the Camino Finisterre are updated regularly and contain much useful information. They include a general introduction to the Camino; a quick guide to preparation; practical, mystical, and personal reflections for each segment; notes on places of interest along the way; detailed maps; elevation charts; and a list of selected accommodations.

Miam Miam Dodo (title translation: *Yummy Yummy Nighty Night*), by various authors, is a series of French guides to several of the routes to Santiago. If you can read basic French, they are very helpful. These guides include detailed maps of each segment and of the villages and towns. Also included is a very comprehensive list of accommodations from albergues ("*gites*") to B&Bs ("*chamber d'hôtes*"), hotels, and camp sites along with email addresses and phone numbers, as well as information about a wide range of facilities along the way. The guides are updated annually.

Camino Blogs

Katharine B. Soper, "Been There, Done That?" *Crazy Wisdom Community Journal (blog)*, 2015, / www.crazywisdomjournal.com/

Soper, "Danger on the Camino: Trust in Allah and Tie Up the Camels," *Crazy Wisdom Community Journal (blog)*, 2015, / www.crazywisdomjournal.com/

Soper, "Creature Comforts on the Camino, Part 1: Do Real Pilgrims Take Cold Showers?" *Crazy Wisdom Community Journal (blog)*, 2016, / www.crazywisdomjournal.com/

Soper, "Creature Comforts on the Camino, Part 2: Are Smartphones, Email, and Apps Existential Threats?" *Crazy Wisdom Community Journal (blog)*, 2020, /www.crazywisdomjournal.com/

Steps Out of Time

Steps